MEL BAY'S

Basic Concepts of

ARRANGING AND ORCHESTRATING MUSIC

BY TOM BRUNER

CONTENTS

ABOUT THE AUTHOR

After graduating from North Texas State University in 1967 with a Bachelor of Music degree in jazz performance and composition, Tom Bruner served on the arranging staff of the United States Air Force Academy Band (1967 to 1971). In late 1971, he moved to Los Angeles where he began to make his living as a studio musician, performing on the following productions:

Hawaii Five-O	The Mary Tyler Moore Show	Dirty Sally
The Merv Griffin Show	The Bob Newhart Show	The Dukes of Hazard
Police Story	Movin' On	Laverne & Shirley
Police Woman	Cannon	Happy Days
Shaft	Gunsmoke	The Rich Little Show
Matt Helm	Barnaby Jones	The Hardy Boys
The Wonderful World of Disney	The Streets of San Francisco	
Medical Center	The F.B.I.	

In 1975, Tom formed his own production company for the purpose of composing and arranging music for television and radio commercials. For the next four years, he composed, arranged and produced over 150 music tracks for commercials for various clients such as:

Coca Cola	KFI Radio	L.A. Civic Light Opera
Sumitoma Bank	KCOP Television	Gulf Oil
Carnation	Miller Beer	Mattel Toys
Buick	Brittania Sportswear	Avocado Growers
Hughes Supermarkets	McDonnell Douglas Corp.	Kenwood Stereos
Playgirl Magazine	Lowenbrau Beer	U.S. Forest Service
Los Alamitos Race Track	Sanyo	Frontier Hotel
State Mutual Savings	Pizza Hut	Dunes Hotel
Pup & Taco	Zacky Farms	International House of Pancakes

Tom's primary role in the music business from the late 1970s thru 1987 is one of musical director for television variety shows. He has served in this capacity (arranger/conductor) on over six dozen television productions, some of which are listed below:

The Golden Globe Awards—1980, 1983, 1984, 1985, 1986, 1987
The Academy of Country Music Awards—1976, 1977, 1978, 1979, 1980, 1981, 1982, 1983, 1984, 1985, 1986, 1987
Betsy Lee's Ghost Town Jambouree (13 episodes of children's shows)
The Great American Sing Along (2 hour variety special starring Steve Allen)
The US Magazine Awards—1982, 1983
Slapstick Studio (13 episodes of children's shows)
The Lou Rawls Parade of Stars—1982, 1983, 1984
Great Moments in History (13 episodes of children's shows)
12 cable TV shows for the Playboy Channel—1983
The 40th Anniversary Salute To Ray Charles—1983
I Love Men (2 hour special starring Donna Mills)—1983
Celebrity Fun Cruise (2 hour special starring Andy Gibb & Engelbert Humperdinck)

Aerobics With The Playmates (Playboy Channel)—1984
The Black Gold Awards (starring Lou Rawls)—1984, 1985, 1986, 1987
All Star Caribbean Cruise (2 hour special)—1986
Thanks For Caring (2 hour special saluting C.A.R.E.)—1987

Over the course of years in his role as Musical Director for television shows, Tom has arranged and conducted music for the following recording, motion picture and television artists:

Kenny Rogers	Freddy Fender	Marilyn McCoo	Ann Jillian
Pat Boone	Mel Tillis	A Taste of Honey	Engelbert Humperdinck
Loretta Lynn	Jerry Reed	Denise Williams	Roger Miller
Sarah Vaughan	Ronnie Milsap	Conway Twitty	Lacy J. Dalton
Crystal Gayle	Peaches & Herb	Lee Greenwood	Larry Gatlin
Robert Goulet	Gloria Gaynor	Gary Morris	Tom Wopat
Charlie Rich	Milton Berle	Gloria Loring	Tom T. Hall
Glen Campbell	Rudy Valle	Leslie Uggams	Joe Williams
Debbie Reynolds	Anthony Newley	Nell Carter	Debbie Boone
The Oak Ridge Boys	Paul Williams	Lisa Hartman	Gladys Knight
Steve Allen	Dottie West	Diahann Carroll	Nancy Wilson
Terry Gibbs	Tammy Wynette	Frank Stalone	Melba Moore
Herb Ellis	T.G. Shephard	Andy Gibb	The Judds
Micky Gilley	Roy Clark	Susan Anton	Toni Tennille
Patti Page	George Jones	David Frizzel	Bill Medley
Charlie Pride	Eddie Rabbit	John Schneider	Natalie Cole
Janie Fricke	Lou Rawls	Barbara Mandrell	

In 1980, Tom composed and conducted a large music package for the Chris Craft Broadcasting Group using a 50 piece orchestra comprised of members of the London Philharmonic Orchestra and recorded this music at the Music Center in London, England. In 1984, he composed a large music production package for the Dick Clark Company and has composed and conducted music for corporate films for the Miller Brewing Company, McDonnell Douglas and the U.S. Navy. Tom as also composed music for two feature films. In addition, he gives periodic seminars and lectures on music composition, arranging and production at various universities and schools of music across the U.S.

BASIC CONCEPTS OF ARRANGING
AND ORCHESTRATING MUSIC

Forward

Hearing music which you create as you play an instrument is a joy, to say the least. But hearing music which you have intricately woven for other instruments to play in combination is pure exhilaration! It is not unlike an artist, who has only drawn line drawings with a charcoal pencil to suddenly be given a pallet of unlimited colors with which to paint the pictures that are so vivid in his mind. As an arranger and orchestrator, you will not just be dealing with the one color of your instrument (the black and white charcoal pencil of our example), but rather an unlimited assortment of colors and textures, taken from the limitless possibilities of instruments and instrument combinations you, as an arranger/orchestrator have at your disposal.

Learning basics of how to deal with these instrumental colors and textures is what this book is about. If you are a beginner to the techniques of arranging and orchestrating music, this book will be very beneficial. And for those musicians who are at the Intermediate and Advanced levels of arranging and orchestrating, this book will serve as a reference source and review.

It is my full intention that the student will have a thorough understanding of the "basics" of arranging and orchestrating music after studying this book and that teachers find it a useful supplement/workbook to primary arranging and orchestrating classes. I am very motivated to make this study all I have said, for nothing could please me more than to know I have had a part in introducing students of music to the extremely exciting and aesthetically rewarding world of arranging and orchestrating music.

PART I
THE ARRANGER / ORCHESTRATOR'S
USE OF THE PIANO

In order to have a specific reference point as we enter our study of arranging and orchestration, I will be referring to the piano and the piano keyboard. By doing so, the entire range of the piano keyboard will become a reference point for such things as register colors relating to instruments, chord voicings, chord progressions and an aid in my teaching you such techniques as transposition and counterpoint.

I must emphasize that you DO NOT have to to be a piano player to study arranging in this book. Neither will you learn how to play the piano from studying this book. But you will start to form some concepts about registers, chord voicings, chord progressions and music theory in general by starting to play what is affectionately known as "Arranger's Piano". Consequently, you should make a point to have a piano nearby to use to help you understand some of the basic information about arranging and orchestrating. Pianos are relatively plentiful. If you have to go to a school, a church or even a friend's house to use their piano (in the event you don't own a piano yourself), I strongly suggest you do so. There is nothing "wrong" with using a piano as an aid to your learning how to arrange and orchestrate music. Many of the great composers of music always wrote their scores at the piano keyboard (of course, many did not), so you shouldn't feel like you are leaning on a crutch by doing so either. And, after basic principles have been learned about arranging and orchestration, you might find you can learn to write "away from the piano" as so many "advanced" arrangers do.

The Grand Staff As It Relates To The Piano

The "grand staff" is a name give to the bass and treble staff combination that contain all the pitches which can be written for instruments of Western music (music from the traditions of Europe and America as opposed to music from China, India or the Middle East). It extends from the very lowest note to the very highest note instruments can play. Generally, the eighty-eight key piano encompasses all the notes in the "grand staff".

The Grand Staff
As It Relates to Instrument Registers

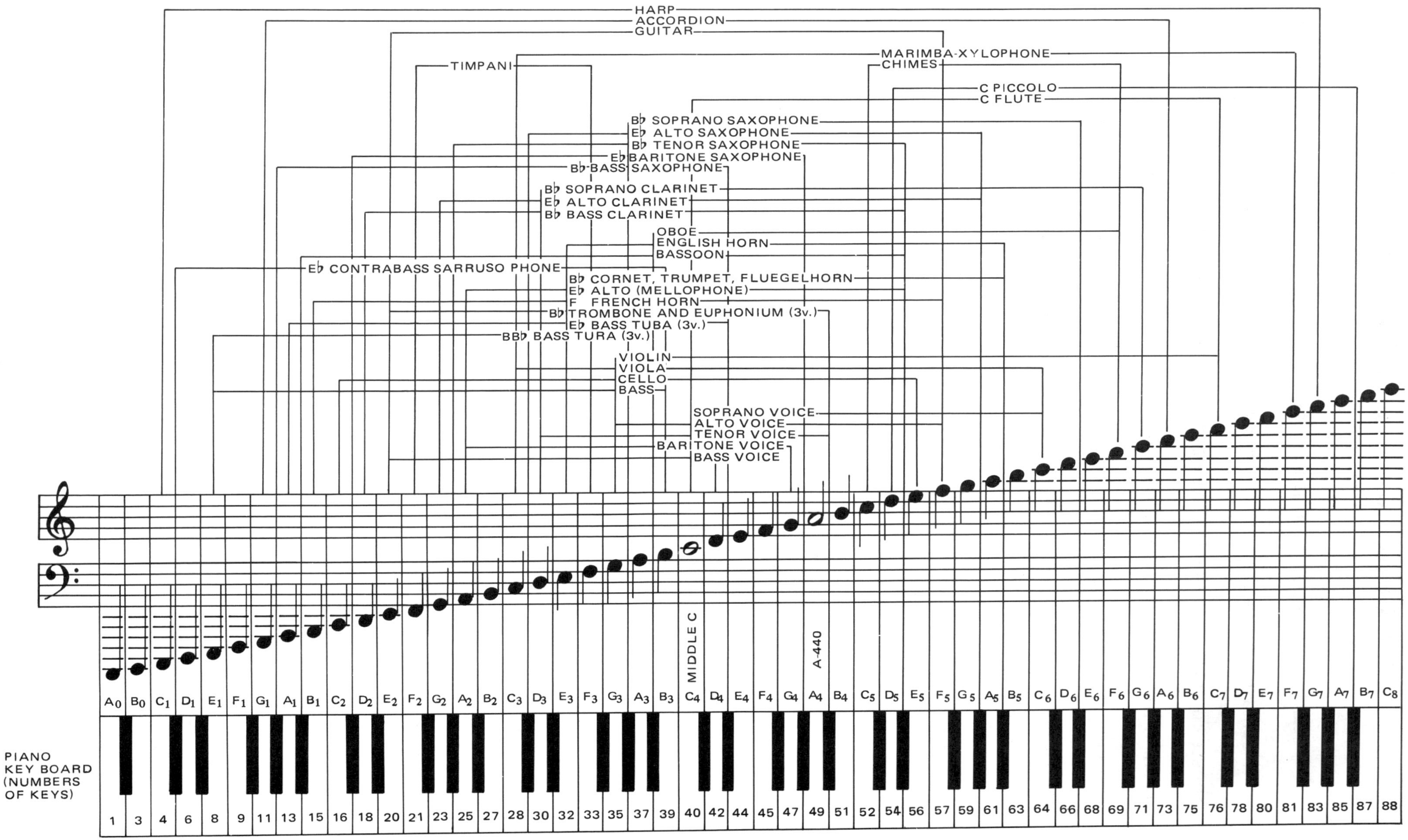

8

As you can see by the preceeding illustration, ranges of various instruments can be directly related to the Grand Staff or the grand "scope" of the piano keyboard.

1. Concert Pitch

All of the notes in the preceeding example are notes of CONCERT PITCH. CONCERT PITCH means the "actual" pitch which an instrument sounds. Look at the preceeding chart of the Grand Staff. You will see that each of the note's names have a number by it as it relates to a specific octave. For example, middle C is labeled "C4" (as it is the fourth octave C on the Grand Staff). Consequently, that "pitch" is always called CONCERT MIDDLE C, no matter what instruments play it. Some instruments which are called TRANSPOSING INSTRUMENTS would play that pitch (Concert Middle C), but would call it by another name on their particular instrument (the transposed note). But no matter what the pitch may be named (on any number of different instruments) it is ALWAYS, in CONCERT PITCH, middle C.

Write the concert pitch note for the following:

Exercise #1

PART II

THE BASICS OF MUSIC THEORY

Knowing the rudiments of music is an absolute prerequisite to the study or arranging and orchestration. While this book is not a "Theory" book, we will at least look at the fundamental concepts of music theory in order to begin our study of arranging and orchestration. There are two ways you should study this chapter: (1) intellectually...with paper and pencil; (2) practically...playing and relating everything to the piano keyboard.

1. The Staff and Clefs

Below is an example of the four clefs which we will be using as arrangers and orchestrators.

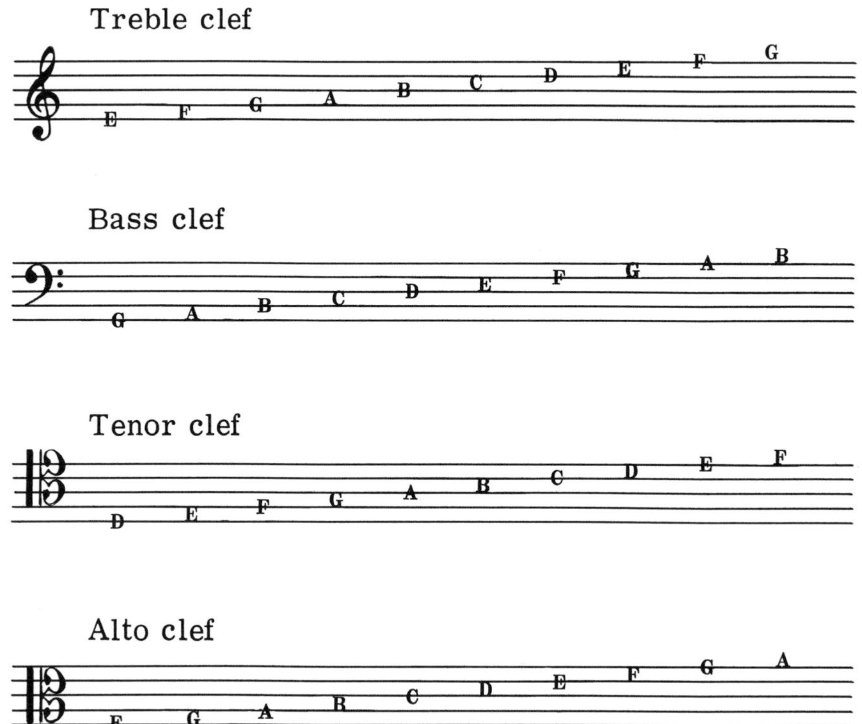

In order to "group" patterns of rhythms together, bar lines are used on the staff. Double bar lines usually separate a specific phrase of music.

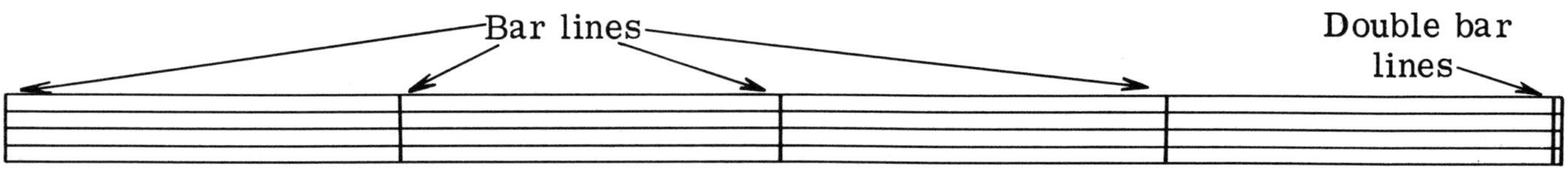

2. Fundamental Principles of Notation

To draw a note, you must consider that it has three elements: the head, the stem and the flag.

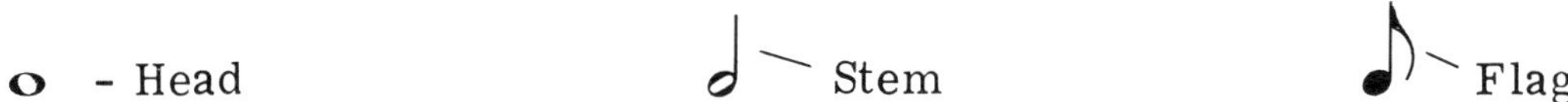

When the stems are going UP, you always put the stem on the right side of the note.

When stems are coming DOWN, you always put the stem on the left side of the note.

When placing notes on the staff, put the stems UP on any notes on or below the middle line.

Place stems DOWN on any notes above the middle line.

When writing TWO SEPARATE PARTS on one staff, put stems UP on the top part and stems DOWN on the bottom part.

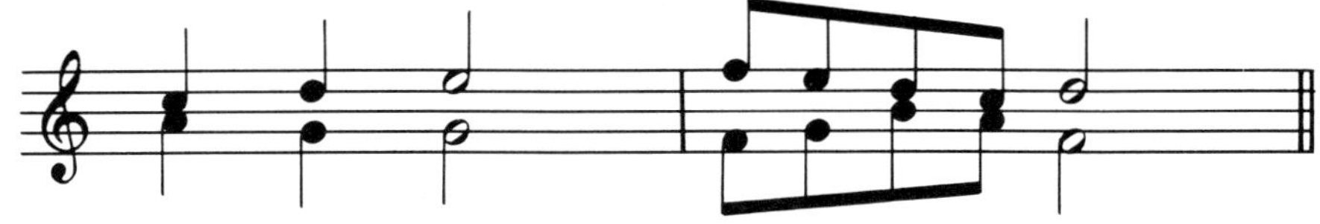

If you were to want two DIFFERENT PARTS performing the same note, put stems UP and DOWN.

Ledger Lines:

When writing ledger lines, care must be taken in spacing. Make all ledger lines the same

distance apart.

Placement of Accidentals:

ALWAYS place accidentals on the line or space preceeding the note to be altered.

Vertical Arrangement of Notes:

It is essential that orchestrators and arrangers form the habit of placing notes and rests

in the proper vetical line up, one under the other (whether it be on two staffs or on score

paper). ALL NOTES SOUNDING SIMULTANEOUSLY MUST BE WRITTEN SO THAT A

VERTICAL LINE COULD BE DRAWN THROUGH THE HEADS OF THE NOTES.

Notes & rests
all line up
Correct vertical placement of notes
Piccolo
B♭ Clarinet
B♭ Clarinet
Bass
Clarinet
Trumpets
1
2
3
Trombones
1
2
3

Wrong! nothing lines up vertically

Piccolo
Bb Clarinet
Bb Clarinet
Bass Clarinet
Trumpets 2
Trombones 2

You will notice that the first preceeding example has notes lining up perfectly in a vertical manner, with the correct amount of bar space allowed for the corresponding rhythm, where as the second example is TOTALLY CONFUSING! NEVER write a score like this! SPACE BETWEEN NOTES IN A GIVEN BAR SHOULD ALWAYS BE PROPORTIONATE TO THEIR TIME VALUE.

3. Rest, Ties and Dotted Notes

Below are listed rhythmic notations and their corresponding durations of silence (known as rests).

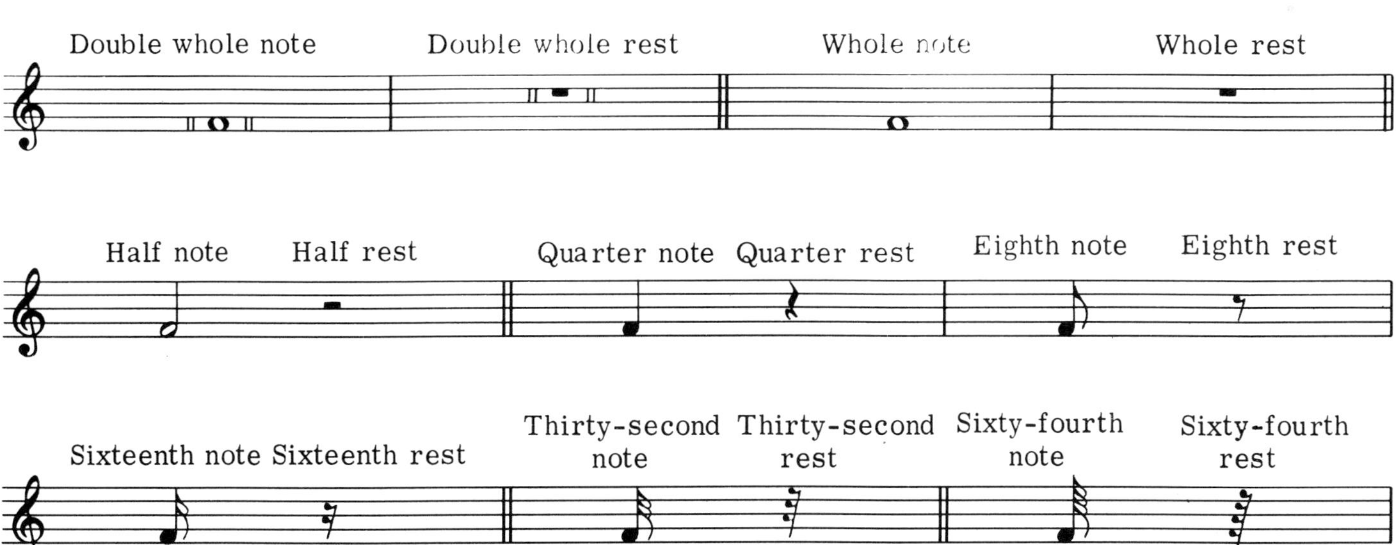

A WHOLE note equals two HALF NOTES or four QUARTER NOTES or eight EIGHTH NOTES or sixteen SIXTEENTH NOTES.

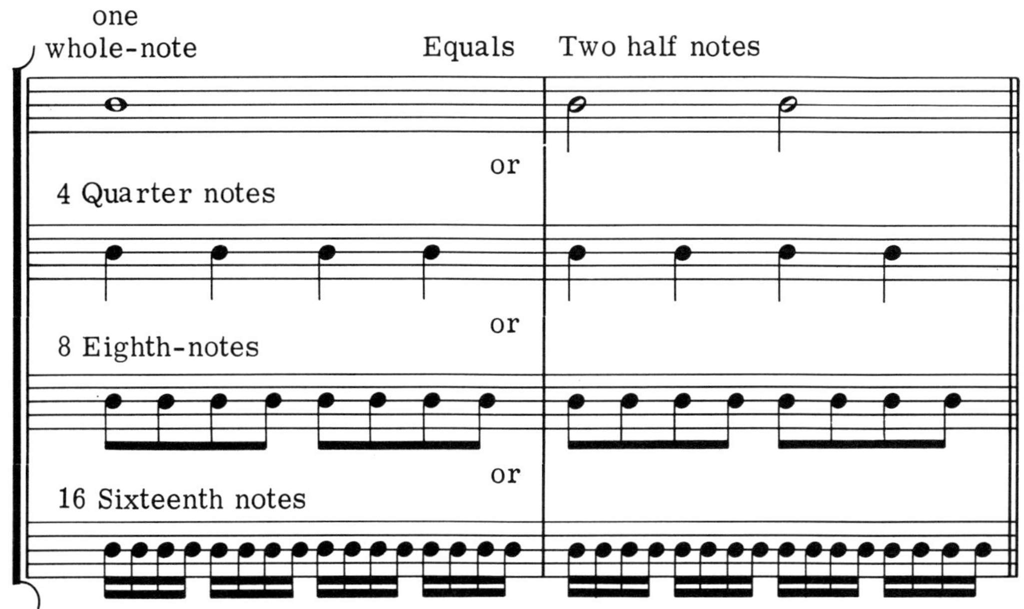

A Tie is acurved line which joins two notes of the same pitch. These two notes then sound as ONE PITCH. Thus, ♩♩ would sound as ♩ . A DOTTED NOTE: Placing a dot behind a note increases its value by one-half. ♩. = ♩♩♩

4. Intervals

An INTERVAL is the distance between two notes. The smallest interval in Western Music is the HALF-STEP (from C to C♯ would be a half-step). A WHOLE STEP is made up of two half-steps (from C to D would be whole step). Write above each of the following intervals if it is a HALF STEP or a WHOLE STEP.

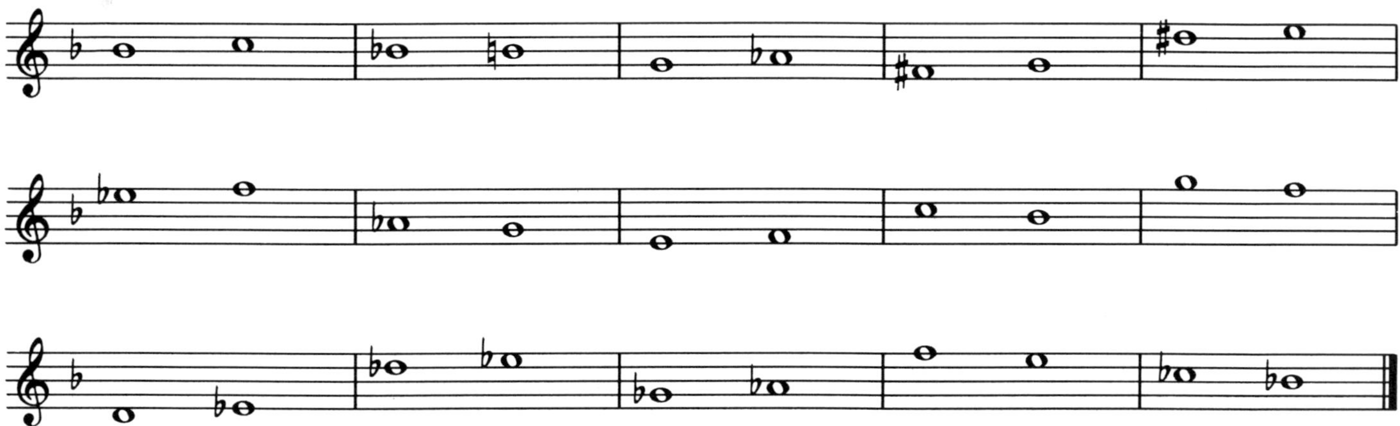

A. Interval Names

Intervals are named by the number of letter names within the interval. For instance, C up to G is a "fifth", as five letters are included within the interval: C, D, E, F, G. Intervals may be called major, minor, diminished, augmented and perfect. Here is an example of major, minor and perfect intervals as they relate to C.

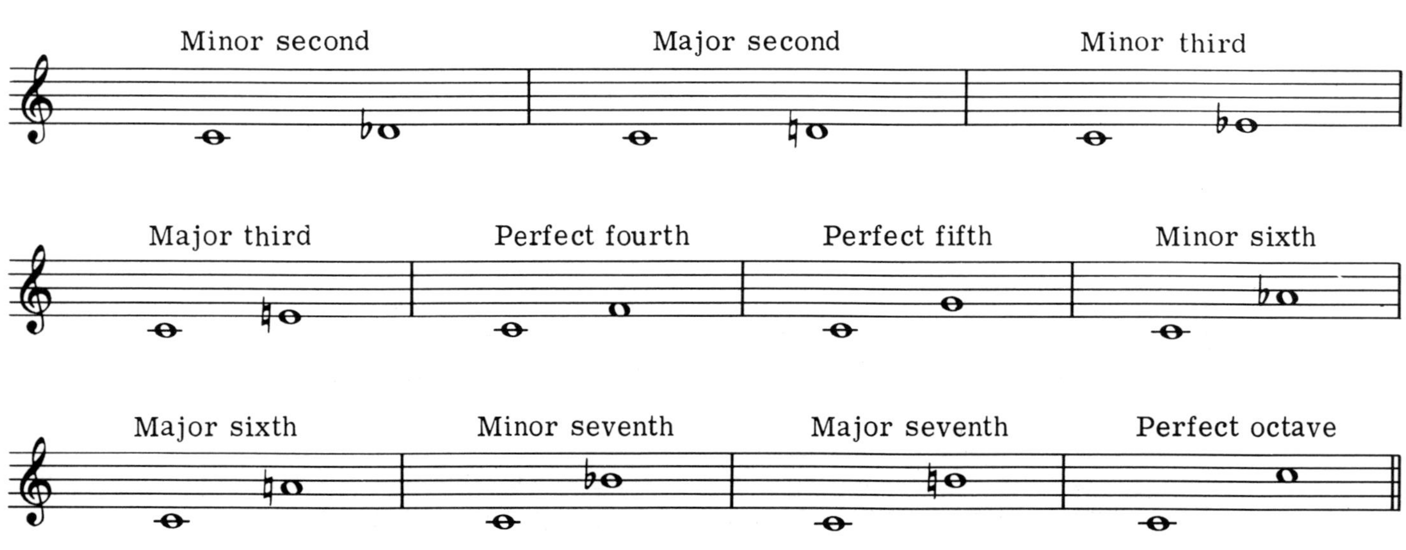

By inverting intervals (placing the lower note one octave higher or the higher note one octave lower), major intervals become minor while minor intervals become major. Perfect intervals remain "perfect".

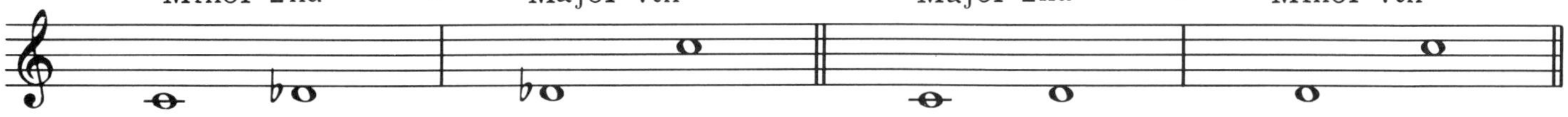

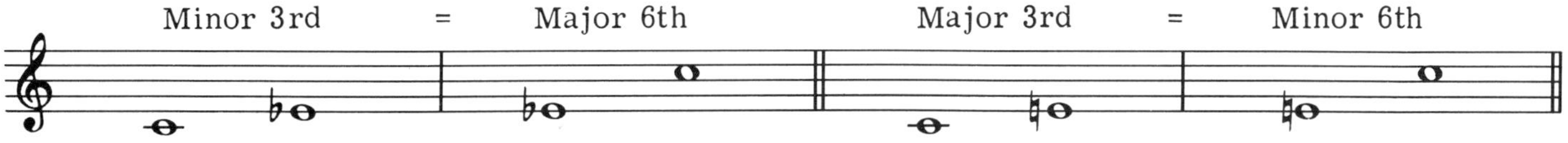

Interval Inversions

Minor 2nd = Major 7th | Major 2nd = Minor 7th

Minor 3rd = Major 6th | Major 3rd = Minor 6th

Perfect 4th = Perfect 5th | Perfect 5th = Perfect 4th

Minor 6th = Major 3rd | Major 6th = Minor 3rd

Minor 7th = Major 2nd | Major 7th = Minor 2nd | Perfect octave= Perfect prime

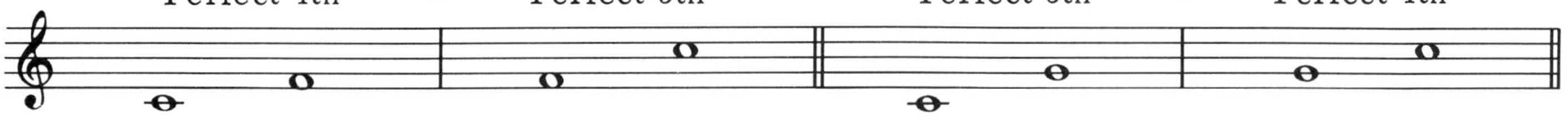

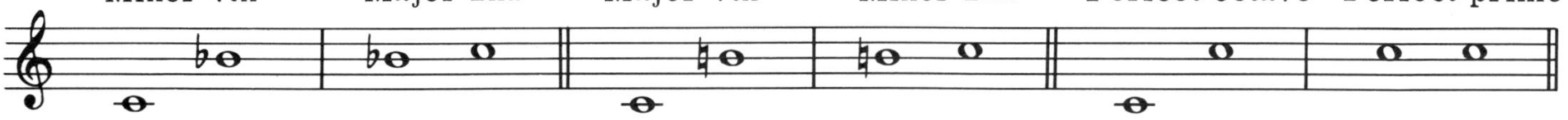

B. Intervals - A Review

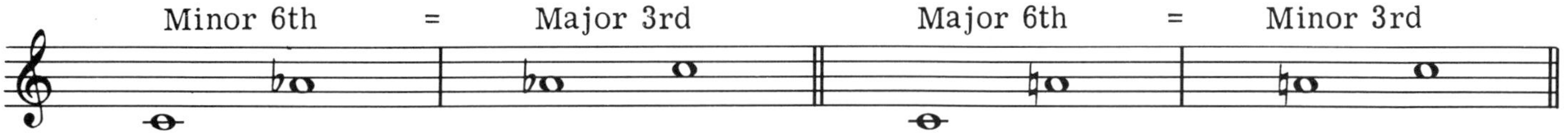

Again, an INTERVAL is the distance between two notes. The smallest interval is a HALF STEP, from one note to the next consecutive note.

1/2 step

Two half-steps make a WHOLE STEP.

Whole step

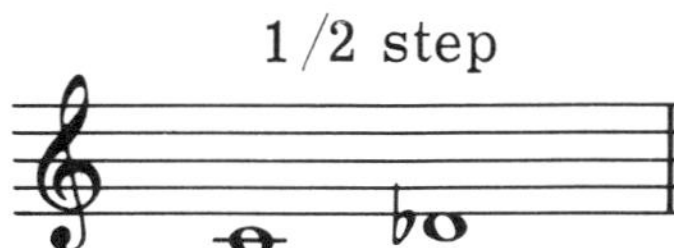

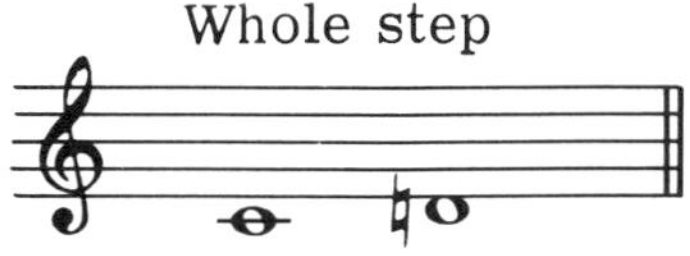

Interval distances are made up of the following half-step, whole step combinations:

> second - 1 whole step
>
> third - 2 whole steps
>
> fourth - 2 whole steps, 1 half-step
>
> fifth - 2 whole steps, 1 half-step, 1 whole step
>
> sixth - 2 whole steps, 1 half-step, 2 whole steps
>
> seventh - 2 whole steps, 1 half-step, 3 whole steps
>
> octave - 2 whole steps, 1 half-step, 3 whole steps, 1 half-step

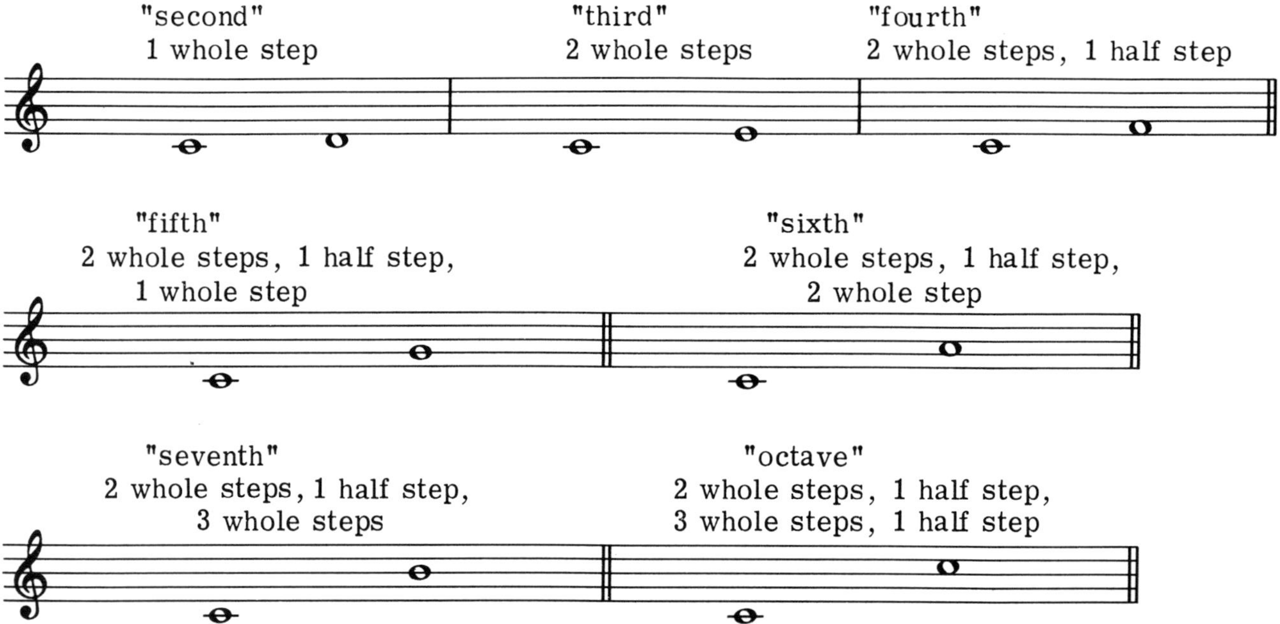

If we count up a C major scale using C as our starting point, we can thus learn interval distances. Look at the following example of intervals as they relate to a C major scale as well as the piano keyboard.

Intervals

one octave
6th
5th
3rd
2nd
4th
7th

Piano Keyboard
octave
7th
6th
2nd
3rd
4th
5th

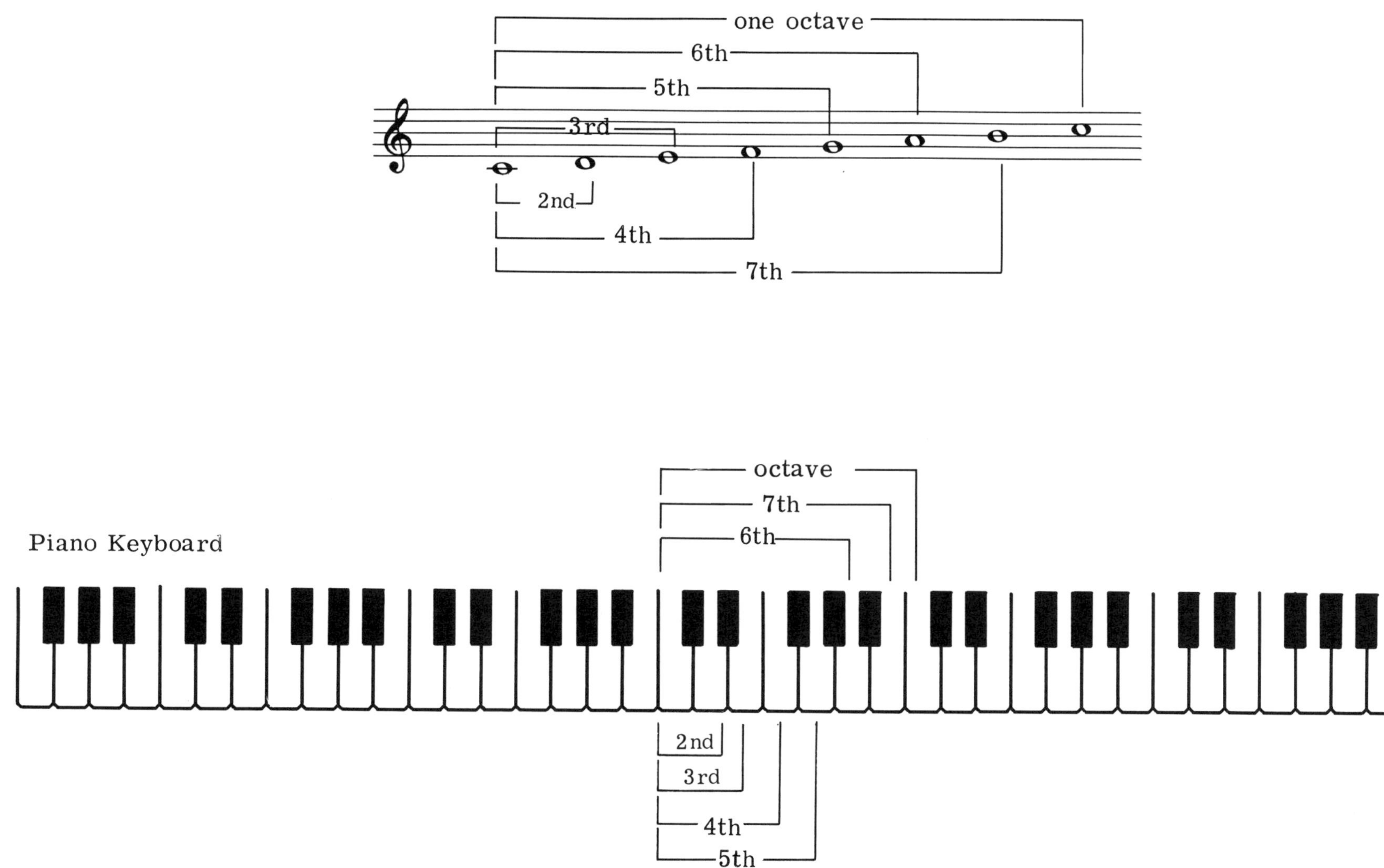

Exercise #2: Name the following intervals.

Exercise #2

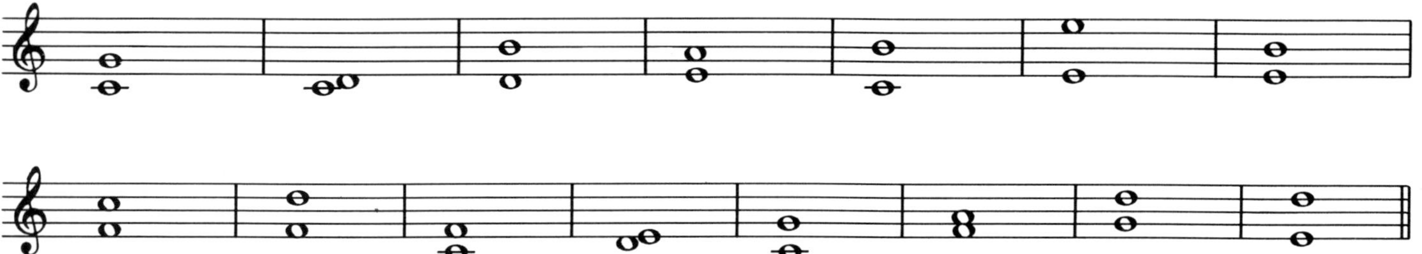

Play the preceeding intervals on the piano to begin to train your ear as to their sound.

Play them melodically first (from one note to the next), then play them harmonically

(both notes at the same time). You should soon begin to recognize intervals both melodically

and harmonically.

Major and Minor Intervals:

We have seen that to go from a C to E is an interval of a third. This interval is called a

MAJOR THIRD.

If we were to flat the E, we would be taking our major third interval and

making it a MINOR THIRD.

The half-step, whole step relationship then in a MINOR THIRD would be:

whole step, half-step

Thus, to: flat a major second interval would make a MINOR SECOND

flat a major third interval would make a MINOR THIRD

flat a major sixth interval would make a MINOR SIXTH

flat a major seventh interval would make a MINOR SEVENTH

The intervals of seconds, thirds, sixths and sevenths are considered either MAJOR or MINOR.

Diminished Intervals:

To alter fourths or fifths by flatting them, we would then call those intervals DIMINISHED. Thus,

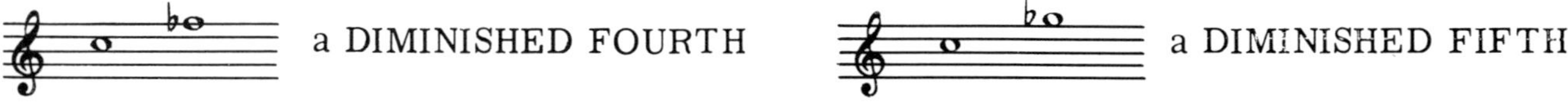

a DIMINISHED FOURTH   a DIMINISHED FIFTH

Augmented Intervals:

TO AUGMENT an interval means to SHARP the interval.

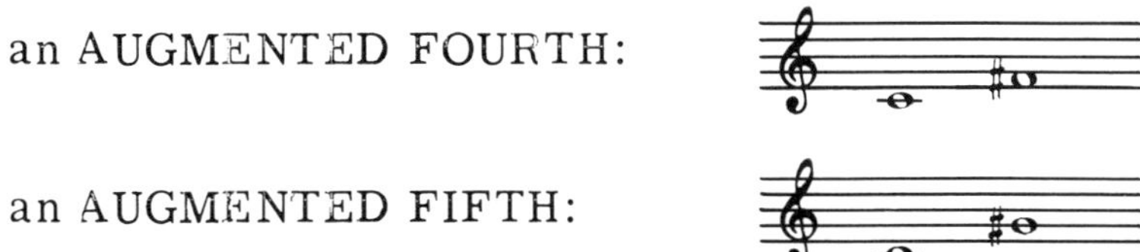

If we were to AUGMENT one of the other intervals, we would be creating a new interval.
For example, to AUGMENT a third (C to E), we would be creating a fourth (C to E♯ or,
enharmonically C to F). Enharmonic means "the other name" for the same note. Example
of enharmonic notes: E♯ or F, G♯ or A♭, A♯ or B♭, B♯ or C, C♭ or B, F♯ or G♭, C♯ or D♭,
D♯ or E♭. Consequently, if we were to AUGMENT intervals of a third, sixth or seventh,
we would ENHARMONICALLY be creating other intervals.

Compound Intervals:

Intervals that occur beyond an octave are called COMPOUND INTERVALS. They are called
by a new name, although they are repetitions of intervals within the first octave but,
because they occur IN ADDITION TO one octave, their name changes. For example, even
though C to D is an interval of a SECOND, because we go from C to D over an octave higher,
we call this interval a NINTH.

In other words, to count up a C major scale NINE places, from C to D would be the interval
of a NINTH. In a C scale then, COMPOUND intervals would look like this:

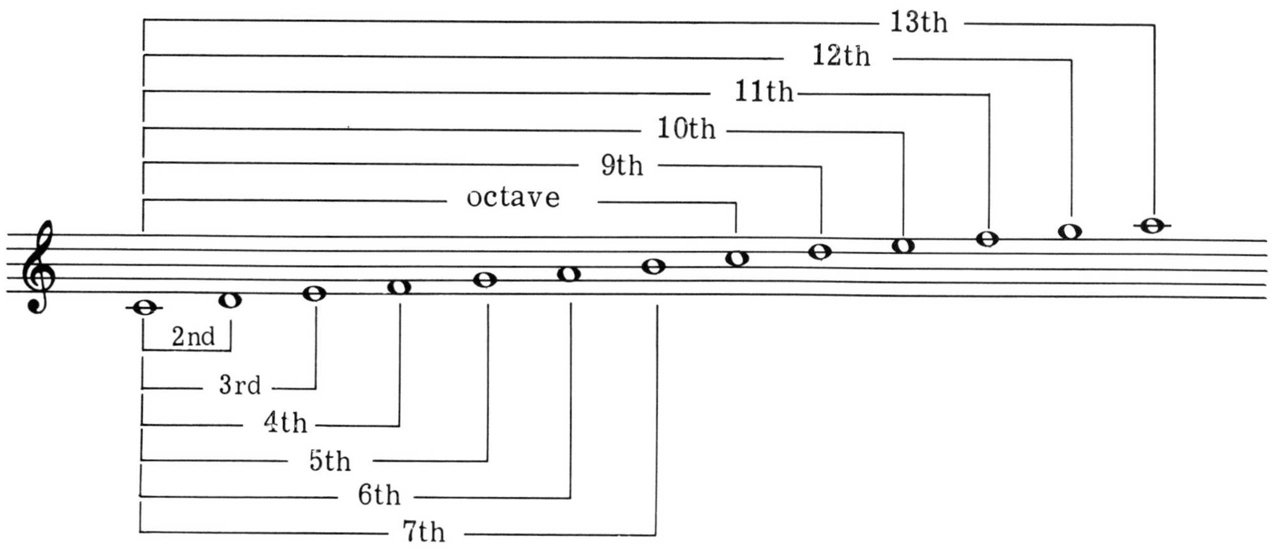

Generally, the most prevelant COMPOUND INTERVALS which you will deal with as an arranger/orchestrator will be NINTHS, ELEVENTHS and THIRTEENTHS.

Exercise #3: Name the following intervals:

Exercise #3

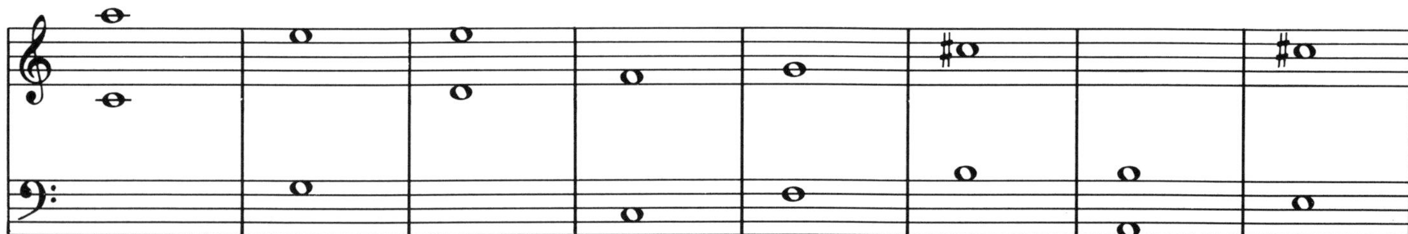

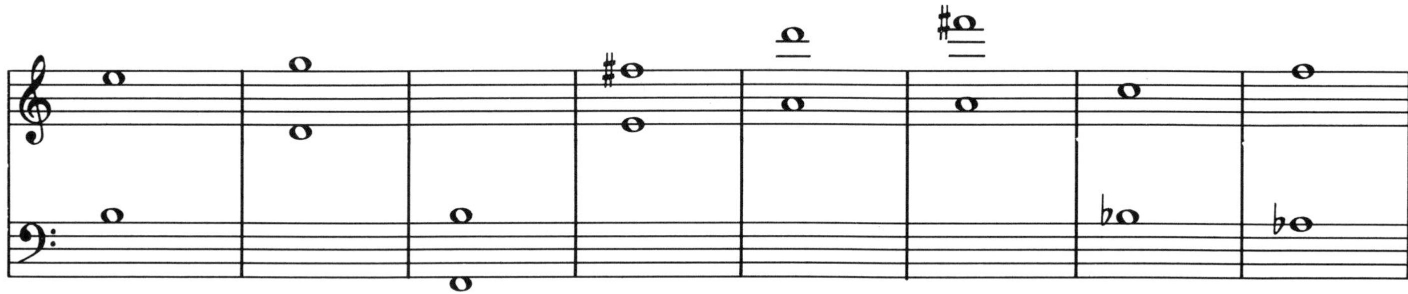

5. Scales

A scale is a series of half-steps and whole steps in different configurations. Here is the breakdown of a MAJOR SCALE.

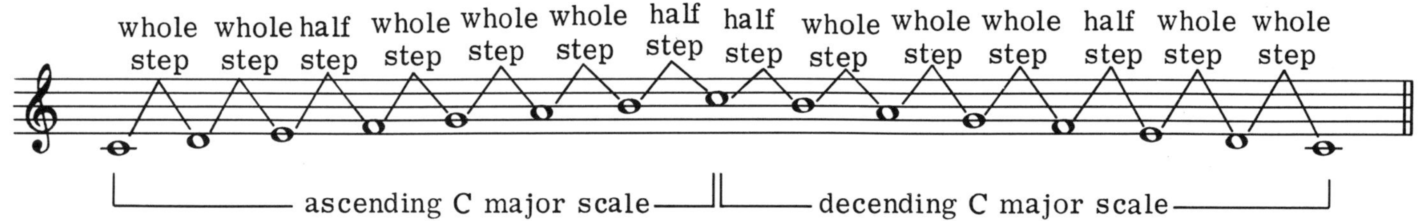

There are THREE types of MINOR SCALES:

Pure Minor

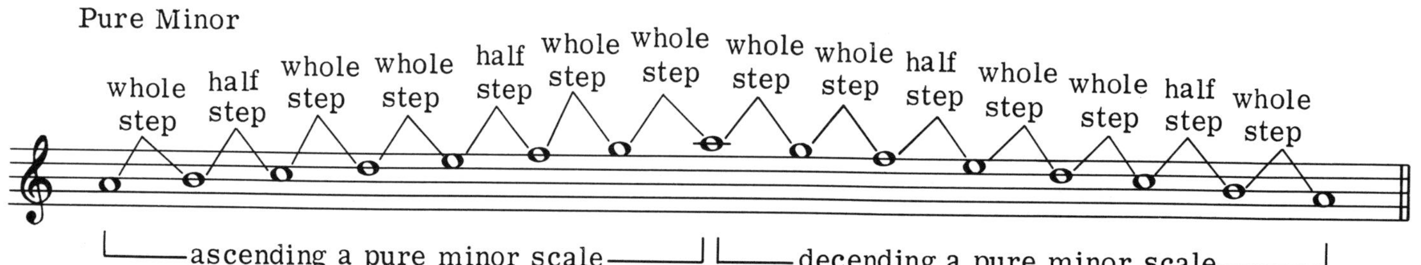

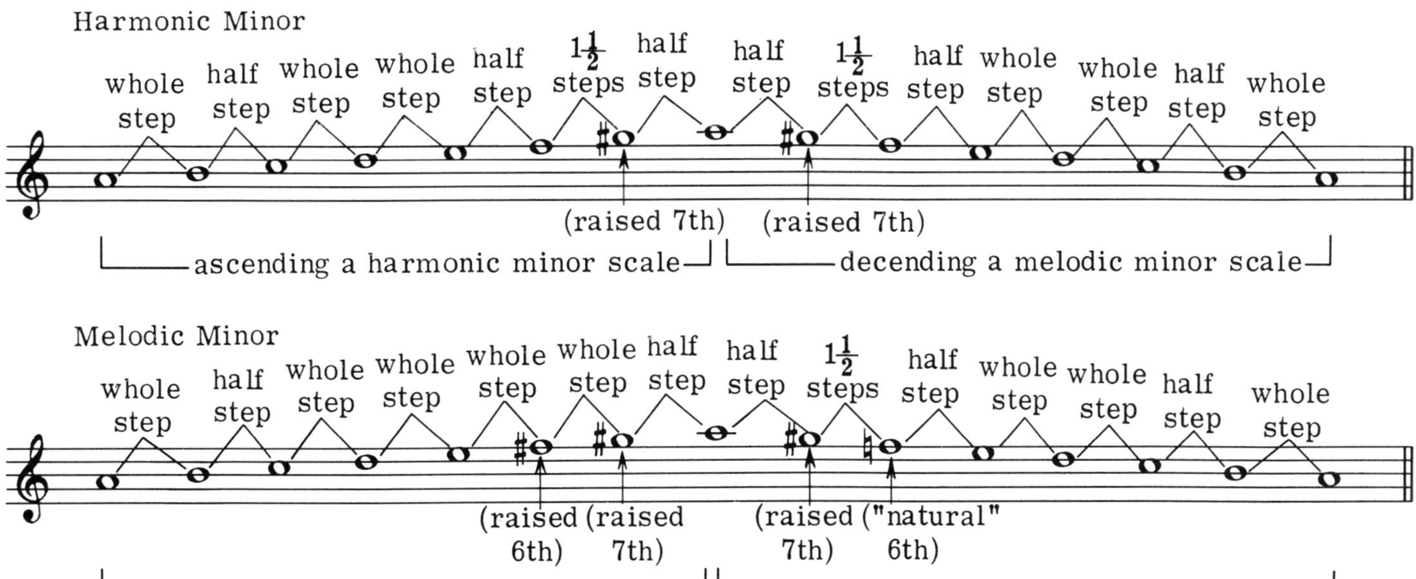

As you can see in the preceeding example, the pure minor scale is altered to make the harmonic minor (by raising the 7th scale step) and the melodic minor (by raising the 6th and 7th in ascending form but only the 7th in descending form).

6. Key Signatures

A key signature is the instruction placed at the beginning of a piece of music which indicates which notes are to be SHARPED (raised) or FLATTED (lowered). The key signature for the C MAJOR SCALE (and thus the key of C) is NO SHARPS OR FLATS. It has a RELATIVE MINOR key, that being the key of A MINOR, which uses the same key signature (no sharps or flats). Below are listed the other 14 MAJOR KEYS with each one's corresponding RELATIVE MINOR KEY. A relative minor key has the same key signature as its relative major key.

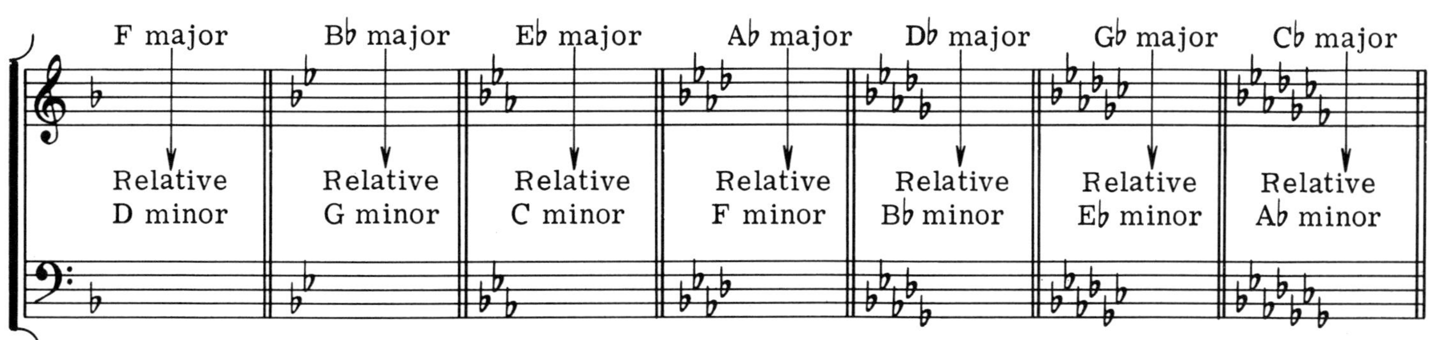

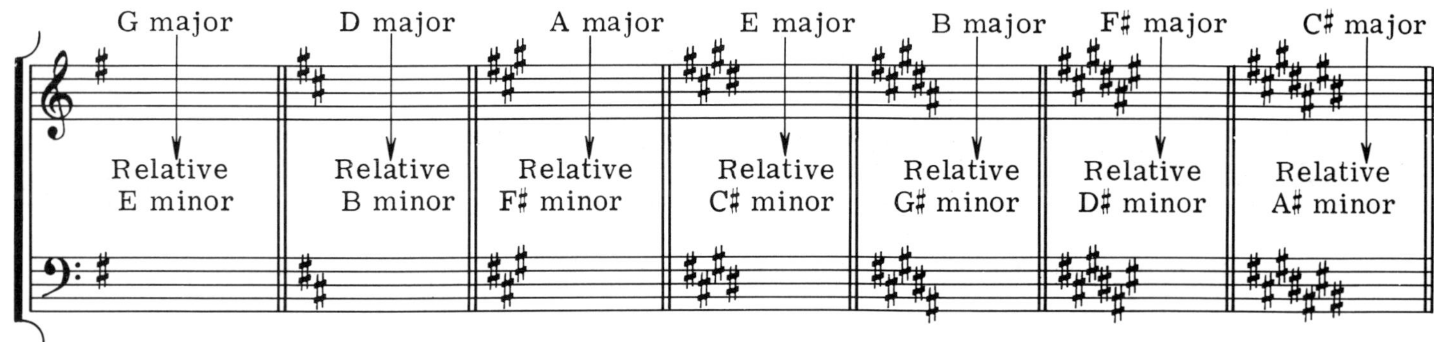

PARALLEL KEYS are different major and minor keys with the same letter name (Example: D major and D minor).

7. Time Signatures

Time signatures are found at the beginning of a piece of music and may occur throughout it as well. They consist of two numbers, one over the other. The BOTTOM number denotes the "kind of note" getting the beat (count) while the TOP number denotes "how many" of these beats occur in each bar. TEMPO is the speed at which these counts or beats occur.

Two quarter notes per bar with the quarter note receiving the beat.

Three quarter notes per bar with the quarter note receiving the beat.

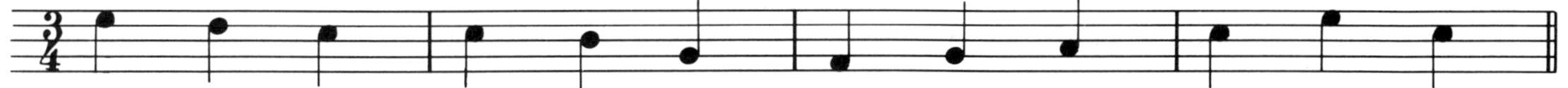

Four quarter notes to the bar with the quarter note receiving the beat.

Five quarter notes to the bar with the quarter note receiving the beat.

In the preceeding example, the QUARTER NOTE ♩ received the beat (count). A HALF NOTE ♩ would equal TWO quarter notes and receive TWO COUNTS. A WHOLE NOTE o would equal FOUR quarter notes and receive FOUR counts. An EIGHTH NOTE ♪ would equal ONE HALF of a quarter note count, thus there would be two eighth notes in one beat in a time signature of 4. A SIXTEENTH NOTE ♪ would equal ONE FOURTH of a

quarter note count, thus there would be four sixteenth notes to a beat in a time signature

of 4. There are many times when time signatures contain notes OTHER than quarter notes

that are the unit of beat (unit of count). Here are a few examples:

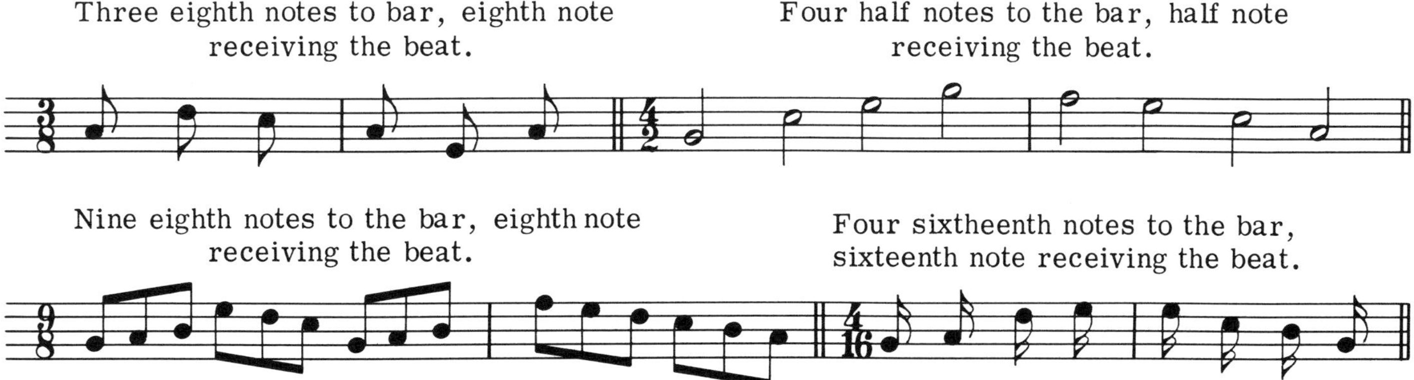

Duple and Triple Time Signatures:

Time signatures which contain THREE BEATS (or multiples of three) in each bar of music

are said to be in TRIPLE TIME. Time signatures which contain TWO BEATS per bar (or

multiples of 2) are said to be in DUPLE TIME.

8. Scale Degree Names

The major scale (as we have seen) consists of 8 notes. We will now number and name

each scale step.

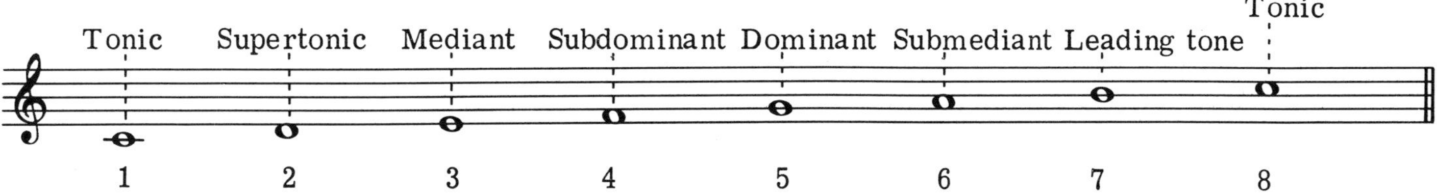

9. Chords

Chords are groups of notes which are sounded together or in rapid succession (as in

arpeggios or broken chords).

Triads:

Triads are chords consisting of three different notes and are spelled in thirds. If we took

a major scale and built triads on each scale step, they would thus be numbered and named

like this. Notice major triads use large Roman numerals while minor triads use lower

case Roman numerals.

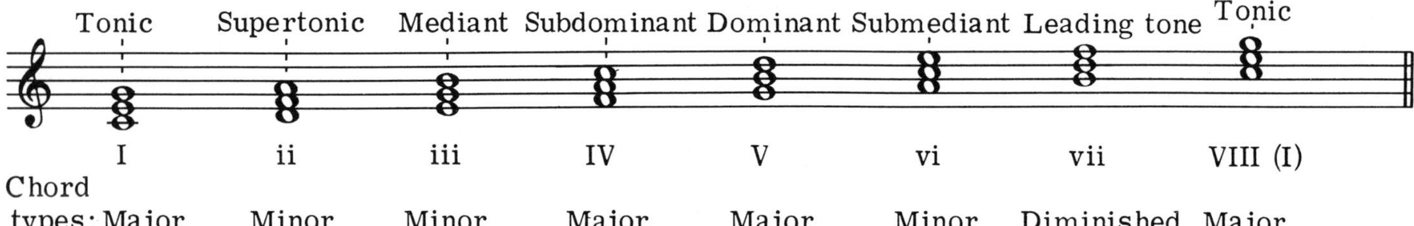

Notice the above example contains notes which are ONLY from the key signature (there are no accidentals, no sharps or flats). These notes (and triads) are called DIATONIC. If sharps or flats (accidentals) were used in the make-up of any of these triads, the chords would then contain CHROMATIC notes.

10. Voice Leading Principles

Voice Leading is that name given to the technique of creating SMOOTH and LOGICAL melodies or parts for different instruments or voices to execute. For instance, difficult rhythms coupled with consecutive awkward skips can create bad voice leading.

Example of bad voice leading

Good Voice Leading would consist of smooth interval relationships (often times scale-wise or chromatic). If large skips are written, then scale-wise or chromatic intervals should follow.

Example of good voice leading

The best kind of Voice Leading is that which creates a melody which would stand and "musically" make sense by itself. Voice leading which would create "un-musical" or awkward sounding melodies when played alone should be avoided, for if these "awkward" sounding parts (melodies) are combined with other parts (melodies), usually "un-musical" and awkward sounding ensemble writing is the result. Strive to always create GOOD, MUSICAL VOICE LEADING!

REVIEW AND EXERCISES

Complete the following exercises as a review to the principles of fundamental music
theory. After working the exercises, check the appendix to see if you have completed
the exercise correctly.

Exercise #4

Draw the following clefs, naming each's lines & spaces

Bass clef   Tenor clef

Treble clef   Alto clef

Exercise #5

Write a triple time signature and fill in the proper amount of notes

Write a duple time signature and fill in the proper amount of notes

Write a nine/eight time signature and fill in the proper amount of notes

Write a four/four time signature and fill in the proper amount of notes

Write a two/four time signature and fill in the proper amount of notes

Exercise #6

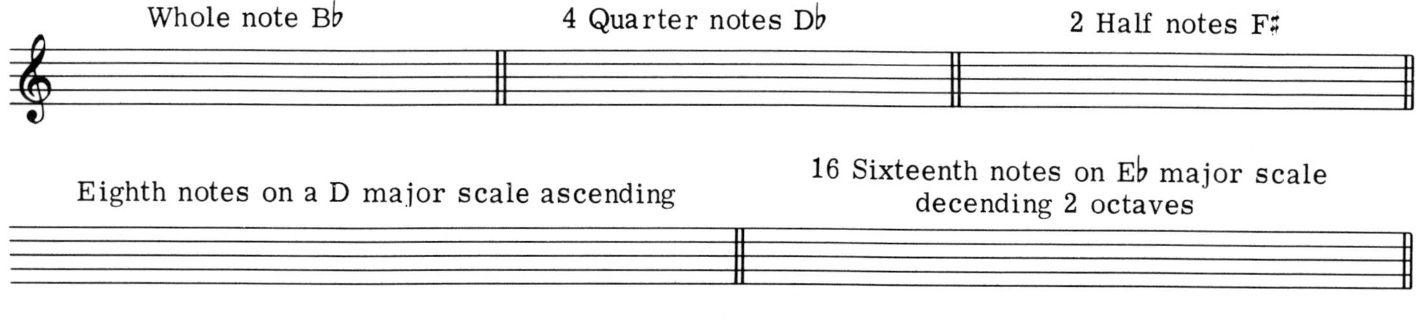

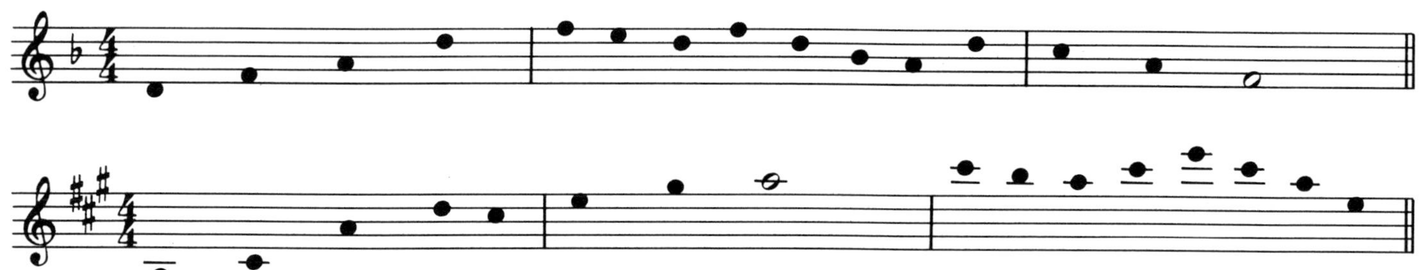

Place stems on the following melody

Exercise ♯7

Fill in the proper rest
Whole rest
Equals
Equals
Fill in the following
Equals
Equals
Equals____Beats
Equals____Beats
Equals____Beat

Exercise #8

Write the following intervals <u>above</u> the following pitches.

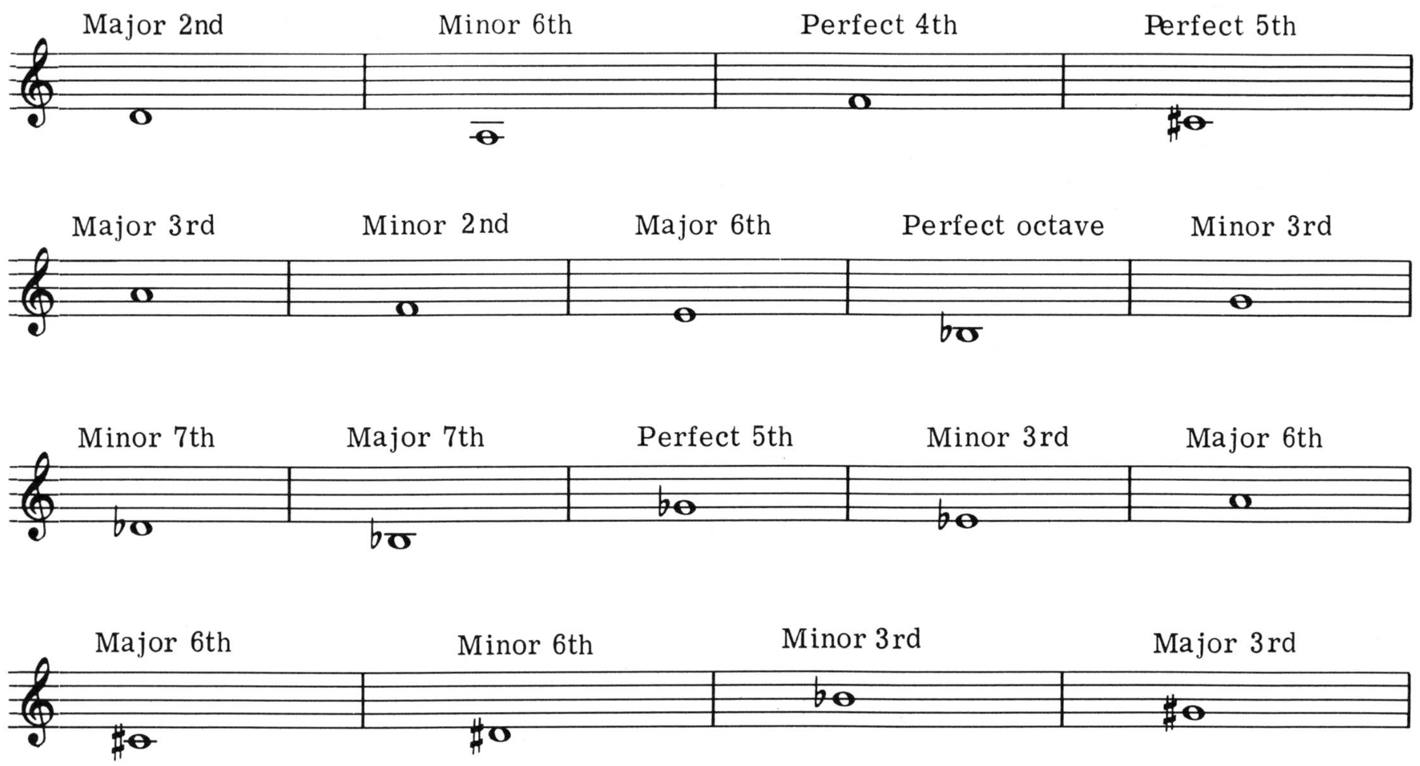

Write the following intervals <u>below</u> the following pitches.

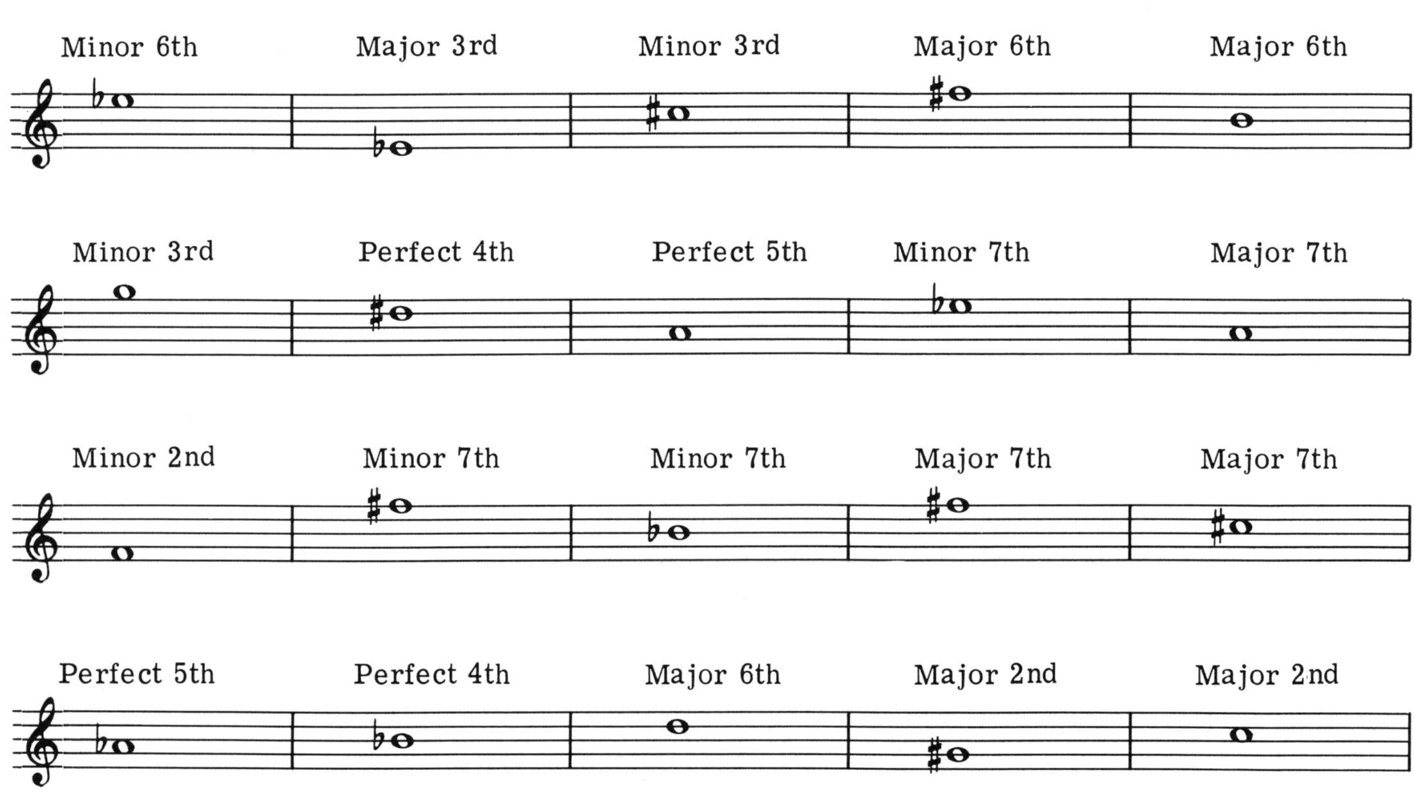

Exercise #9

Invert and name the following intervals.

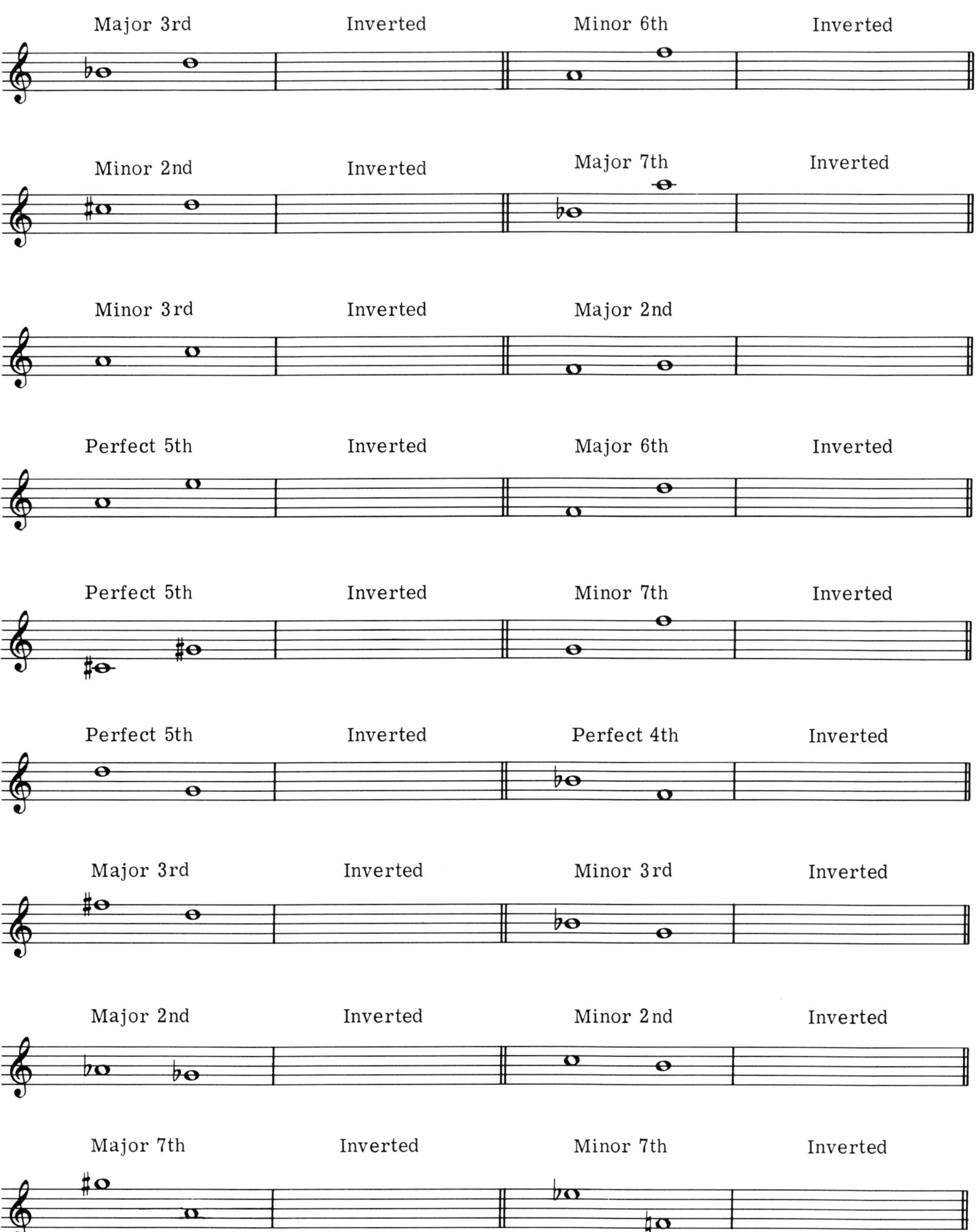

Exercise #10

Fill in the proper key signatures

F# major   B♭ major   D major   F major   G major

E♭ major   C# major   A♭ major   D♭ major   A major

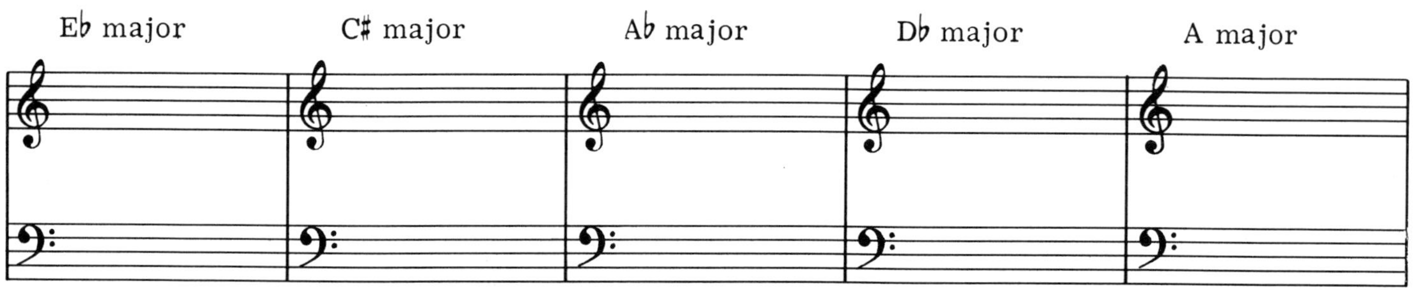

G♭ major   B major   C♭ major   E major   D minor

F minor   A minor   B♭ minor   F# minor   A♭ minor

G minor   E minor   E♭ minor   B minor   C# minor

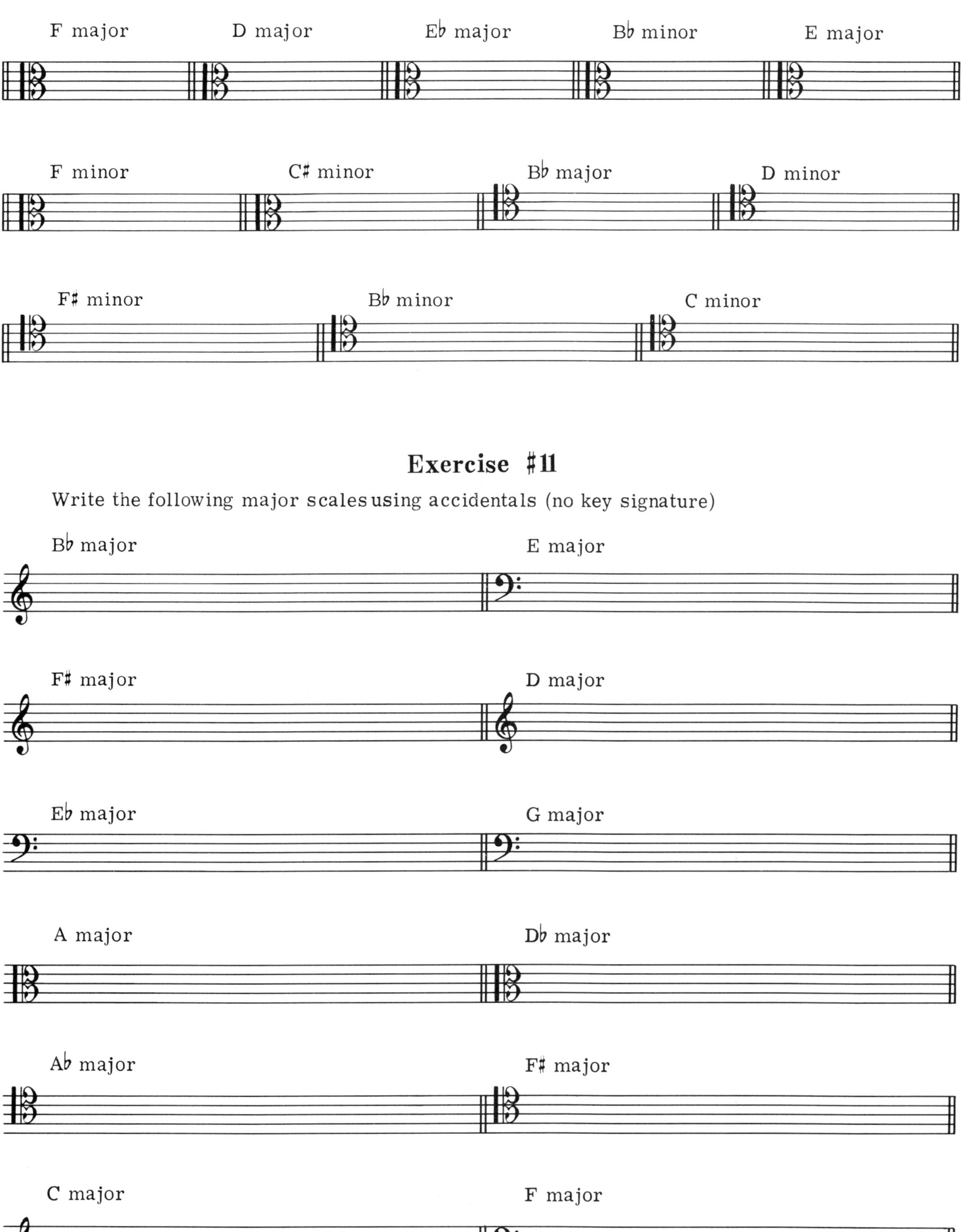

Exercise #11

Write the following major scales using accidentals (no key signature)

Write the following minor scales ascending & decending

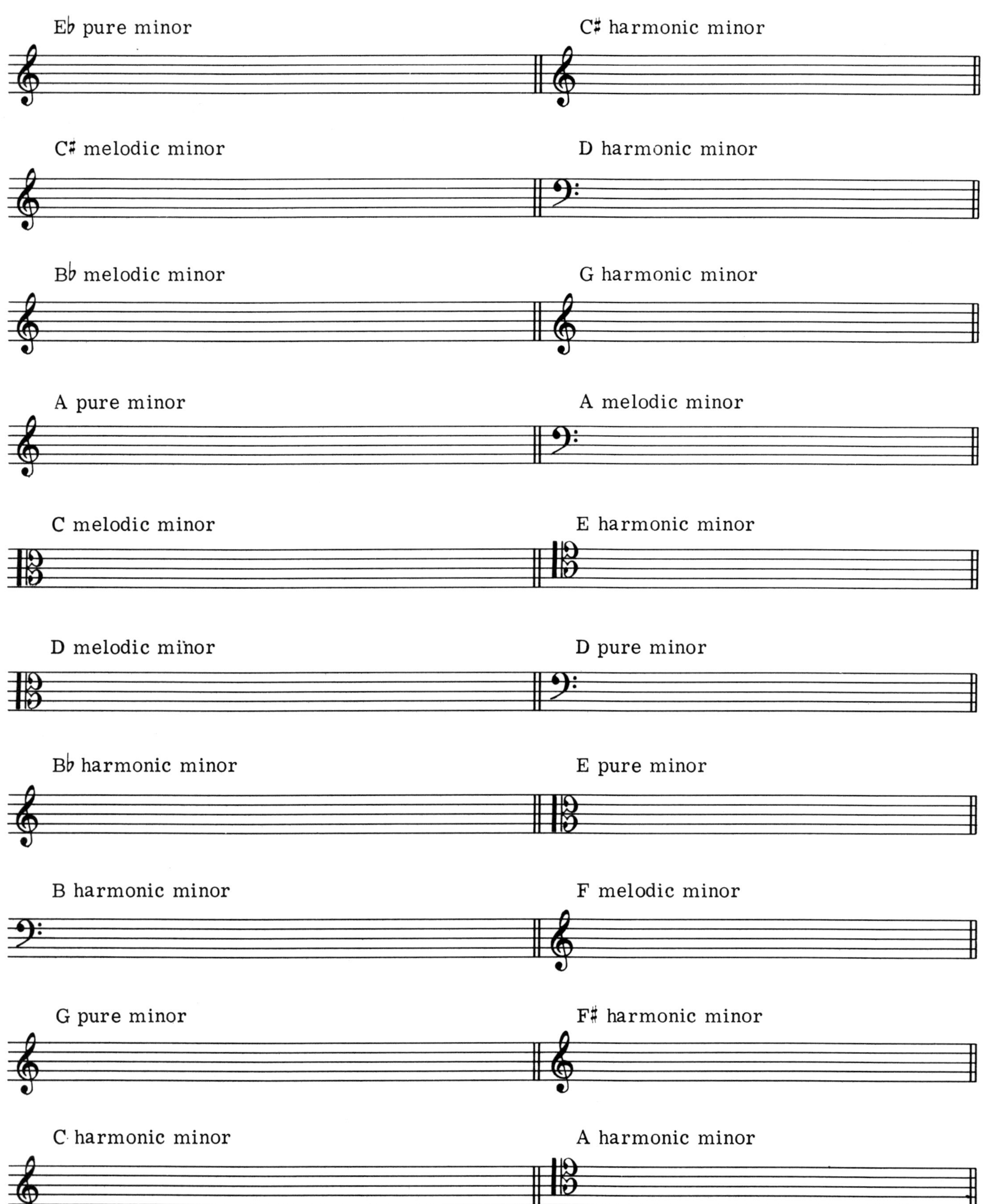

Exercise #12

Number and name the following scale step degrees according to the major key signature
for each.

Exercise #13

Name and write the scale step number according to the major key signature for each and
tell how each functions (major, minor, diminished, etc.)

11. The Inversion and Progression of Diatonic Triads

Triad Inversion:

To invert a triad means to put the notes in a DIFFERENT ORDER from those naturally

occuring in their scale-wise diatonic spelling. For instance, here are the seven ROOT

POSITION diatonic triads occuring in the key of C major.

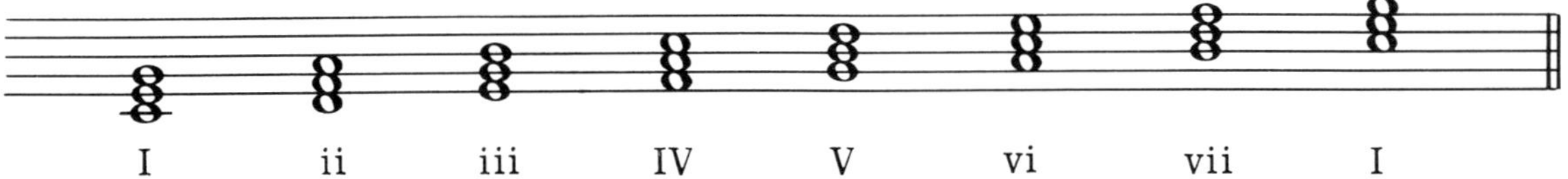

The preceeding triads are in ROOT POSITION, meaning the "root" note of the chord (the

note above which thirds are placed to make the triad) is the bottom note in the chord voicing.

The following example shows a C major diatonic triad in ROOT POSITION with its two

other inversions. The first inversion is with the third in the bottom. The second inversion

is with the "fifth" in the bottom (the third is an interval of a "third" away from the C root

and the "fifth" is a fifth away from the C root).

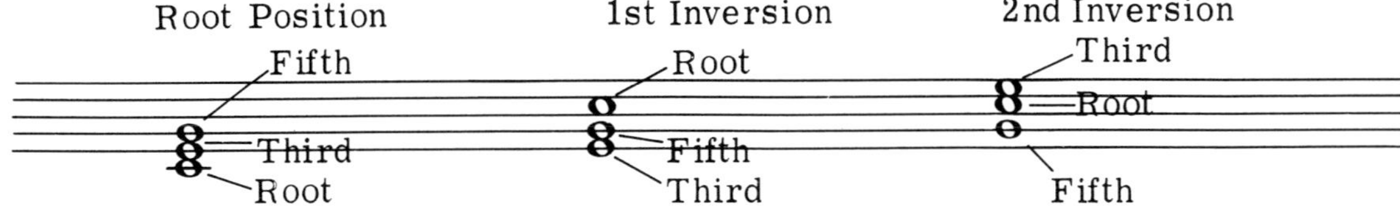

COMPLETE THE FOLLOWING EXERCISE, FILLING IN THE "MISSING" NOTE TO
COMPLETE THE INVERSION SPELLING.

Exercise #14

Diatonic Triad Progression:

Harmonic movement of diatonic triads follows accepted patterns which have come about through hundreds of years of practice in Western Music. We are going to explore several chord progressions of diatonic triads. Study each, then PLAY each one on the piano, so that you can both HEAR the progression as well as intellectually PERCEIVE the progression.

The preceeding harmonic progressions are the most basic in Western Music. But until the fundamental concepts of this "pure" harmonic movement is learned and understood, more advanced progressions will be illusive. As you may have observed in the preceeding example, the V chord (dominant) almost always "leads us to" the I chord (tonic). The Tonic Chord in a key thus represents "home base" while the dominant chord has a tendency to want to "move on", usually to tonic. You should also have noticed that the ii and IV chords have a tendency to progress to the V Chord (dominant) which, in turn, usually progresses to the "gravity" of the key center (the tonic chord). This return to "home base" (tonic chord) is referred to as a CADENCE POINT (or a resting point in a chord progression where the tendency is NOT to "move on").

Here are some additional progressions. Write them out AND play them on the piano, as they are fundamental chord progressions which we must know and understand before we go on with our study of arranging and orchestration.

I ii iii IV V I —In the key of B♭ major

I iii ii V I IV V I —In the key of D major

iii iv iii vi IV V I vi ii V I —In the key of A♭ major

ii vii I vi IV V vi iii IV V I —In the key of E major

12. The Cycle of Fifths

As we previously discussed, the progression from Dominant to Tonic is probably the strongest in music. But what if our tonic harmony became dominant harmony to another tonic, which became dominant to another tonic, which became dominant to another tonic and so on? This would obviously be a "strong" chord progression, by the very nature of DOMINANT to TONIC. This progression is thus known as the CYCLE OF FIFTHS.

Study and play the following exercise to more fully understand the CYCLE OF FIFTHS.

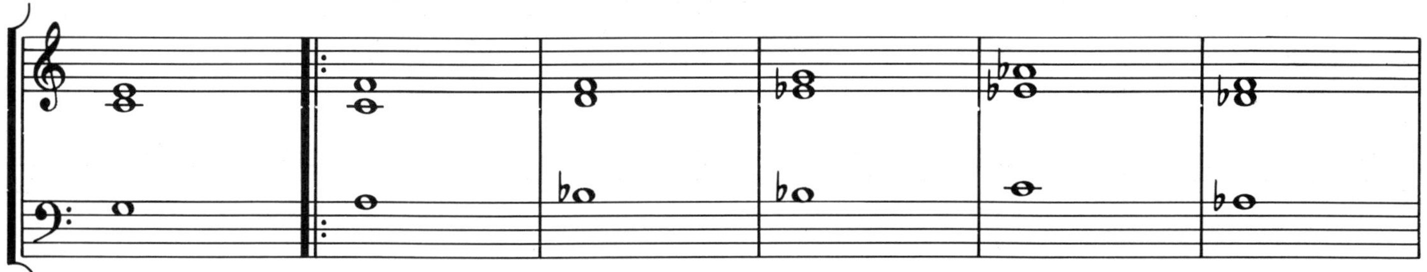

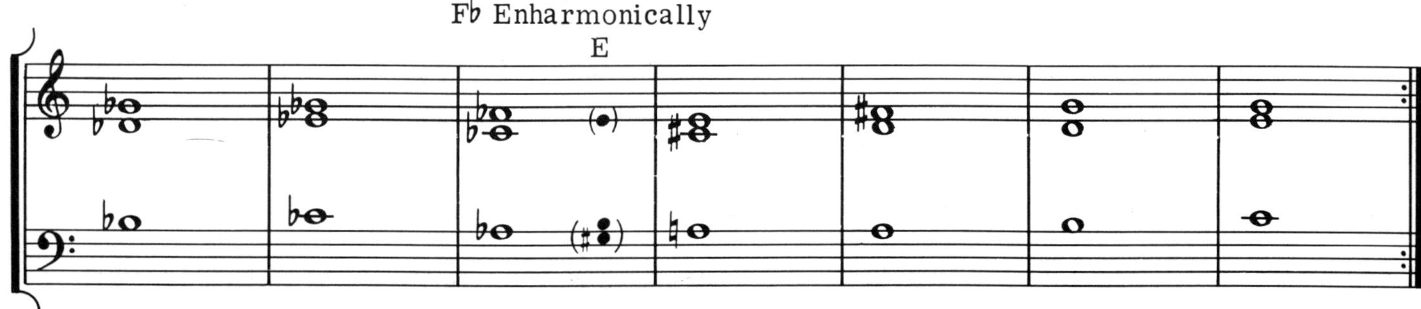

As you can see by the preceeding illustration, the CYCLE OF FIFTHS is an ever going "circular" progression (it would keep repeating over and over). It could thus be illustrated by the following diagram:

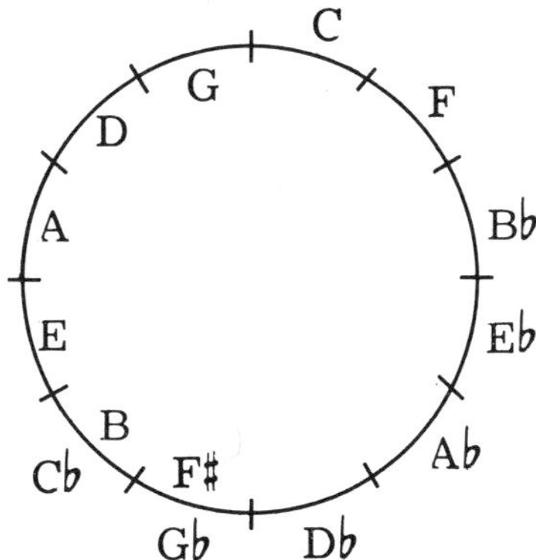

As you can see, we go ENHARMONICALLY from Gb to F#. The CYCLE OF FIFTHS is a very important progression to understand, as many popular **songs** as well as "classical" music is based on its progression. Of course, the entire "cycle" is not completed in the harmonic progression of compositions, but a goodly portion of it can be found in much of the music we all know and love.

Exercise #15

Fill in the following circles with the cycle of fifths.

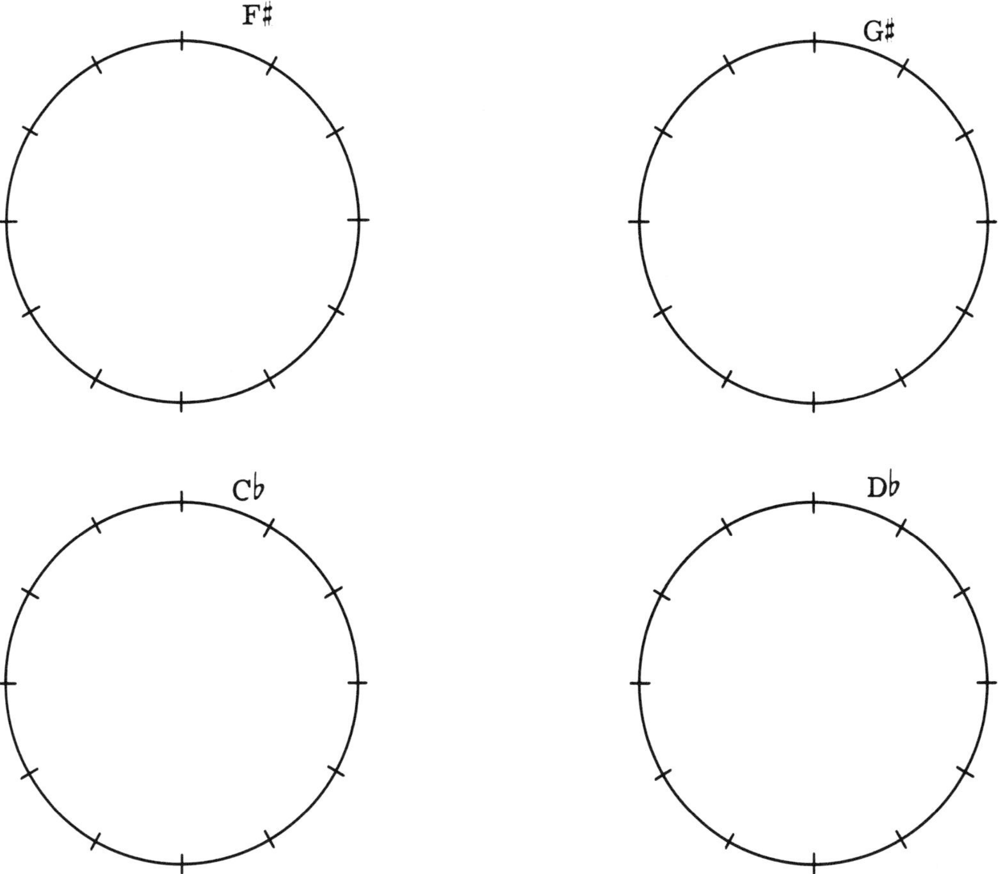

Chromatic Progression of Chords:

By having chords move us from one key to another, we go through a series of CHROMATIC chord progressions, progressions NOT made up entirely of DIATONIC CHORDS.

The following would be an example of CHROMATIC CHORDS taking us through different KEY CENTERS. Study it carefully, then play it (slowly if necessary) on the piano to understand its make-up and harmonic relationships.

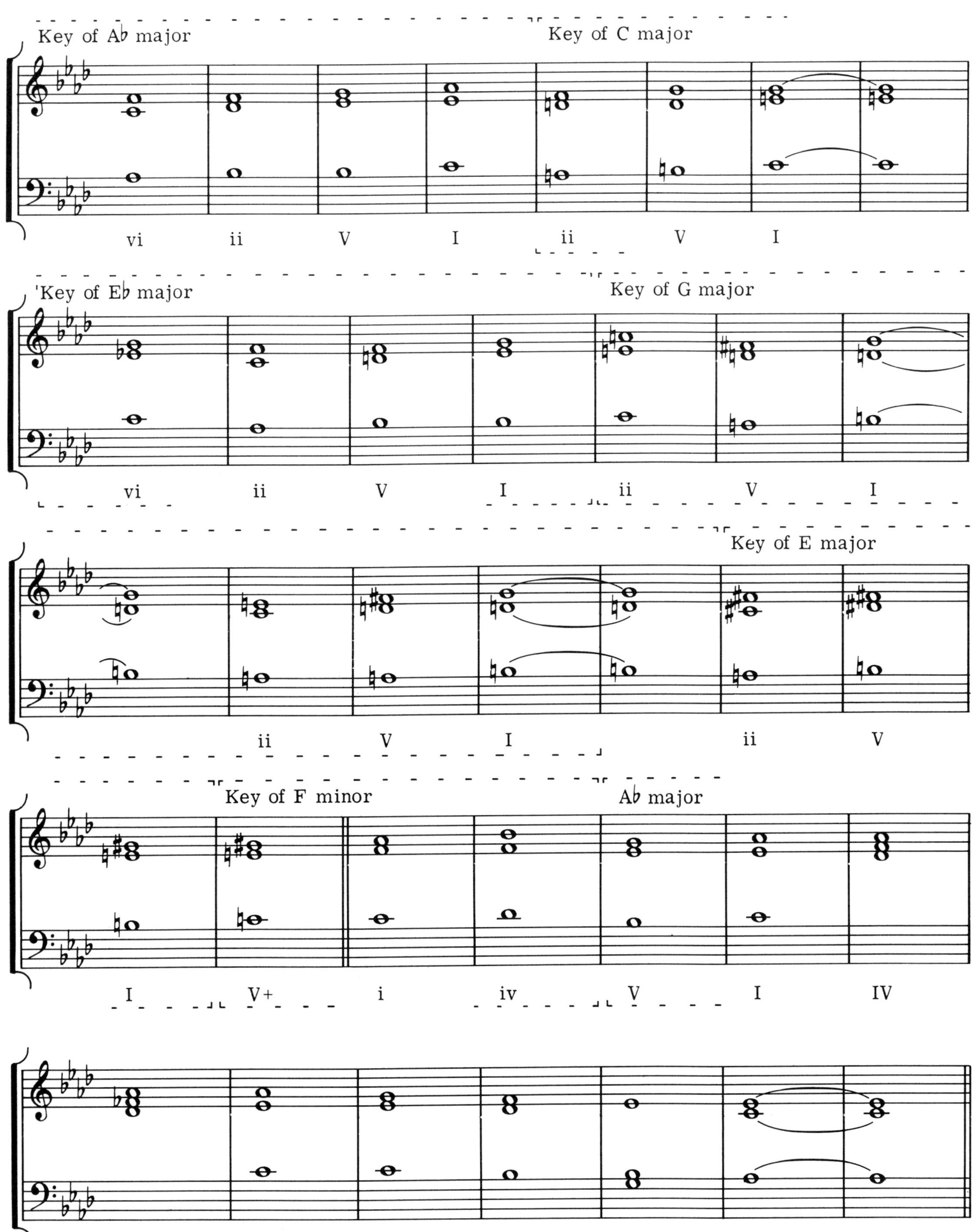

Key of Ab major
Key of C major
vi   ii   V   I   ii   V   I
Key of Eb major
Key of G major
vi   ii   V   I   ii   V   I
Key of E major
ii   V   I   ii   V
Key of F minor
Ab major
I   V+   i   iv   V   I   IV
iv   I   iii   ii   V   I

Even though the preceeding progression contains many CHROMATIC chords (not of the diatonic key), it is fairly simple to understand if we continually consider the MODUAL-TION of a new key to be the guideline for a "diatonic progression". CHROMATIC CHORDS are thus those chords which appear in a harmonic progression that are NOT from the diatonic (unaltered in terms of accidentals) key. Chords from the cycle of fifths would thus be chromatic chords after the initial progression of a fifth.

Exercise #16

Circle any chords chromatic to the key signature.

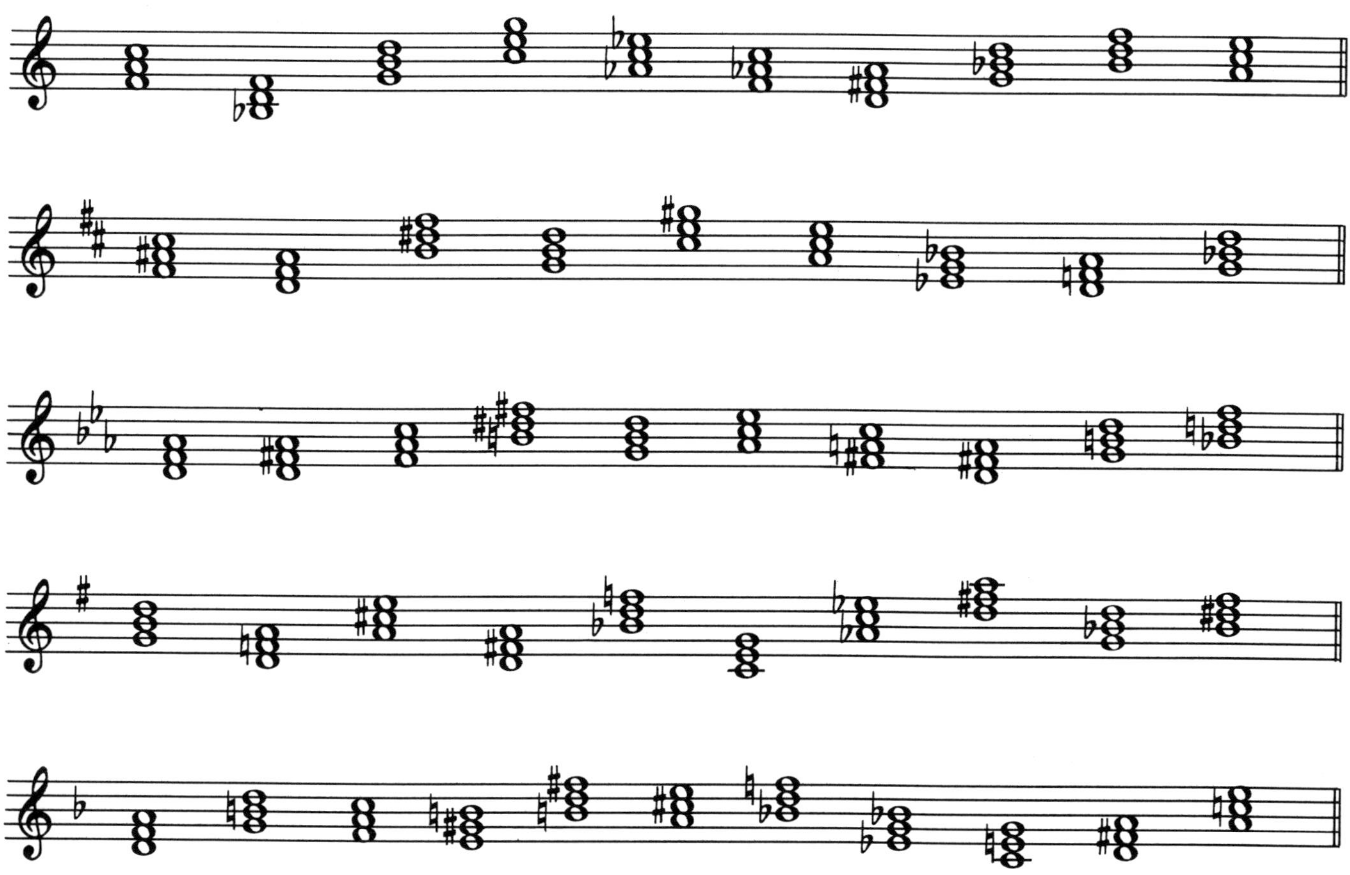

13. Harmonic Extensions and Chord Spellings

Once again I would like to draw your attention to the C major scale (two octaves) with its component members being numbered from the first note upward.

We have previously defined a triad as a 3 note chord built in thirds. Thus, in order to build a C major triad, we would combine the 1st, 3rd and 5th notes of the C major scale (C, E and G).

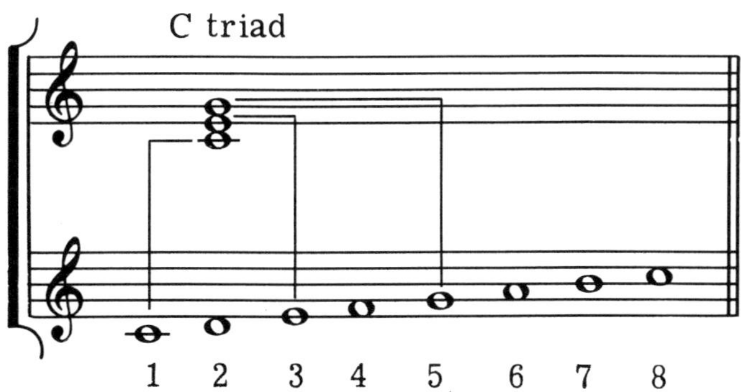

If we were to add the 6th note from the C major scale to the C major triad, we would thus build a C6th chord.

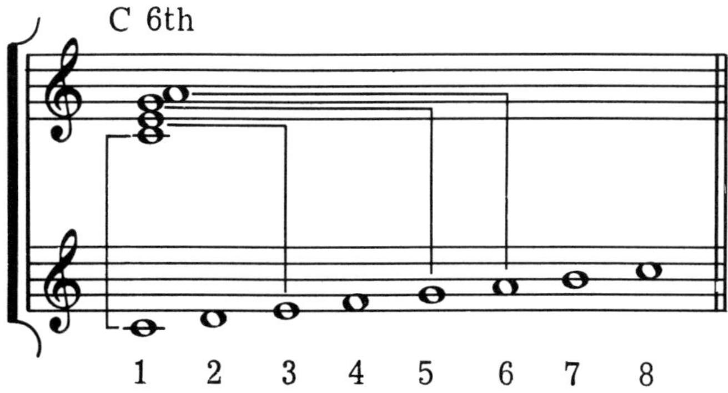

If we added the interval of a major 7th (which is the 7th scale step) to our C major triad, we would then have a C Maj 7th chord.

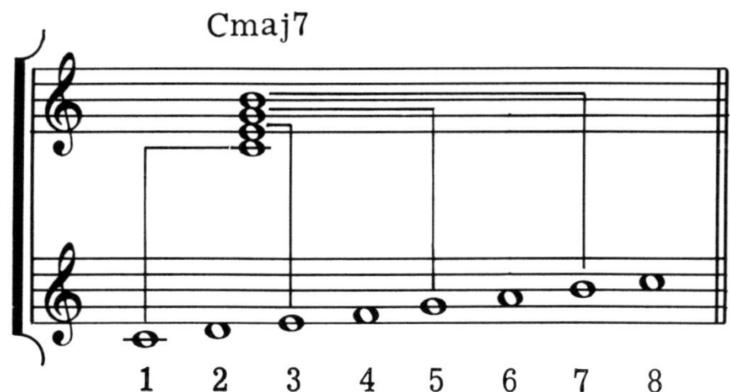

If we were to add the 9th scale step to our C Maj 7th chord, we would thus build a C Maj 9th chord. Notice how this chord is a continuing extension of thirds over our triad.

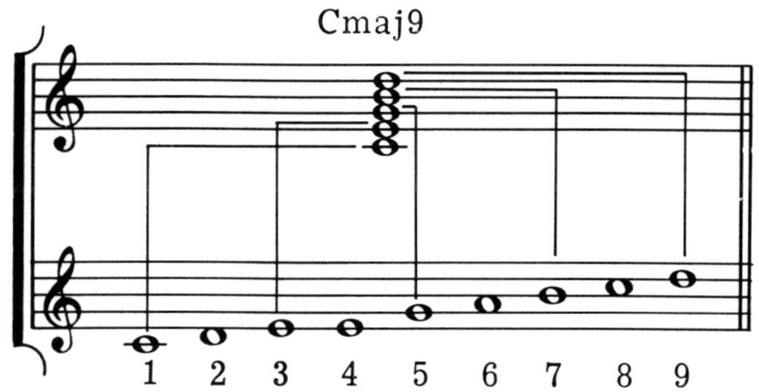

If we continue stacking thirds over the C root, the next third we would come to is the 11th. Over major triads, the 11th IS ALWAYS RAISED (altered). We would thus call the following chord C Maj 9 (#11).

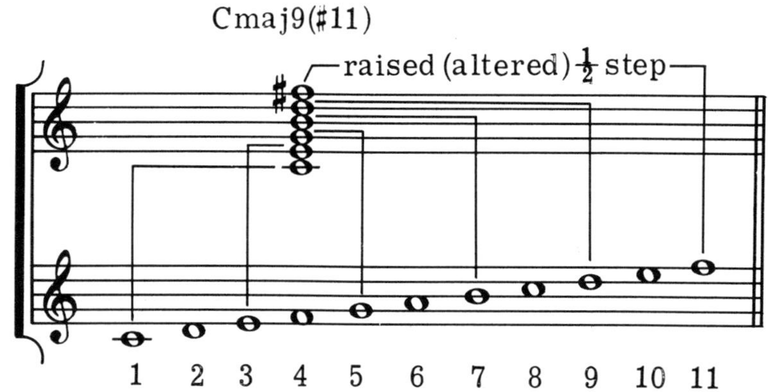

If we add the 13th scale note to a C Maj9 chord, our chord would thus be called a C Maj9 (add 13).

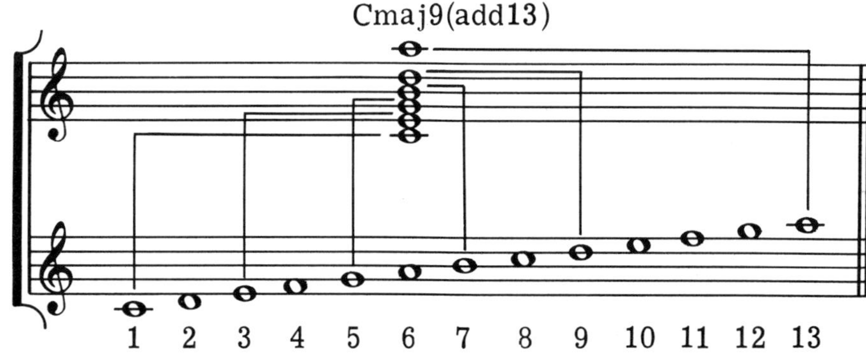

ALL OF THE ABOVE CHORDS FUNCTION AS "TONIC" CHORDS (chords of key center gravity without the inclination in a progression to "move on"). The following chords which we will build function as DOMINANT chords (in a given key, these are usually built off of the 5th scale step) and have the tendency in a progression to want to "move on" or "resolve" to a "tonic" chord.

In the key of C, G is the fifth scale step and is the dominant chord which we will build. Notice that for this illustration, I have RENUMBERED the scale, for purposes of building the chord from a G root. In other words, even though we are still working with scale members from the key of C, we are building a chord in thirds (one, three, five, seven, etc.) from a G root and for that reason, we will number our spelling from G.

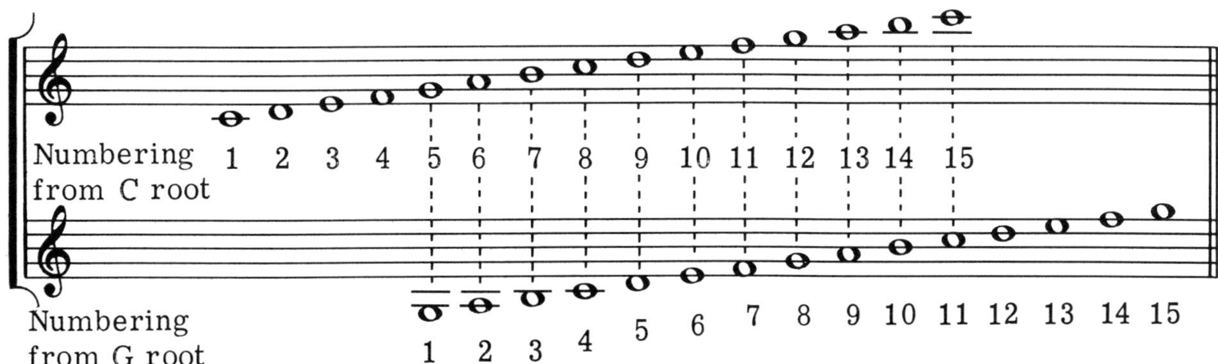

Let us now build DOMINANT 7th chords over a G root. Our first chord is G7.

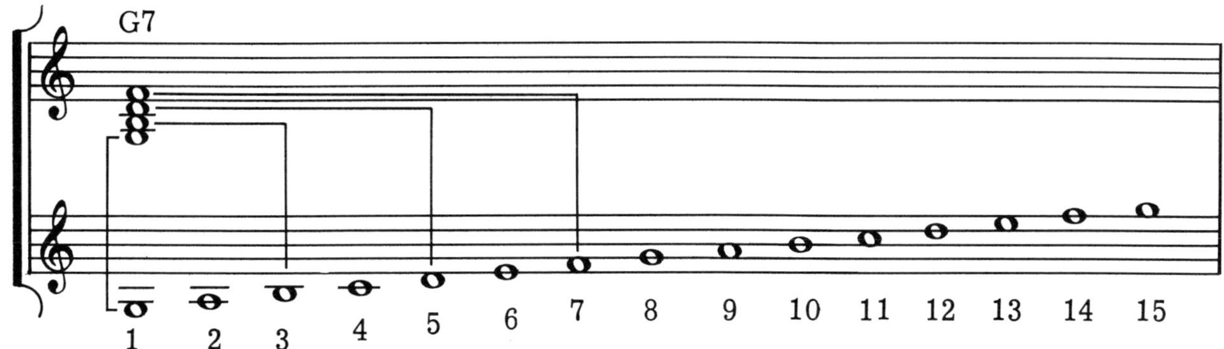

The next chord is a G9.

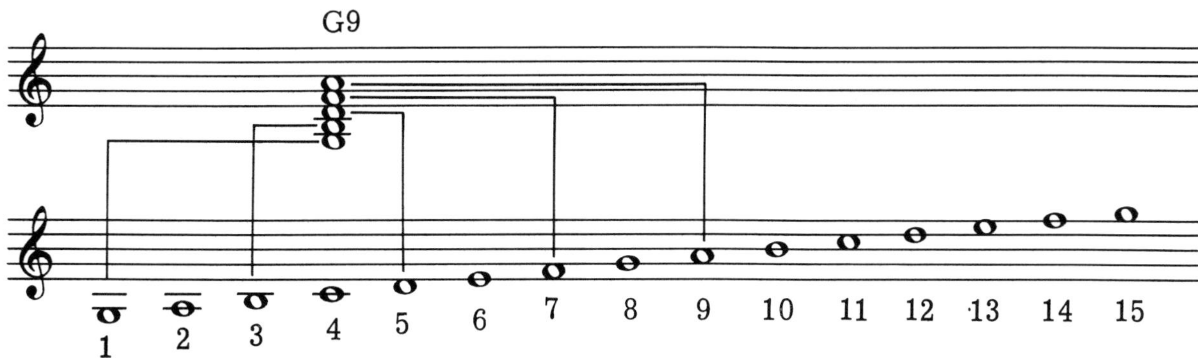

Adhering to the rule that the 11th in major chords is always raised, we thus build a G9#11 chord.

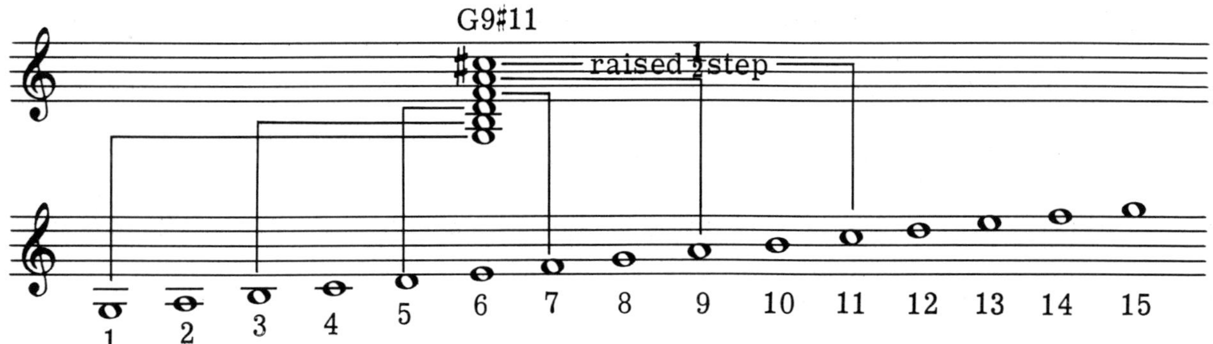

To build a G 13 chord (dominant chord) we usually include ALL notes which occur in thirds above the G root. Thus we would use the 1, 3, 5, 7, 9,#11 and 13 to build a dominant G 13 chord. But, on occasion, the #11 may be omitted in the chord voicing (notice in the TONIC type 13th chord built over the C root, we did not use the #11 at all in the construction of the Maj9 (add 13).

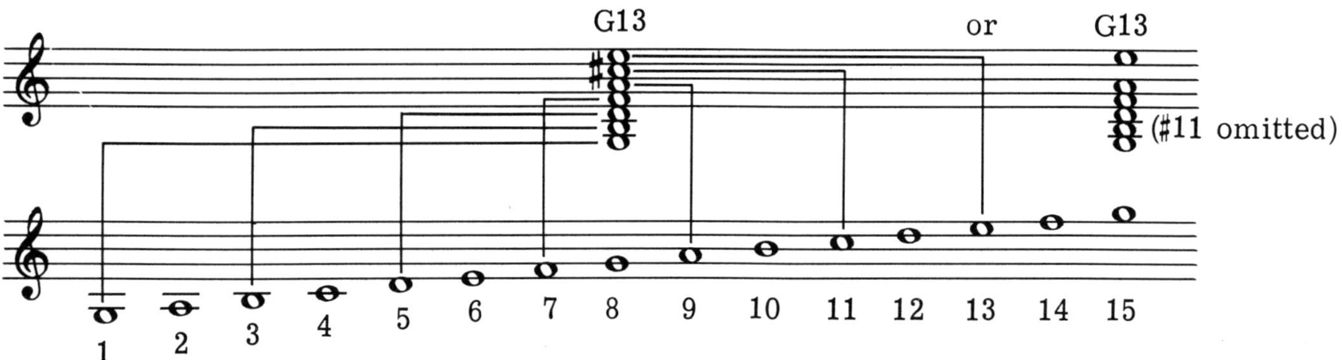

14. Altered Chords

The following are voicings of TONIC functioning and DOMINANT functioning chords whose members (one or more) have been altered. Study these voicings and play them on the piano so that you many understand the principles of building and altering TONIC and DOMINANT functioning major chords.

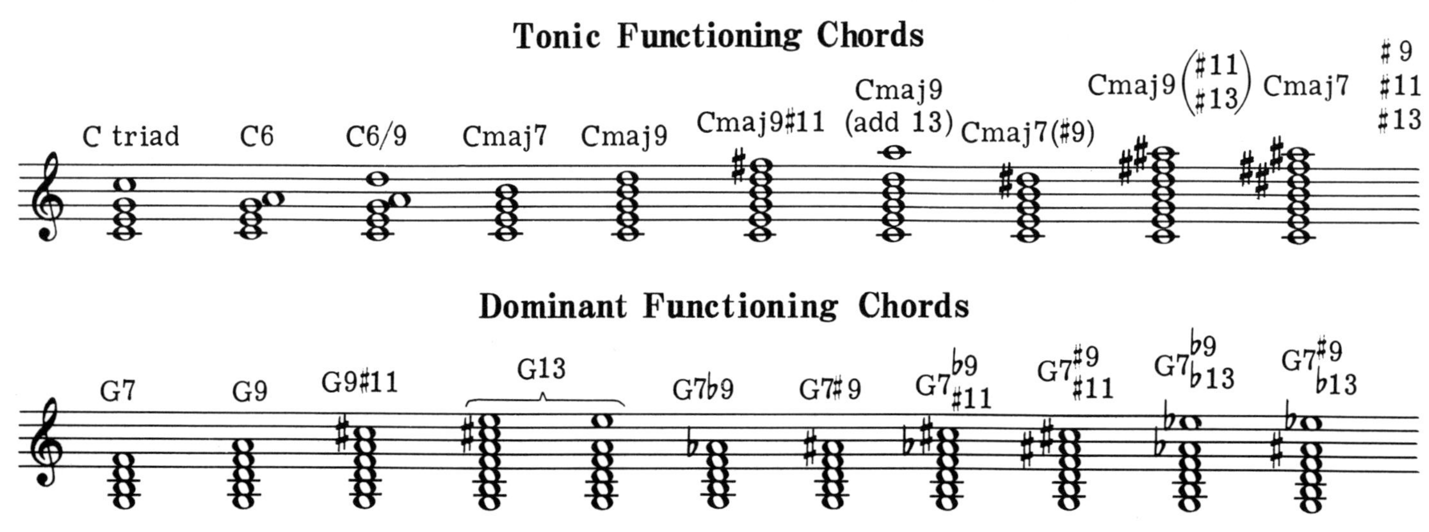

15. Minor Chords

Below is the C Harmonic Minor scale. The same principles of building minor chords apply as they did in major.

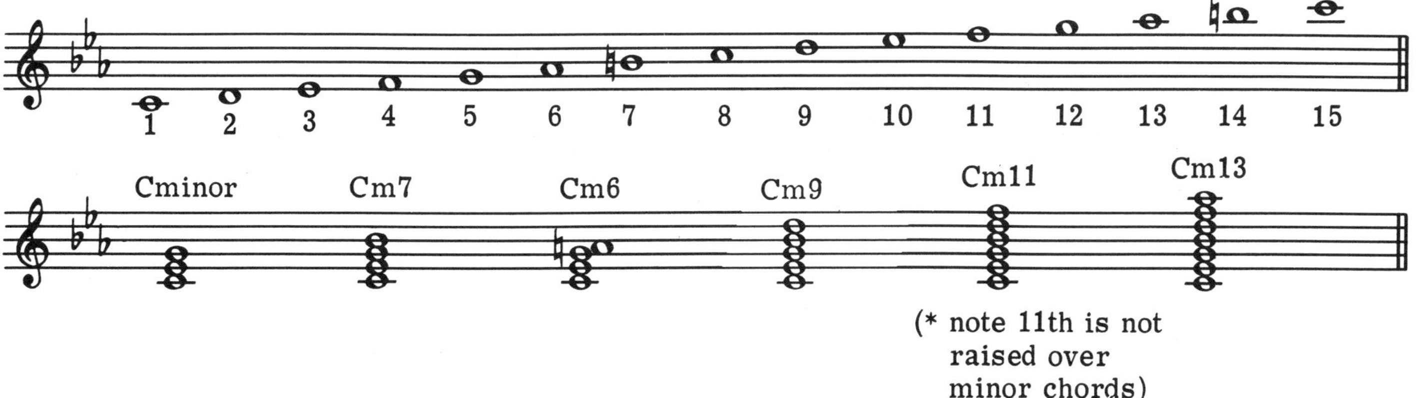

(* note 11th is not raised over minor chords)

Diminished and Half Diminished Chords:

By lowering the 5th scale step of a minor triad, **we create** a diminished chord.

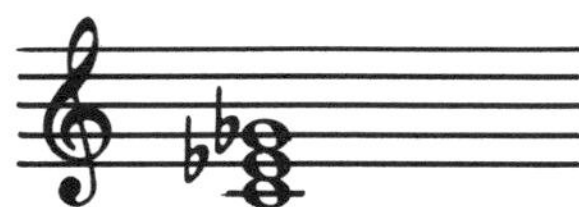

By adding the 7th from the minor scale to the C dim chord we would have a C°7 (C half diminish). This chord is usually called Cm7♭5 - C, E♭, G♭, B♭.

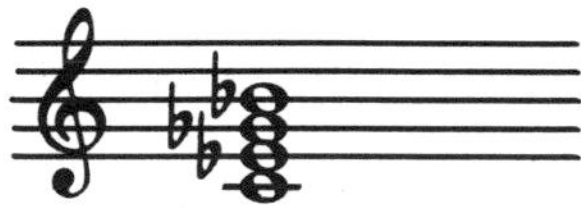

By lowering the B♭ by one half step, we construct the C dim7 chord: C, E♭, G♭, B♭♭.

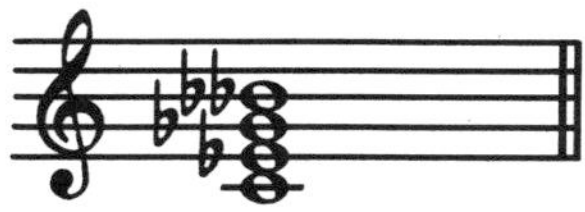

16. Augmented Chords

Raising the 5th scale step in the C major triad - C, E, G♯ creates C aug (also notated C+).

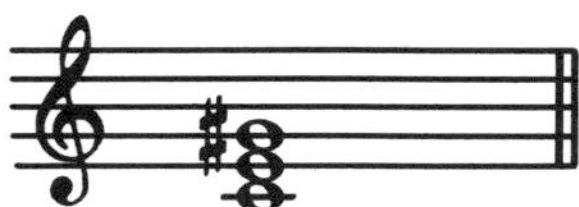

All types of extensions and alterations of those extensions are used with augmented chords. Generally, these type chords function as DOMINANT chords. Below are examples of augmented chords and their extensions. Study them, then play them on the piano so as to understand their construction.

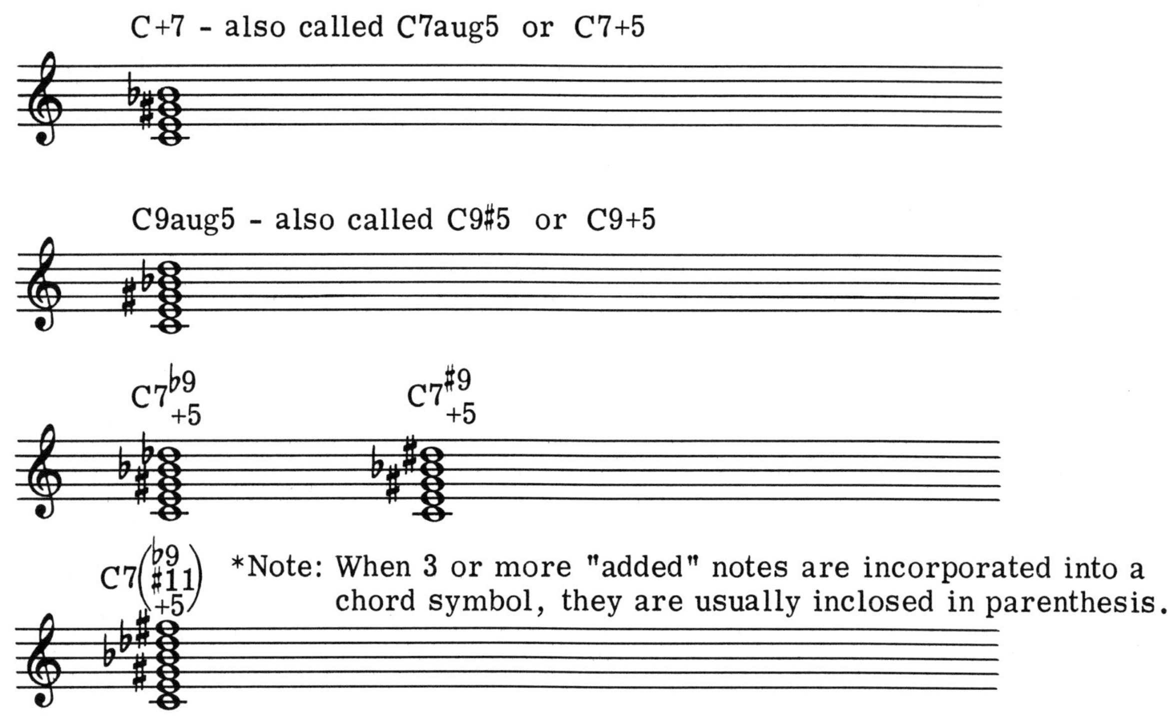

*Note: When 3 or more "added" notes are incorporated into a chord symbol, they are usually inclosed in parenthesis.

17. Suspended Chords

Studying traditional harmony and counterpoint teaches us that a suspension is a "non-chordal" note which is suspended IN PLACE of a chordal note. A 4-3 suspension (in traditional counterpoint) would be a chord containing the suspended 4th in the place of the 3rd: C, F, G.

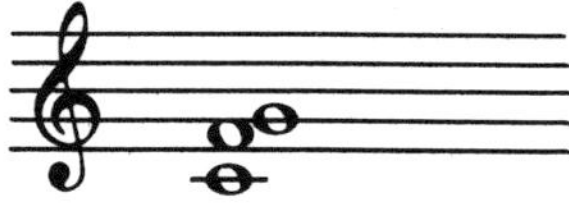

This chord is named C sus4. C, F, G, B♭ would thus be C7 sus 4.

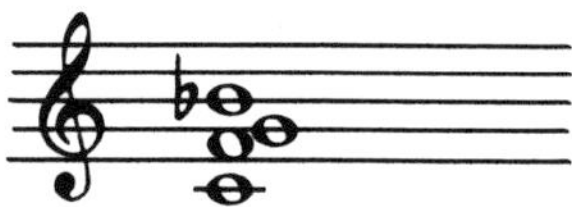

One very common misnomer concerning the suspended 4th (11th) is this chord:

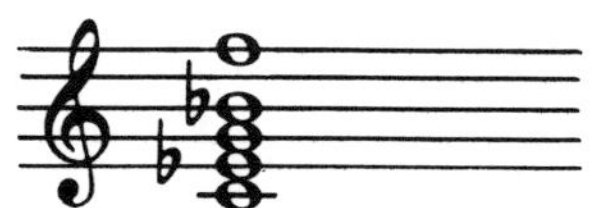

The preceeding chord is sometimes mislabeled C min. 7th sus4. By calling the chord

MINOR, we indicate there is a third present in the chord (a MINOR third above the root).

A suspended chord is a chord with NO THIRD - the 4th is suspended in its place. Thus,

the proper naming of the preceeding chord would be Cm7 add 11. Many times in contem-

porary music this chord is used with the 11th in the bass and is notated Cm7/F . Thus,

any time there is a 3rd and a 4th BOTH present in a chord, the 4th is ALWAYS REFERRED

TO AS AN 11th.

18. Symbols Used When Naming Chords

Here are common symbols used when naming chords with a C root. Note that several

have more than one symbol, although the first one indicated is the most common.

Chord Spelling	Symbol
C, E, G, B	C Maj7* or CΔ7
C, E, G, B♭	C7
C, E, G, A	C6
C, E, G, A, D	C6/9
C , E, G, B♭, D	C9
C, E, G, B♭, D♭, F♯	C7♭9♯11
C, E♭, G	Cm or C - or Cmin
C, E♭, G, B♭	Cm7, C-7 or Cmin7
C, E, G♯	C+ or C aug

*Do not use a capital M by itself for major seven chords, as many times it is hard to

distinguish from lower case m (designating minor) when copied by hand. Also do not use

C7 for denoting C Maj7, as many people make the number 7 when writing - thus a very

confusing symbol.

For complete clarity at all times, the plus sign should only be used with augmented chords -

indicating the 5th scale step is raised by 1/2 step. Sometimes it is used erroneously to

indicate other notes to be raised: Example: C+9. In this example, the intent is almost

ALWAYS to have a spelling C, E, G, B♭, D♯.

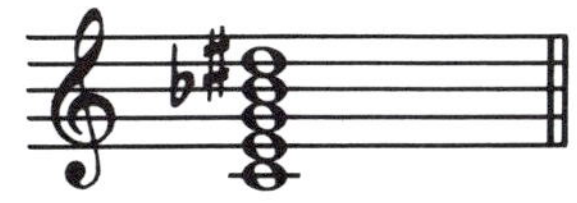

In reality, the symbol C+9 means C, E, G#, B♭, D.

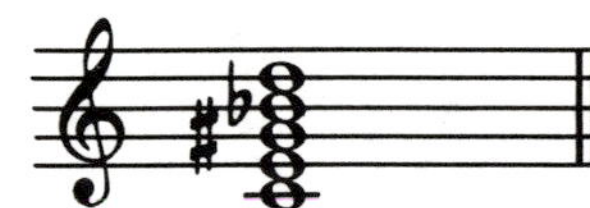

Chord Spelling	Symbol
C, E♭, G♭	C dim or C°
C, E♭, G♭, B♭	Cⵁ or Cm7♭5
C, E♭, G♭, B♭♭	C dim7

Exercise #17

Spell the following chords, making sure all accidentals are properly notated.

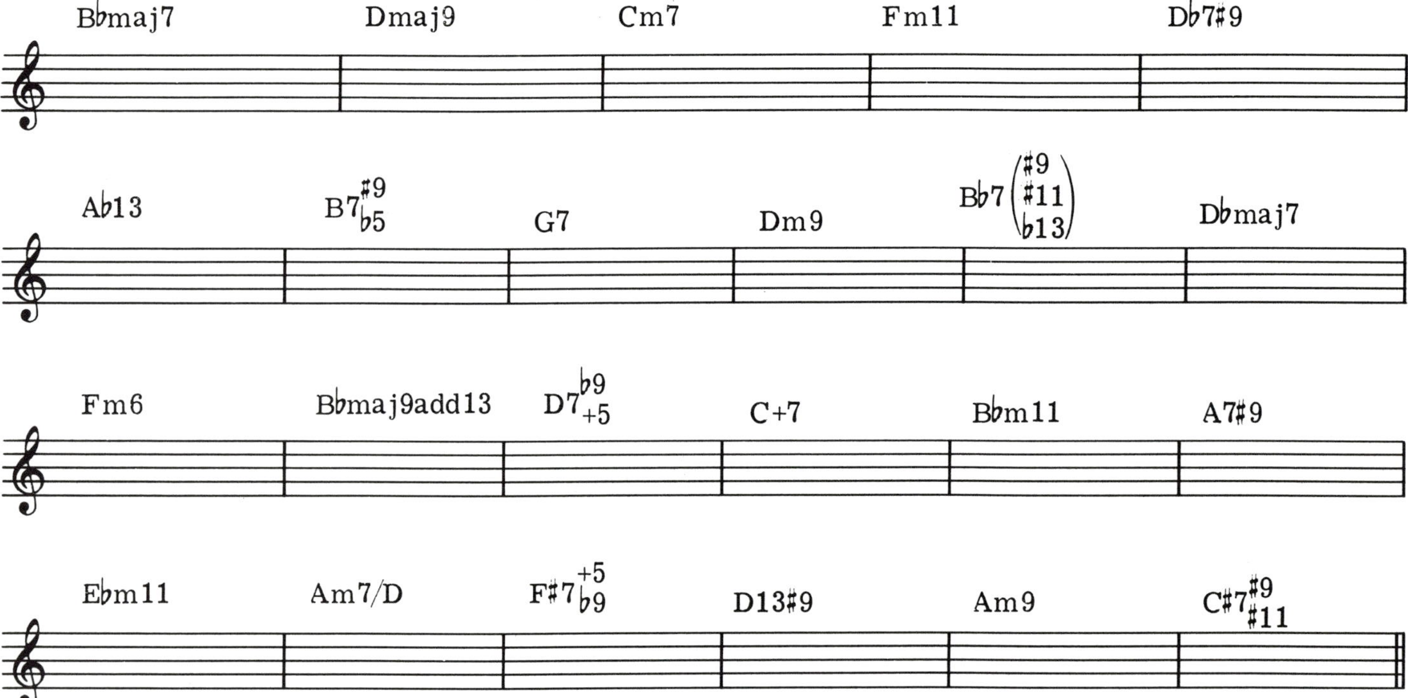

Exercise #18

Put the correct chord symbol above the following chord spellings.

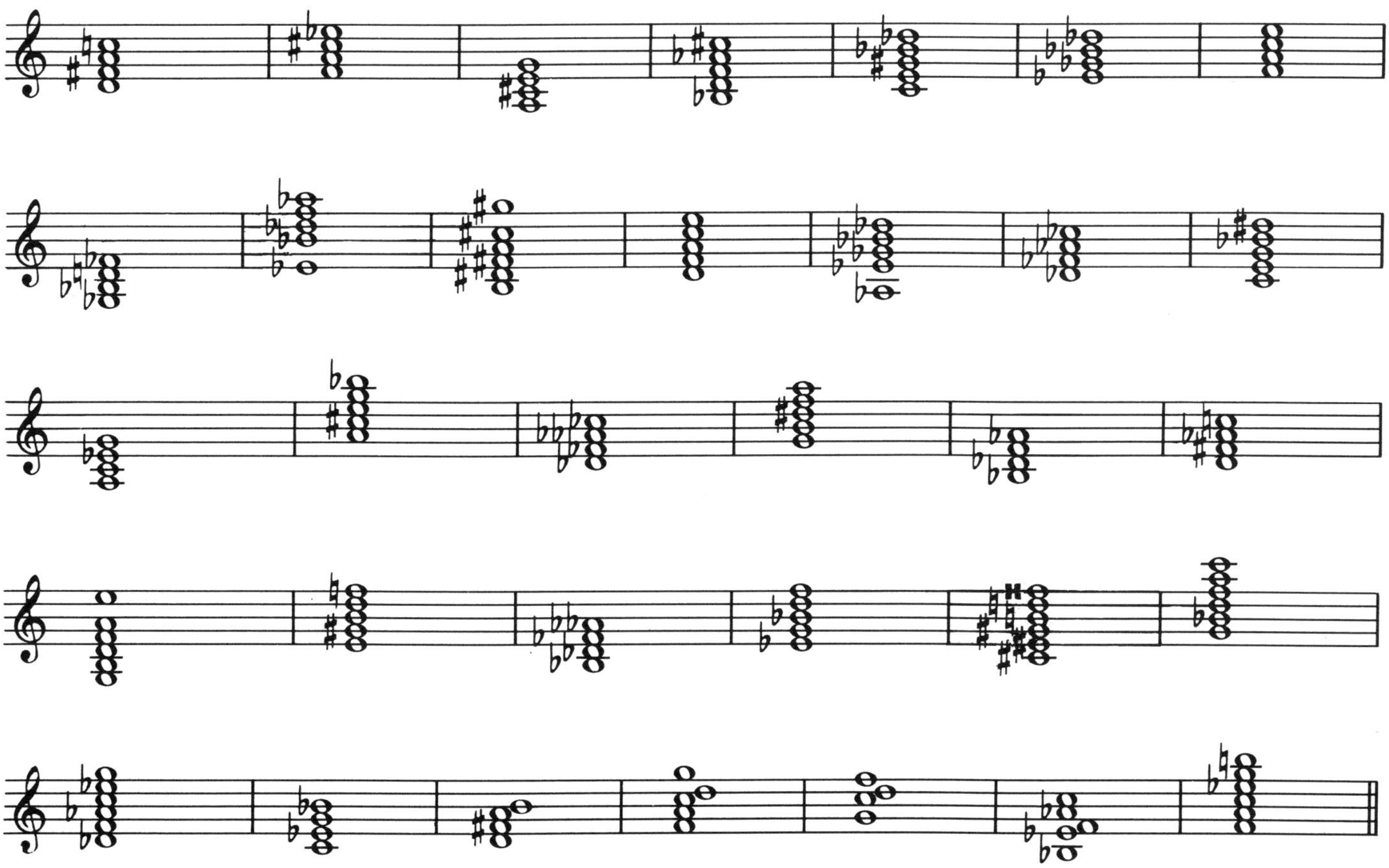

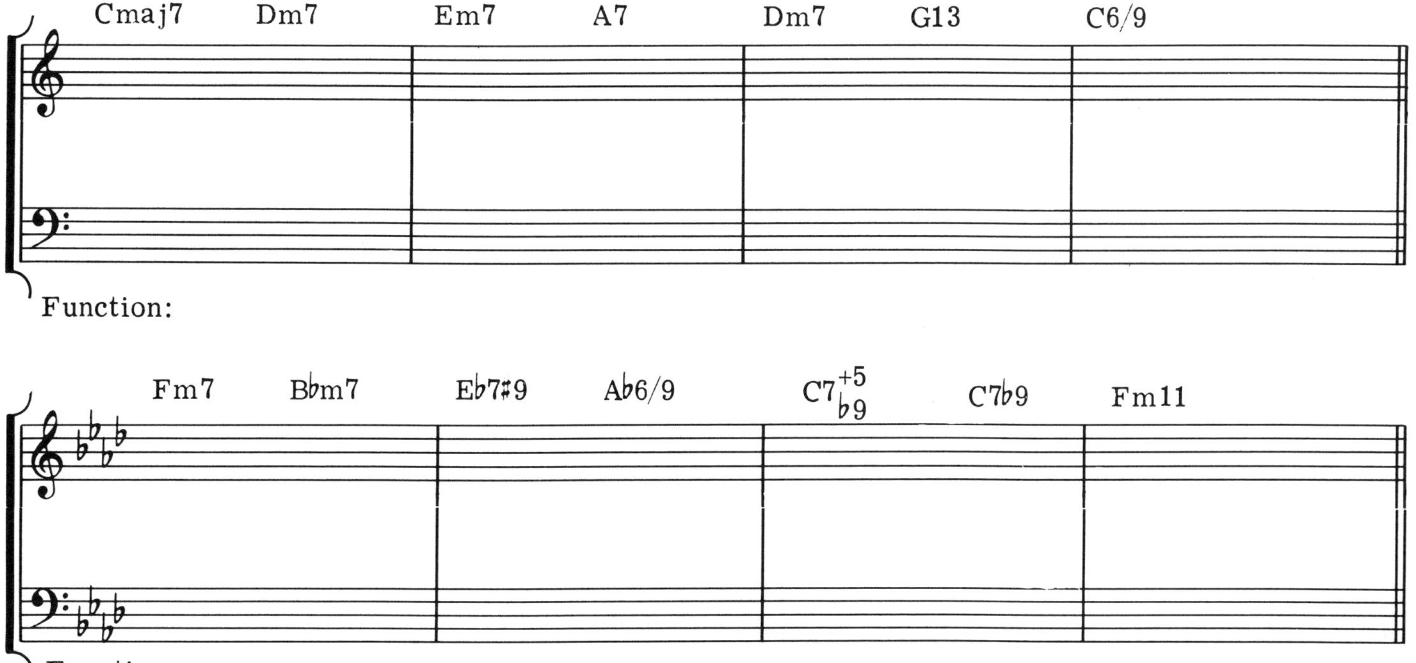

Exercise #19

Spell out the following chord progressions in root position and name by number each chords function. After completion, check your answers in appendix.

Function:

Function:

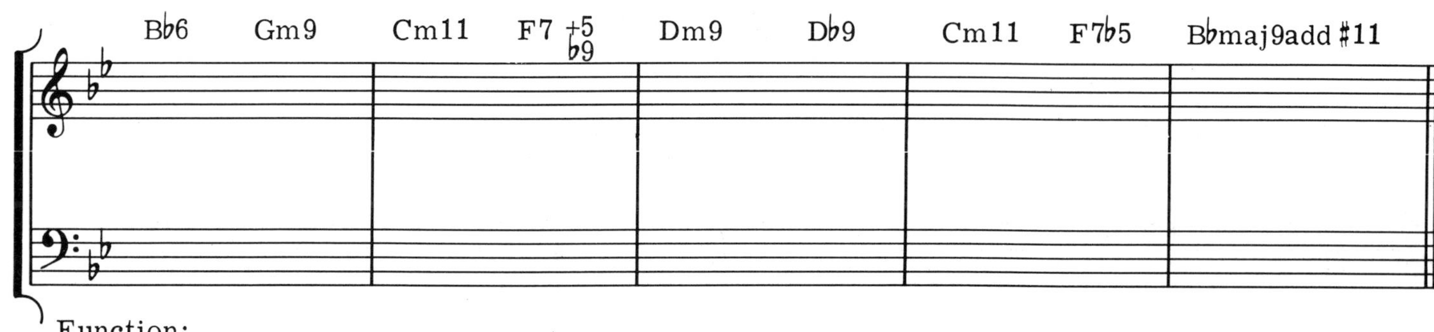

Function:

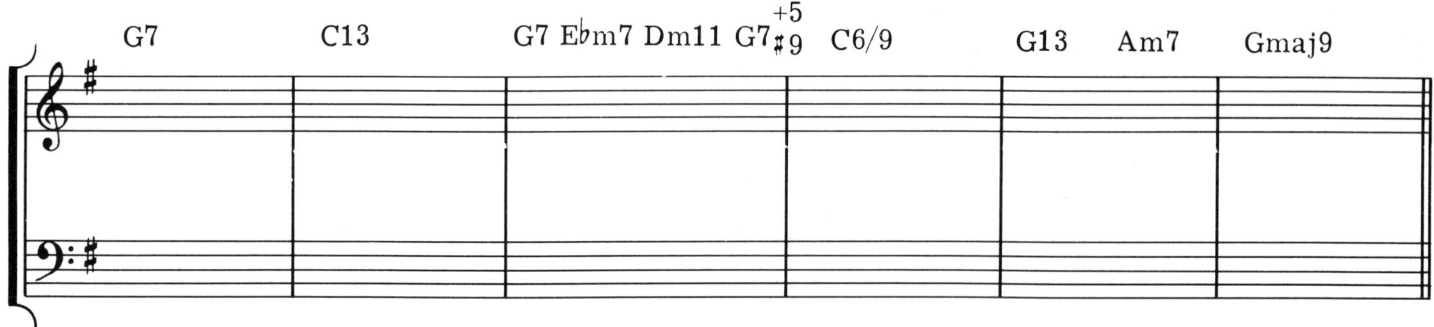

Function

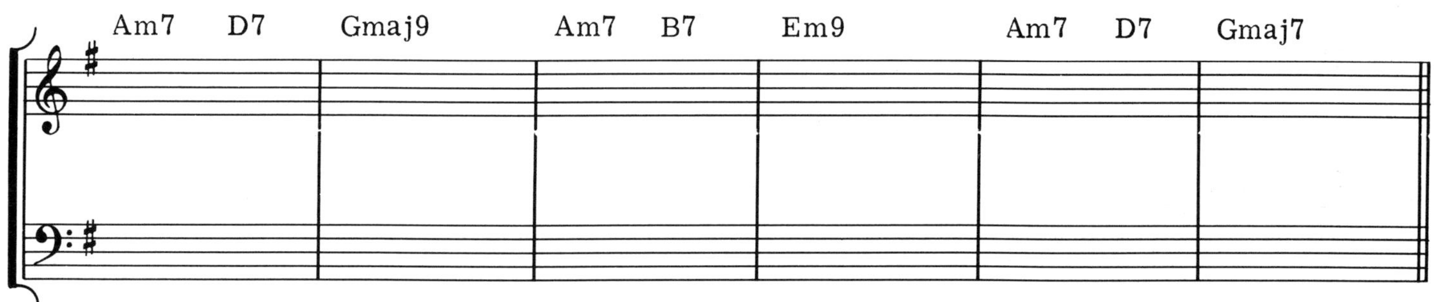

Function

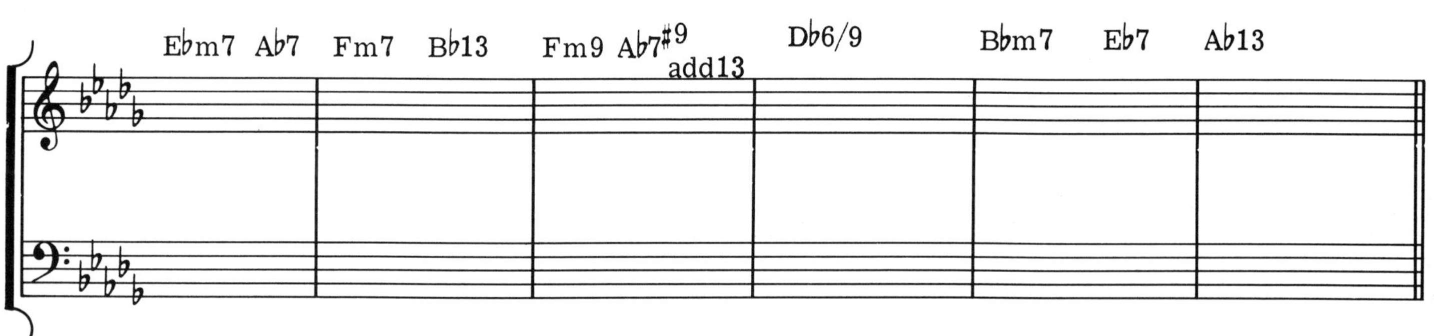

Function

Bm7   F#7   Bm9   F#m7   Em7   A7 +5 b9   Dmaj9   Em7   Eb9   D6/9

Function

PART III

PRINCIPLES OF TRANSPOSITION

Not all instruments are written in CONCERT PITCH, simply because of their physical make-up and registers in which they play. If we were to review the chart on concert pitch as it relates to the Grand Staff, we would notice that every single "concert" note written for the piano is written exactly where that pitch sounds. The piano would then be considered a CONCERT PITCH INSTRUMENT. But many of the other instruments we will need to write for aren't in concert pitch. In other words, we would write notes on a staff for those instruments to play OTHER than the actual concert pitch notes that we would intend for them to play. For instance, the lowest CONCERT PITCH to the highest CONCERT PITCH notes that a B♭ clarinet would play (a clarinet's REGISTER) would look like this on a diagram taken from the Grand Staff.

Practical Range (Register) in Concert Pitch for the B♭ Clarinet

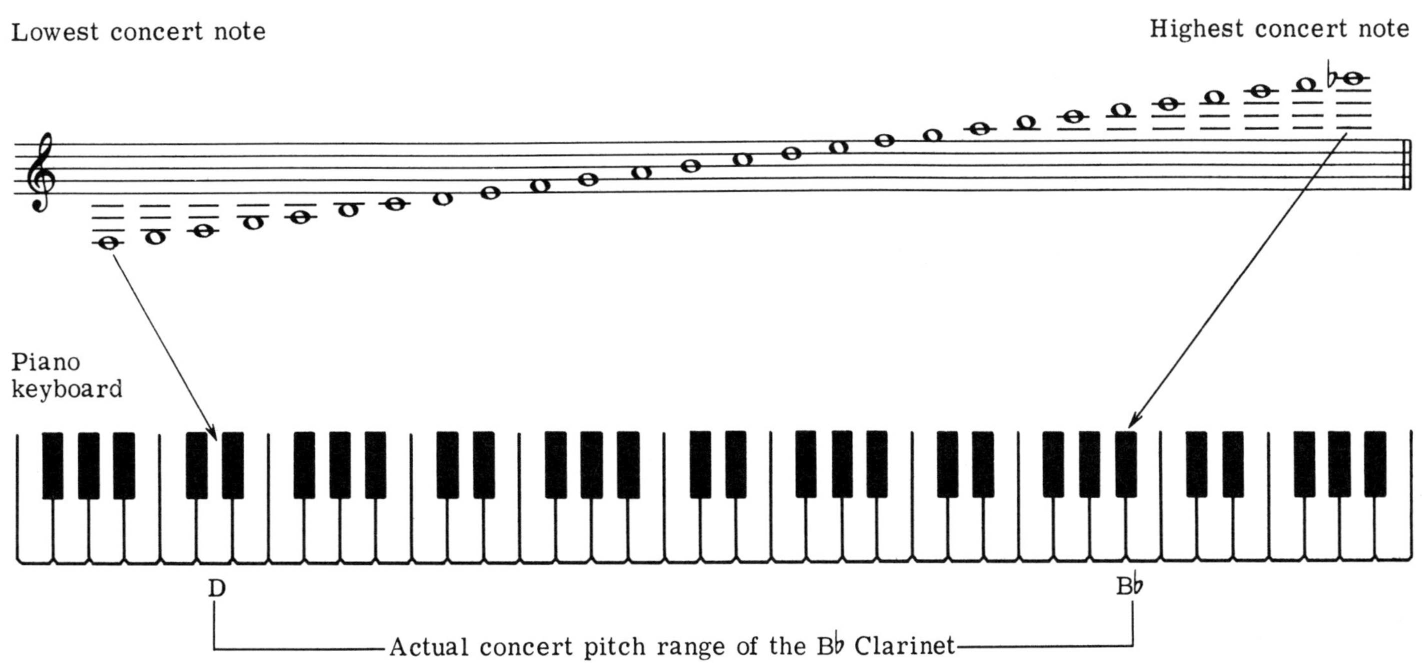

Remember, the preceeding example shows the B♭ clarinet's register (range from lowest to highest notes) as it is heard in CONCERT PITCH. You thus can see as well as play on the piano keyboard where the clarinet's register would lie.

In order to have CONCERT PITCHES sound on the clarinet, we must write TRANSPOSED NOTES for that instrument to play. The clarinet is a TRANSPOSING INSTRUMENT. To have a specific concert pitch to sound on the clarinet, we must write a note A WHOLE STEP higher (an interval of a second). For instance, to have a B♭ concert pitch to sound on the clarinet, we must write a C for the clarinetist to play! This is why it is called a B♭ clarinet (C must be written to get CONCERT B♭ to be heard!).

Consequently, the TRANSPOSED RANGE (register) OF THE B♭ CLARINET IS:

Practical Transposed Range for the B♭ Clarinet

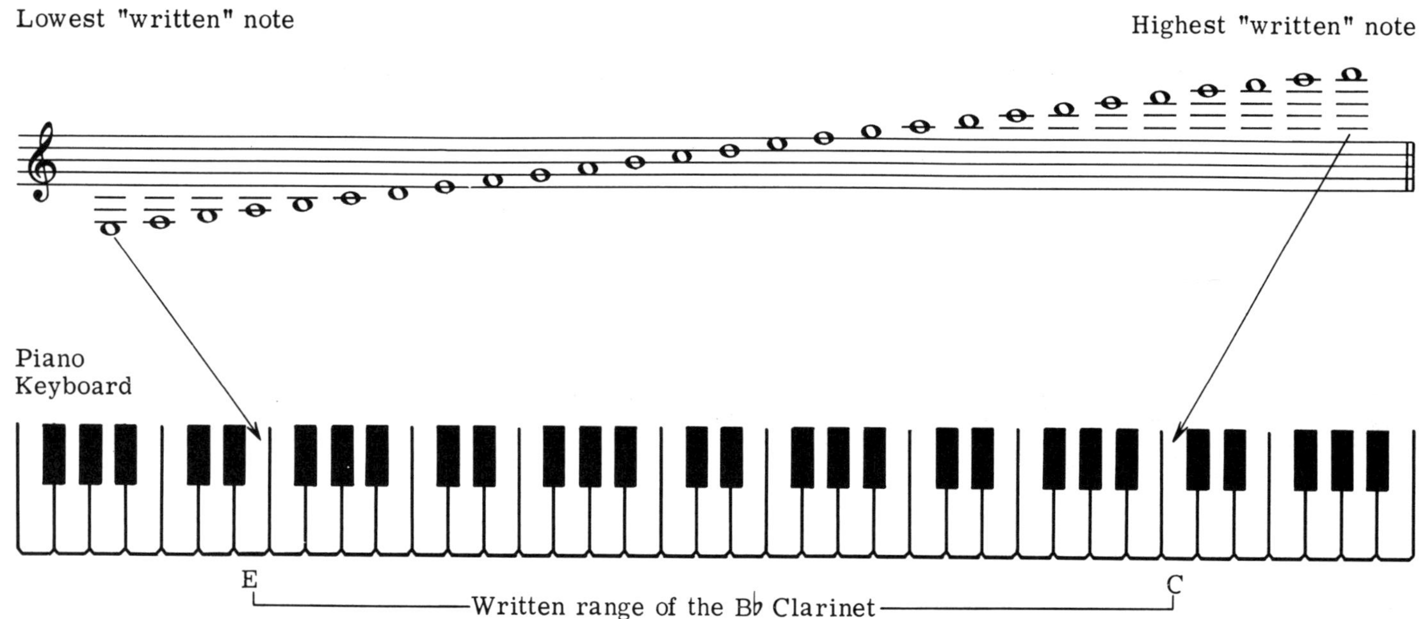

Here is a melody written in CONCERT PITCH:

Now, here is the same melody written for B♭ clarinet. It has been transposed UP A
WHOLE STEP (up a second) so that when the clarinet player reads and plays it, it will
sound the concert pitch of the original melody.

Let us now look at a melody (in score form) which would be played in   unison by a piano
(a concert pitch instrument) and a B♭ clarinet (a transposing instrument).

By examining the preceeding example, you should see that we have TRANSPOSED the
clarinet part UP A WHOLE STEP (up a second) so that when these two instruments play
their respective parts, the melody will be heard in UNISON. Each and every note for the
clarinet was written an interval of a second HIGHER than we wanted it to sound.

It was TRANSPOSED up a second. Even the Key Signature is TRANSPOSED up a second
(from D♭ to E♭).

Write TRANSPOSED B♭ clarinet parts in the following scores.

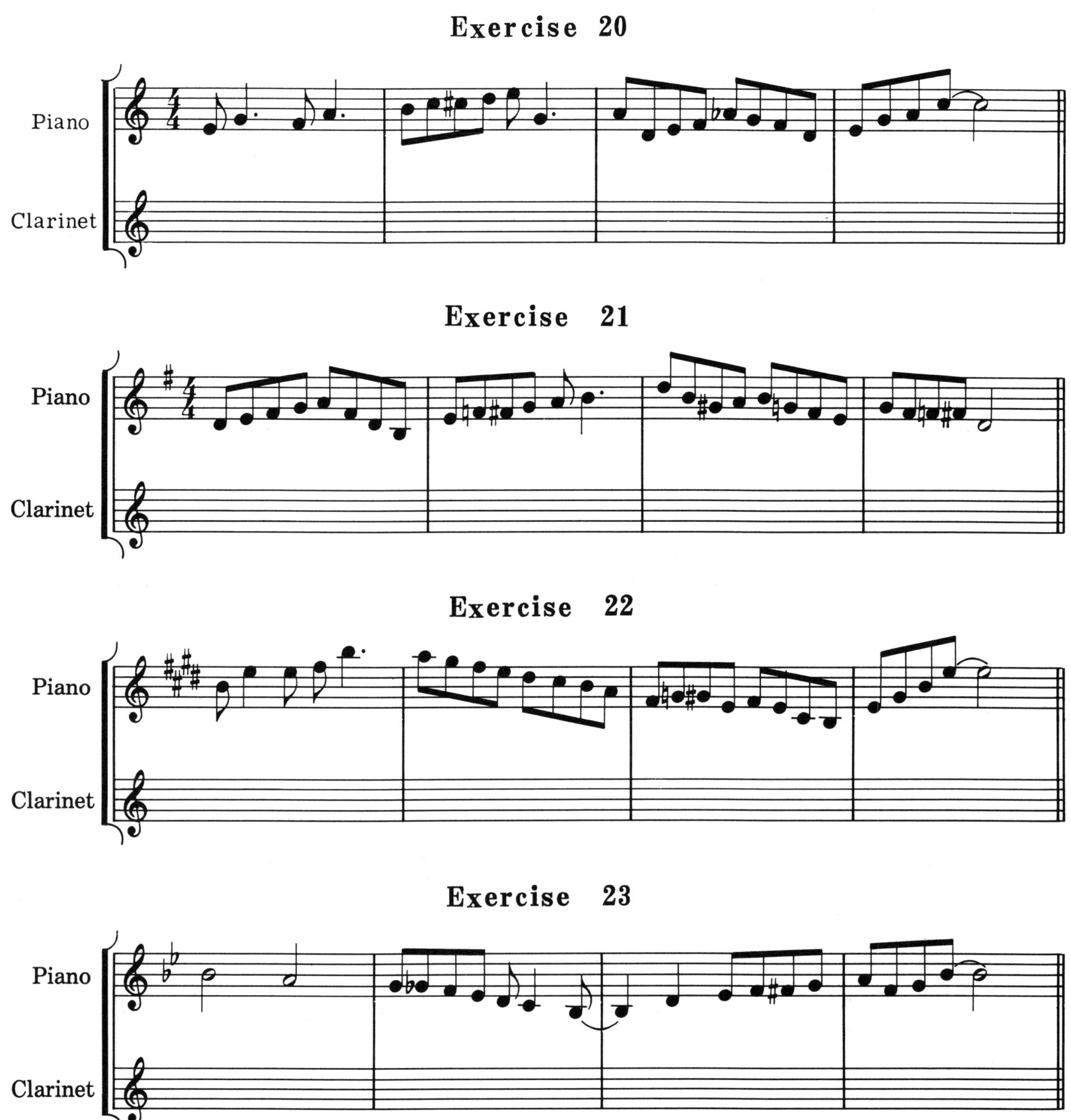

Exercise 24

PART IV

THE RANGE AND TRANSPOSIPION OF INSTRUMENTS

As we saw in the previous chapter, there are two types of instruments which an arranger/orchestrator deals with. These are CONCERT PITCH instruments and TRANSPOSING INSTRUMENTS. Remember, a CONCERT PITCH instrument is written exactly where it sounds in relation to the Grand Staff, while a TRANSPOSING INSTRUMENT is written "in another place" from the actual sounding pitch. This chapter is devoted to learning the range of the different instruments AND where to write for those instruments in order to hear CONCERT PITCHES. Transposition is probably the most basic and important aspect of orchestration which a beginning arranger has to learn! Study this chapter diligently and work all the exercises! Until you can deal with the technique of transposition, you will not be able to orchestrate chord voicings, melodies in the proper register or begin to think in terms of instrumental color.

The Woodwind Family

The woodwind family includes all the flutes, the saxophones, the clarinets, oboe, English horn and bassoons.

1. The Flutes

   A. The Piccolo

   The piccolo plays in the very top registers of the Grand Staff. It is a TRANSPOSING INSTRUMENT in as much as it is written ONE OCTAVE BELOW where it is sounding on the Grand Staff (concert pitch). The following example shows the range of the piccolo in concert pitch AND transposed. Obviously the piccolo can play ALL chromatic notes within its range even though it is only illustrated here scalewise.

Range & Transposition of the Piccolo

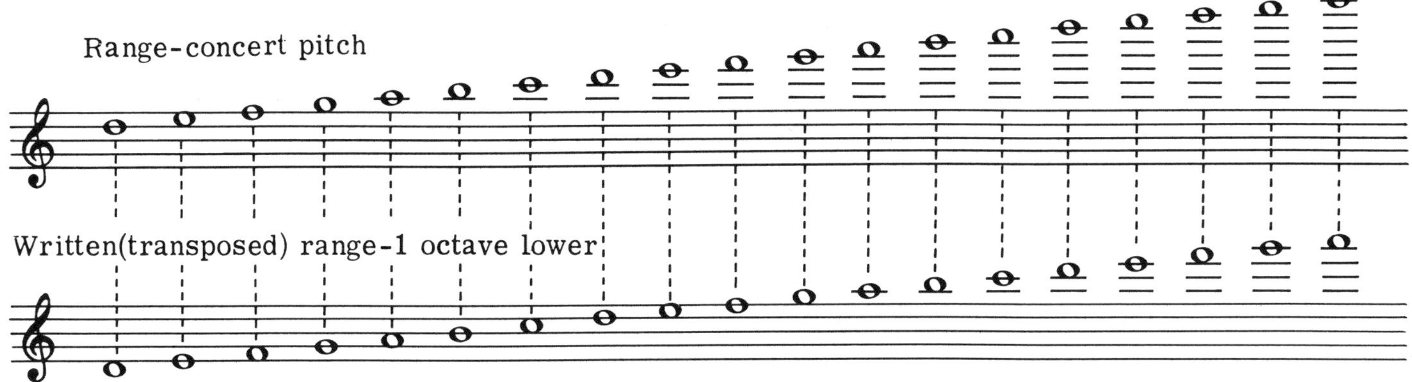

B. The "C" Flute

The "C" Flute is the most common flute which we see and hear. It is a CONCERT

PITCH instrument. In other words, you write the exact concert pitch note which you want

to hear. Here is the range (both concert AND written) for the C Flute.

Range (Written and Concert) of C Flute

C. The Alto Flute (G Flute)

The alto flute is quite a bit larger than the C flute and has a "breathier" tone quality.

It extends the sound of the flute DOWN a fifth below where the C flute can play. It is a

TRANSPOSING INSTRUMENT and is written a fourth higher than it sounds. In other words,

when C is written for the alto flute, G a fourth below it is sounding (thus the name "G"

Alto Flute). The following example shows the CONCERT PITCH range as well as the

WRITTEN (transposed) range of the Alto Flute.

Range and Transposition of the Alto Flute (G Flute)

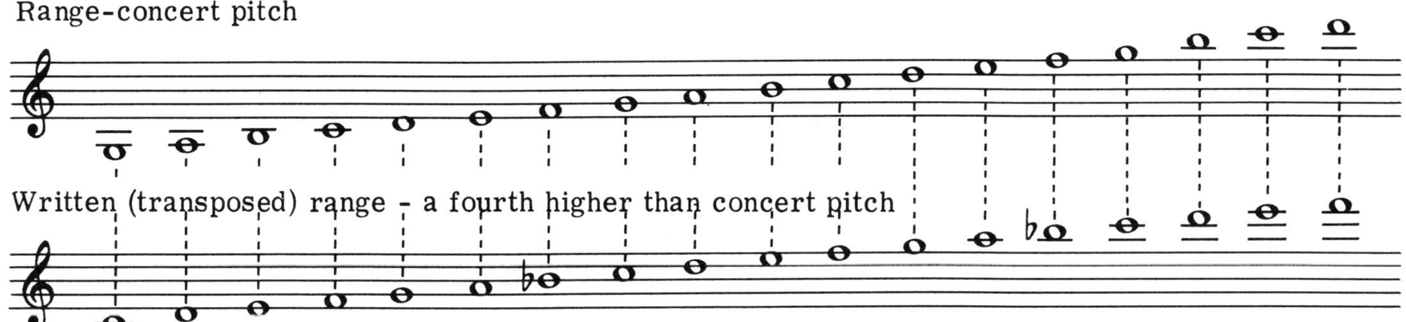

D. The Bass Flute

The bass flute is the largest member of the flute family and is readily recognizable by its size and unique crook in its construction. It extends the flute sound ONE OCTAVE below the C flute and is a TRANSPOSING INSTRUMENT in as much as you write parts for it one octave HIGHER than you want it to sound (in concert pitch).

Range and Transposition of the Bass Flute

Range-concert pitch

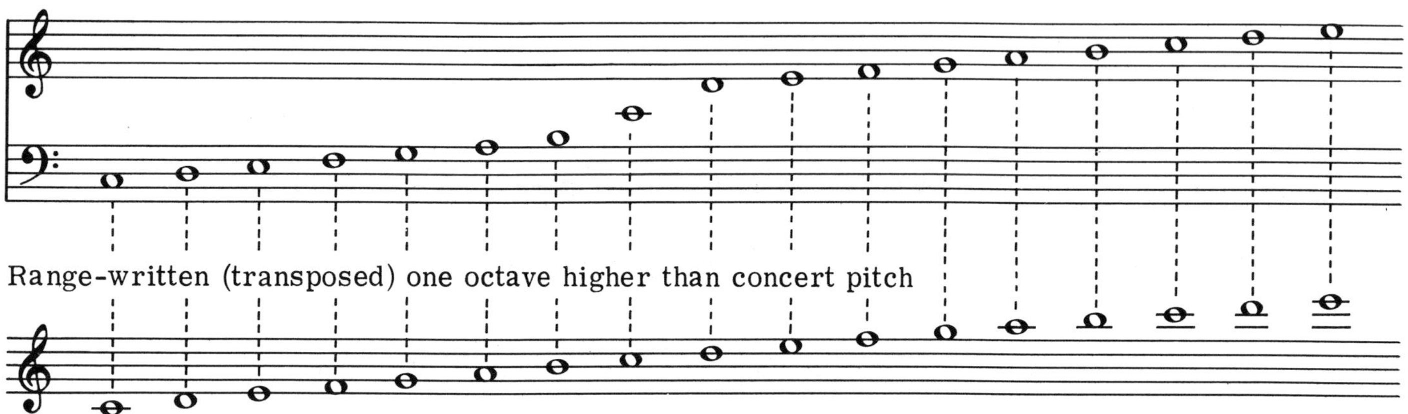

Range-written (transposed) one octave higher than concert pitch

2. The Clarinets

A. The B♭ Clarinet

The B♭ Clarinet is the most commonly seen and heard member of the clarinet family. It is the clarinet we would hear in dance bands and Dixieland bands as well as in the large sections of concert bands. As we discussed in the previous chapter, the B♭ clarinet is a TRANSPOSING INSTRUMENT and you would write parts for it a major second (whole step) ABOVE where you would want it to sound in concert pitch. It should be noted that the B♭ clarinet is written entirely in treble clef.

Range and Transposition of the B♭ Clarinet

Range-concert pitch

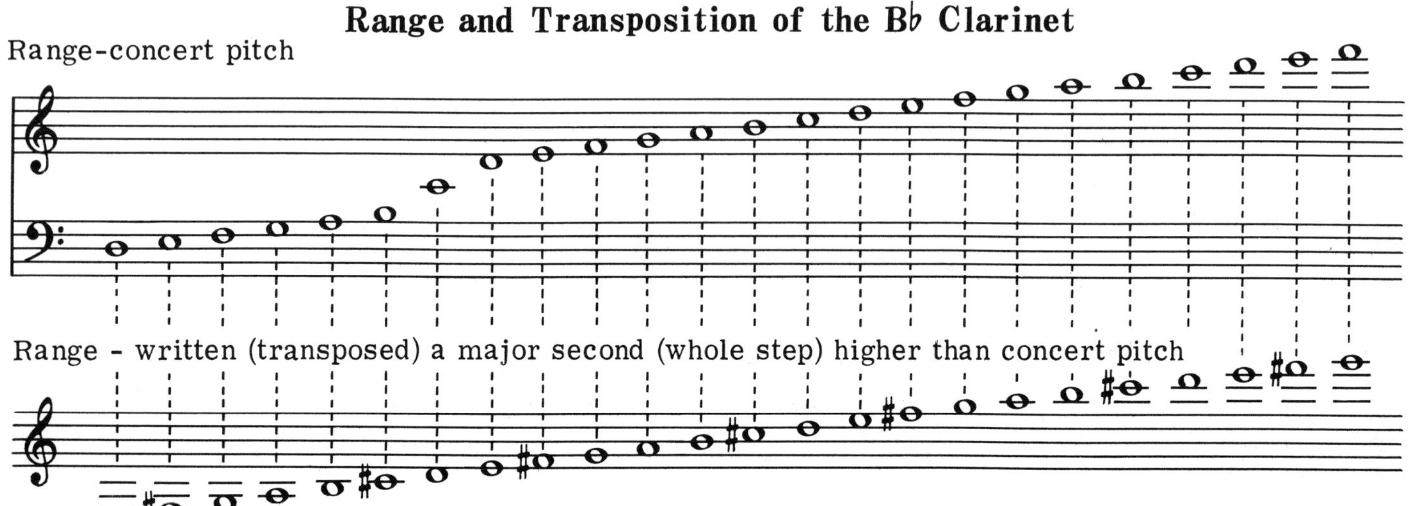

Range - written (transposed) a major second (whole step) higher than concert pitch

B. Other Clarinets

It should be noted that there are "other" clarinets which are used (especially in concert bands and symphony orchestras) which are not quite as common as the B♭ clarinet. They are all written in the treble clef and are TRANSPOSED as illustrated here.

Range and Transposition of the A Clarinet

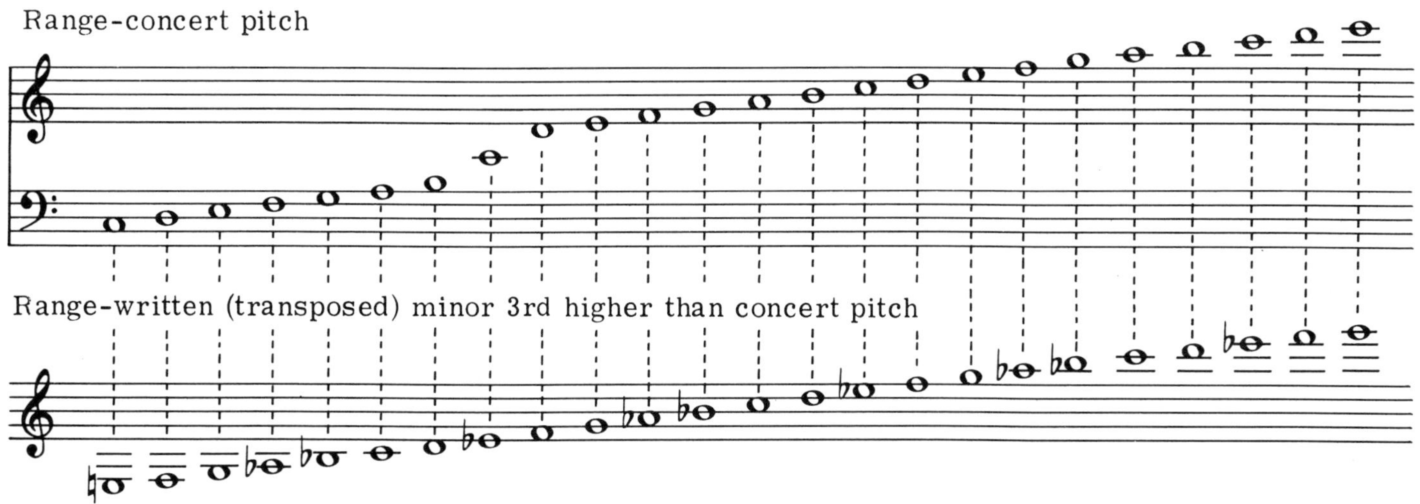

Range and Transposition of the E♭ Clarinet

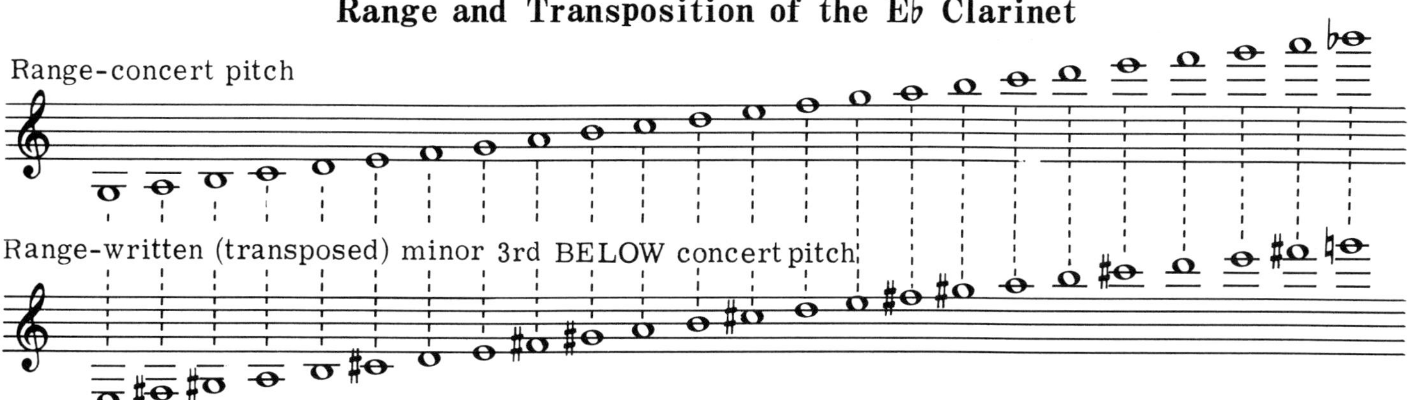

Range and Transposition of the D Clarinet

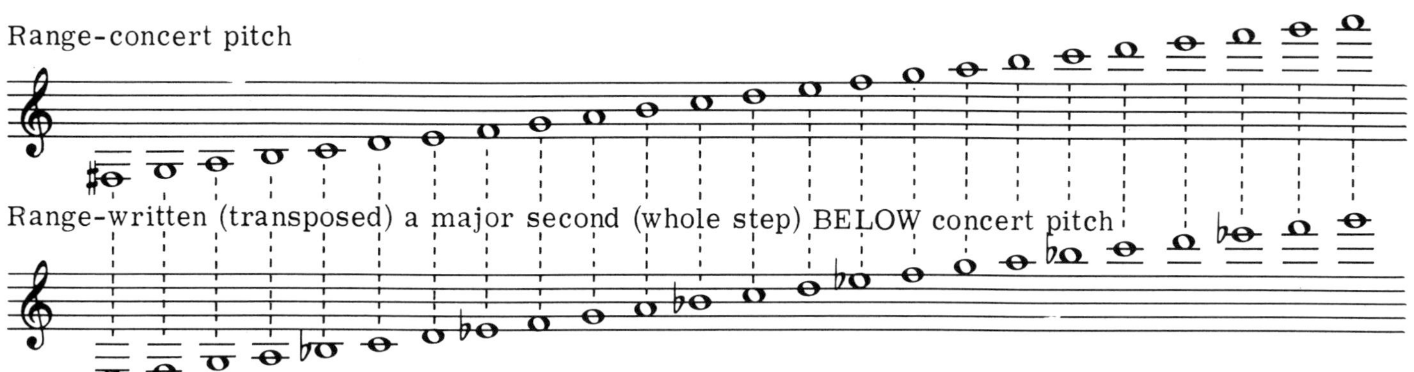

Range and Transposition of the E♭ Alto Clarinet

Range-concert pitch

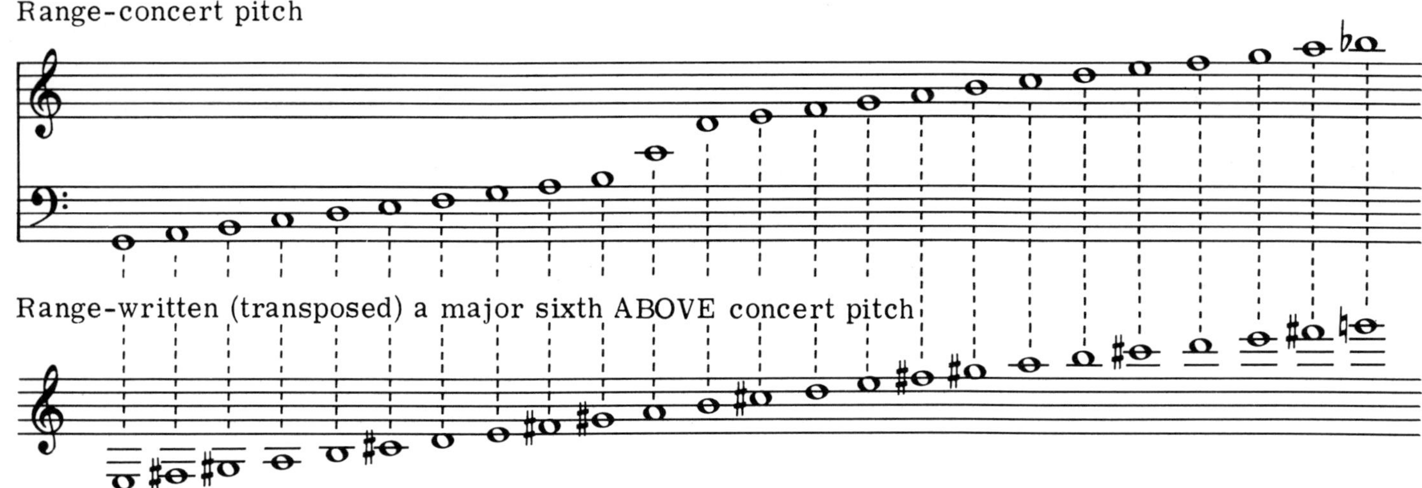

You should notice, by looking at the written ranges of the preceeding clarinet registers,
that all 4 types of clarinets have the SAME written range. What this means is that a competent
clarinetist could play any one of the four instruments, as all the clarinets would have
almost identical fingerings. In other words, fingering a WRITTEN middle C would be the
same for the player, no matter what instrument he would be playing. Of course, because of
the various transpositions, each instrument would be sounding a DIFFERENT concert pitch.

C. Bass Clarinet

The bass clarinet sounds in the lower registers of the concert pitch Grand Staff,
but are ALL written entirely in the Treble Clef. All are TRANSPOSING INSTRUMENTS.

Range and Transposition of the B♭ Bass Clarinet

Range-concert pitch

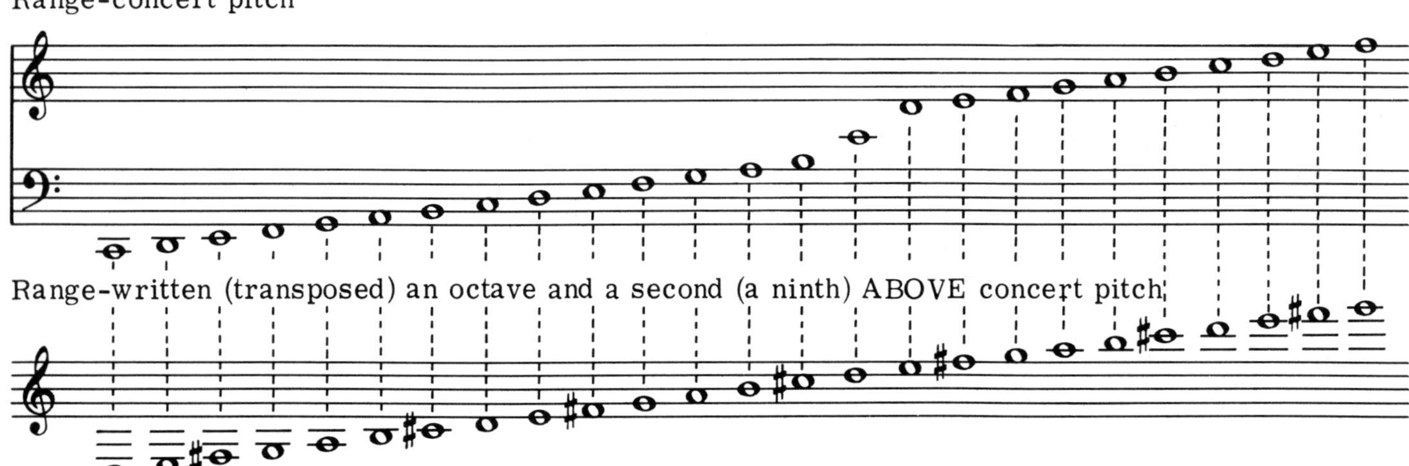

Range and Transposition of the E♭ Contra Bass Clarinet

Range-concert pitch

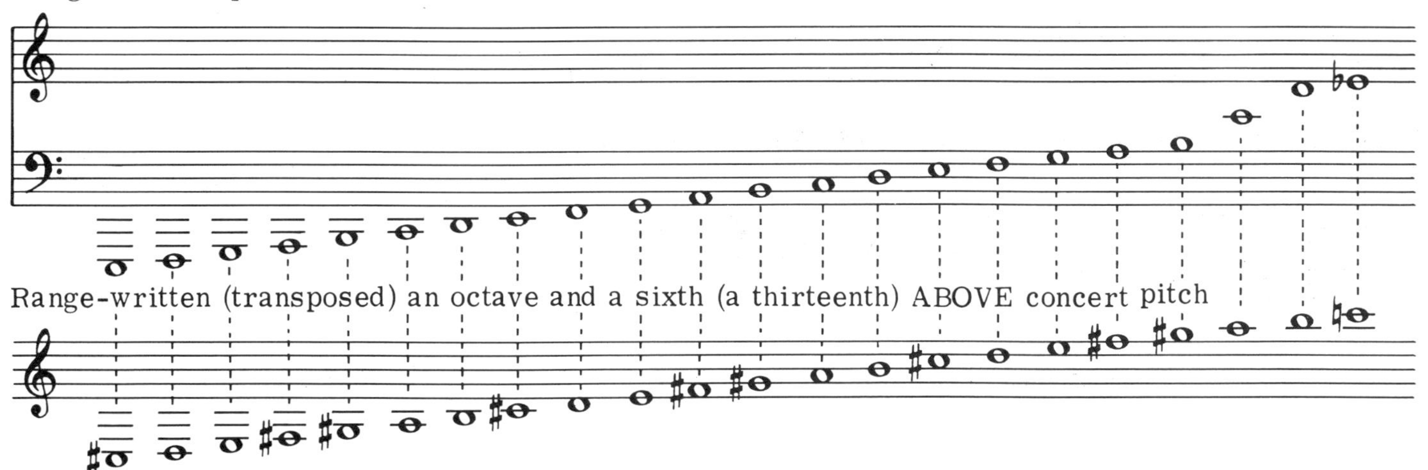

Range and Transposition of the B♭ Contra Bass Clarinet

Range-concert pitch

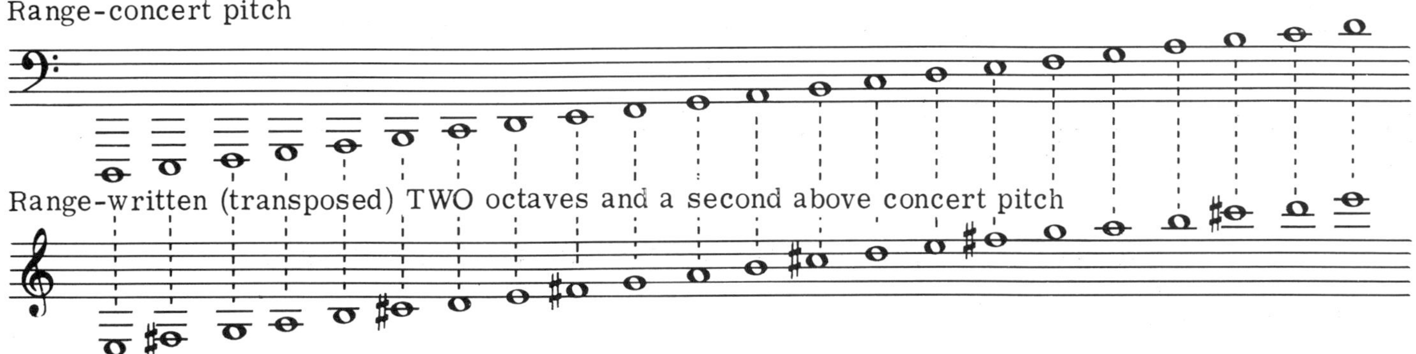

3. The Saxophones

The saxophones are a group of woodwind instruments which are played with a single reed (as is the clarinet). Except for the B♭ Soprano Saxophone, (which is constructed in a straight manner much like a clarinet) all saxophones have the same familiar curvature in their construction. And, except for some Baritone Saxophones which have a special low A key, ALL saxophones have the same written range, from low B♭ to high F (except for the B♭ Bass Saxophone and E♭ Soprano Saxophone which only go to a written E♭ .

Range and Transposition of the E♭ Soprano Saxophone

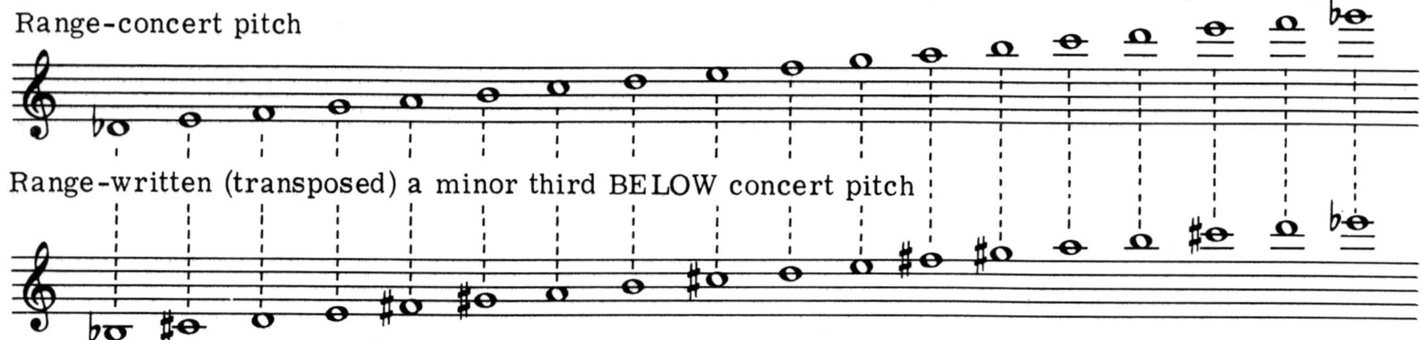

Range and Transposition of the B♭ Soprano Saxophone

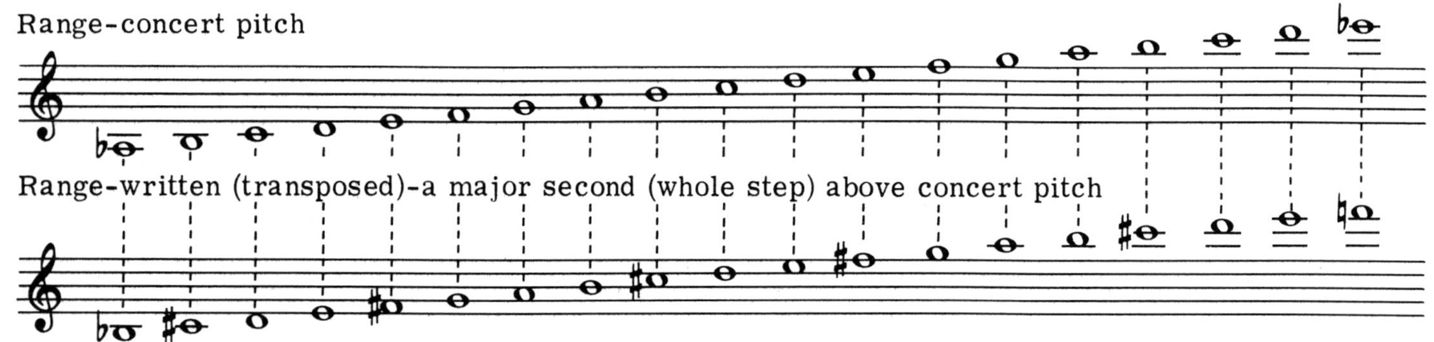

Range and Transposition of the E♭ Alto Saxophone

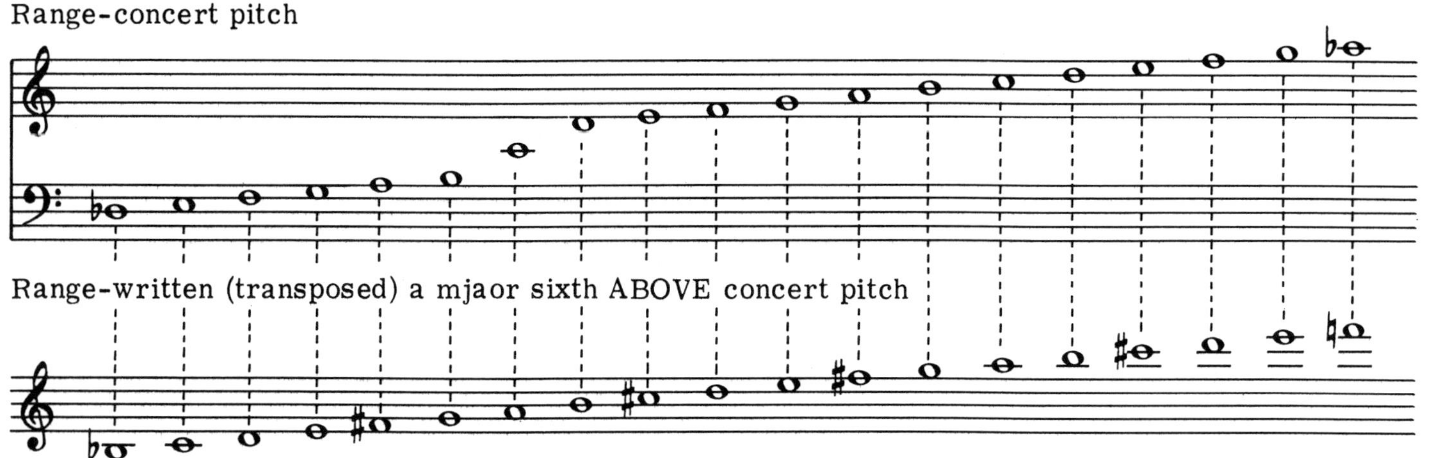

Range and Transposition of the C Melody Saxophone

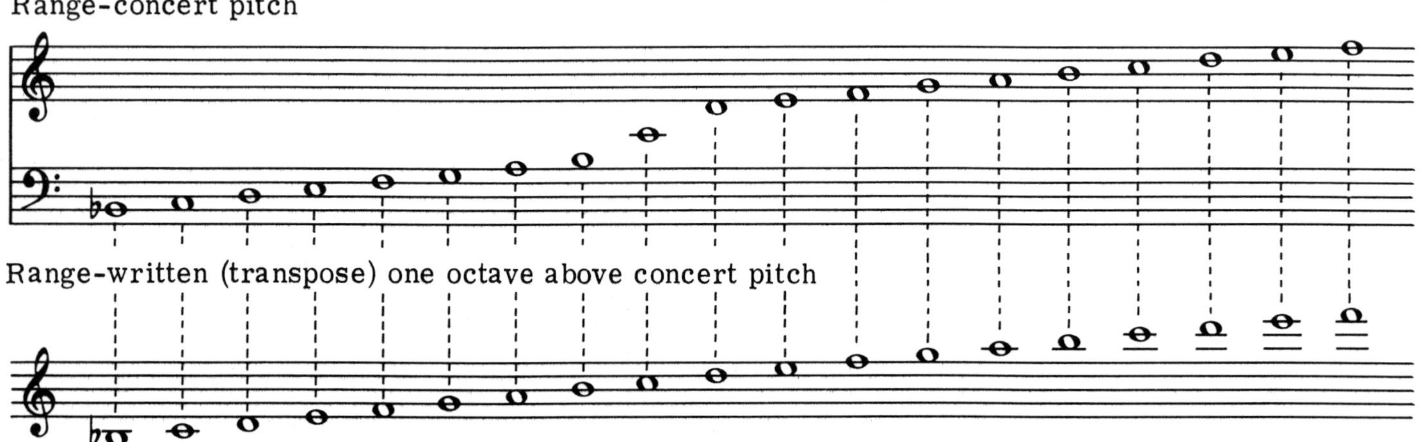

Range and Transposition of the B♭ Tenor Saxophone

Range-concert pitch

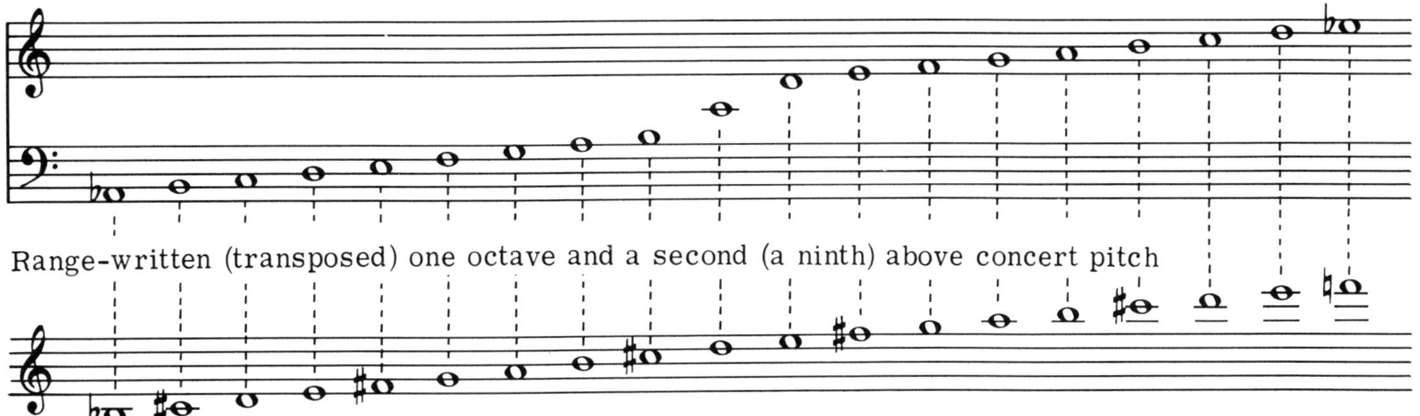

Range-written (transposed) one octave and a second (a ninth) above concert pitch

Range and Transposition of the E♭ Baritone Saxophone

Range-concert pitch

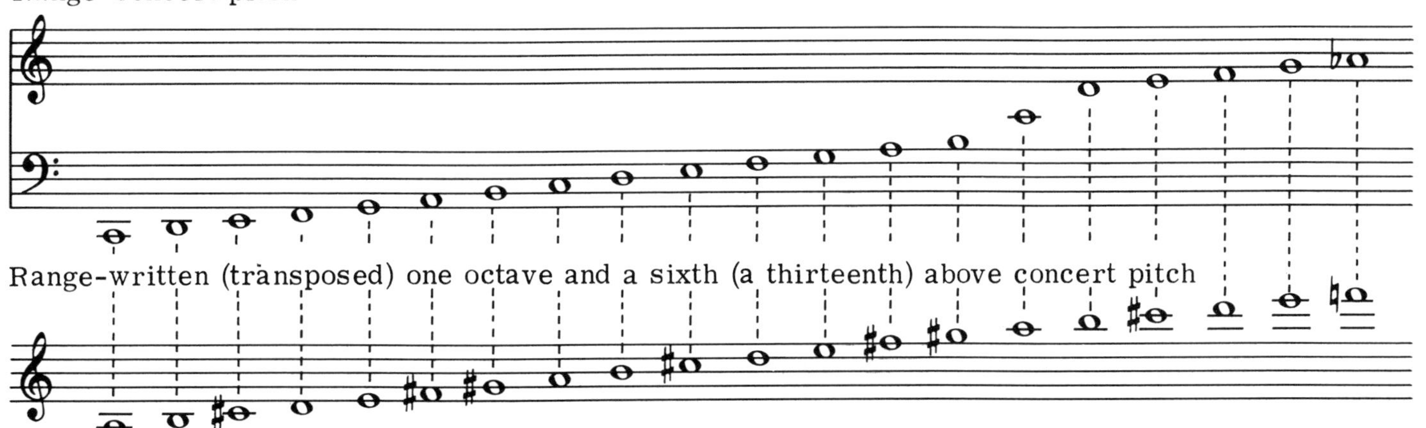

Range-written (transposed) one octave and a sixth (a thirteenth) above concert pitch

Range and Transposition of the B♭ Bass Saxophone

Range-concert pitch

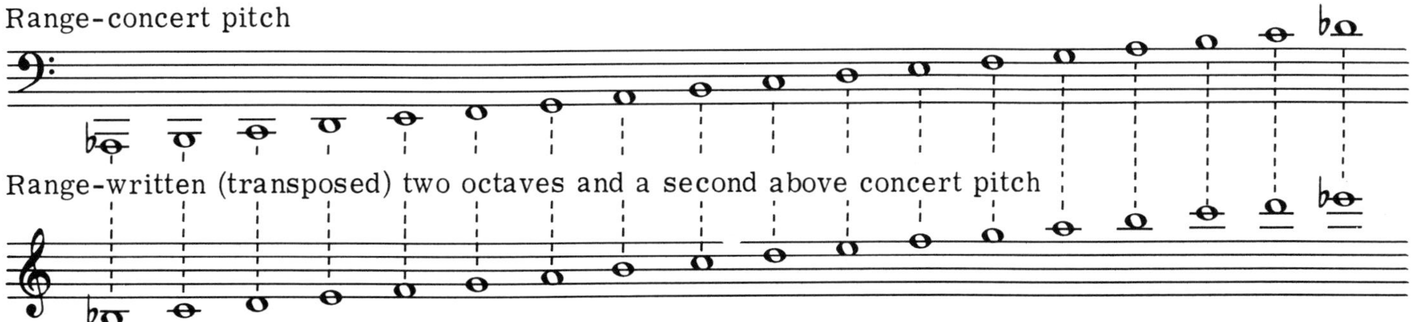

Range-written (transposed) two octaves and a second above concert pitch

4. The Double Reeds.

Instruments of the double reed group are all played with a "tucked lip" type of embouchure (which differs considerably from that of the clarinet or saxophone) and obviously with the use of double reeds (as opposed to single reeds of the clarinet and saxophone group).

A. The Oboe - a CONCERT PITCH INSTRUMENT

Range and (Written and Concert) of the Oboe

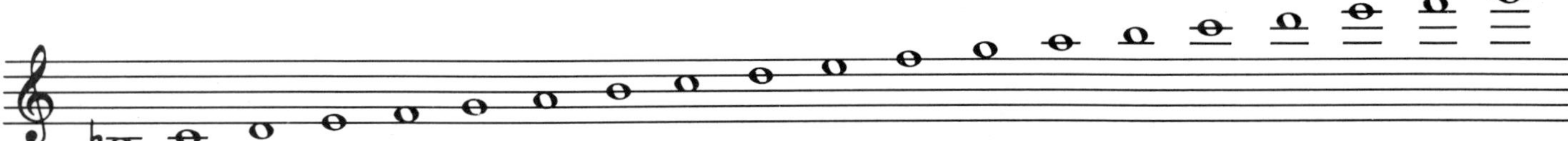

B. The English horn - a TRANSPOSING INSTRUMENT

Range and Transposition of the English Horn in F

Range-concert pitch

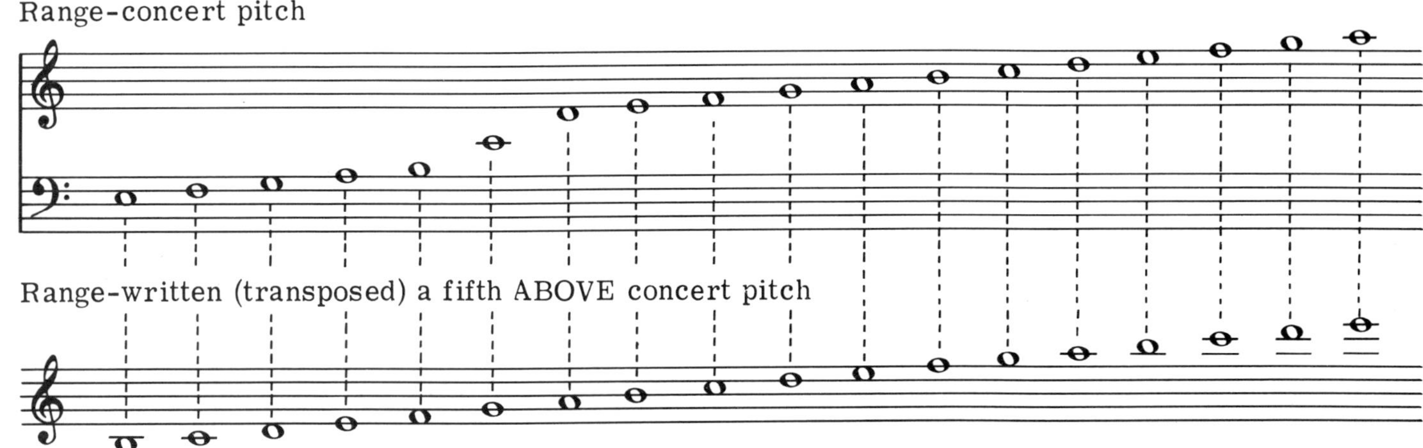

C. The Bassoon - a CONCERT PITCH INSTRUMENT

Range (Written and Concert) of the Bassoon

(Written on one staff-either bass or treble clef)

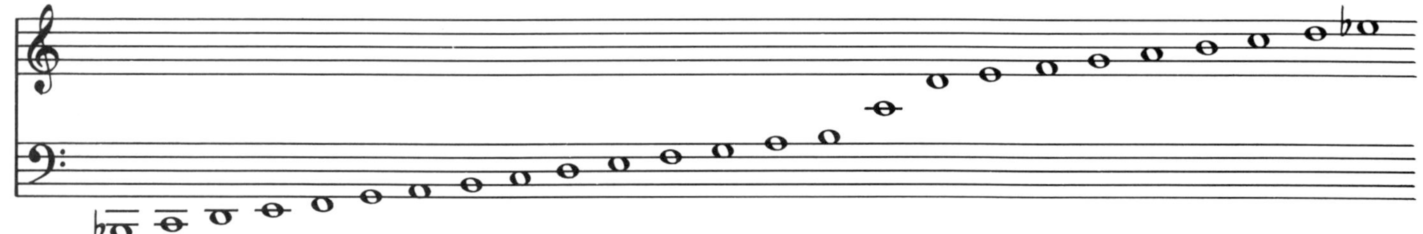

D. The Contra Bassoon - a TRANSPOSING INSTRUMENT

Range and Transposition of the Contra Bassoon

Range-concert pitch

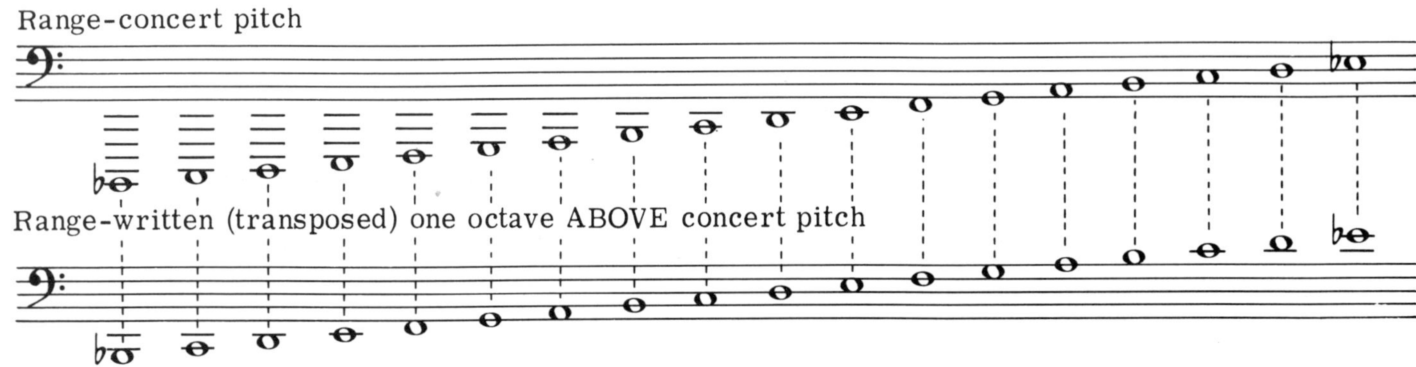

E. Other double reed instruments

1. The Soprano oboe in E♭

Range and Transposition of Soprano Oboe in E♭

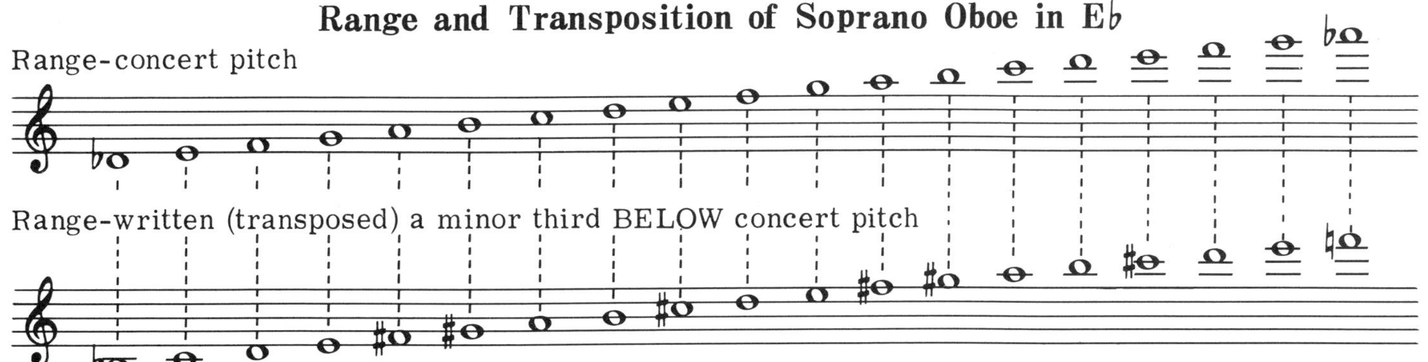

2. The Oboe d'Amore (in A)

Range and Transposition of the Oboe d'Amore (in A)

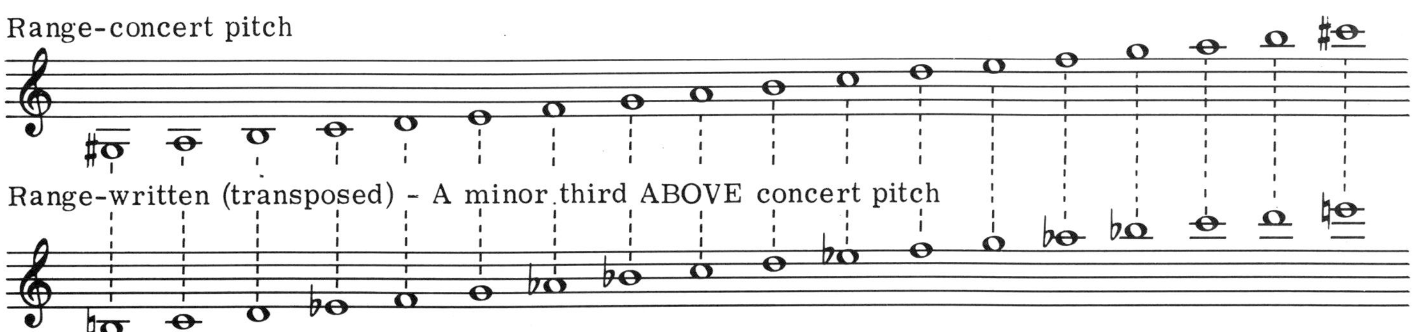

3. The Heckelphon

Range and Transposition of the Heckelphon

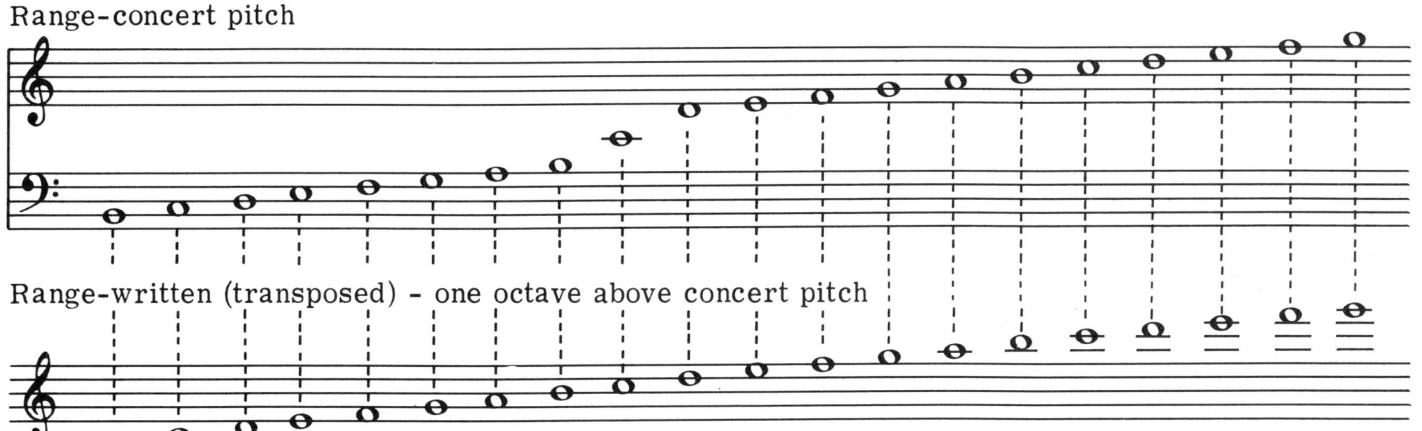

Range and Transposition of the Baritone Oboe in C

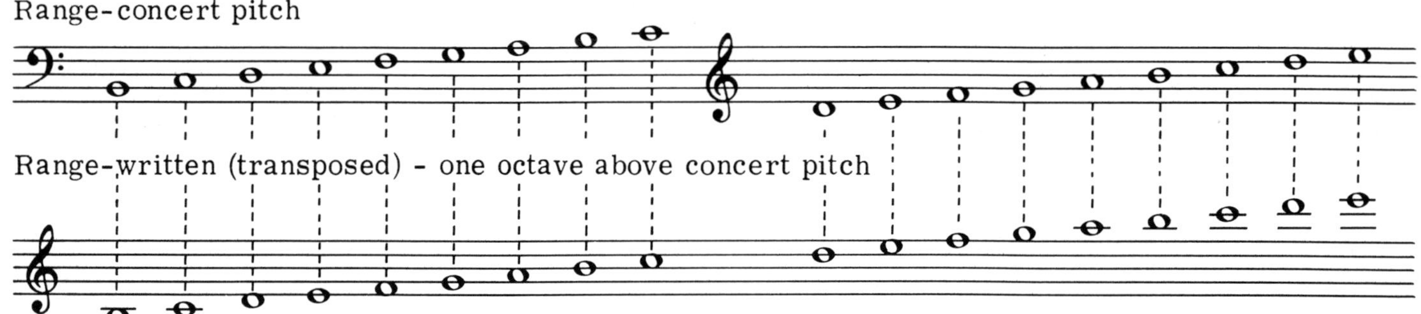

The Brass Instruments

Brass instruments differ from woodwind instruments in several ways. First of all, the sound is produced by the lips vibrating against a mouthpiece, as opposed to a vibrating reed of a clarinet, saxophone or double reed or blowing across a tone hole of a flute. Also brass instruments have valves which lengthen or shorten the stream of air going through tubing in the instrument as opposed to keys, opening and closing air holes on a woodwind instrument.

1. Trumpets

The group of brass instruments called trumpets include trumpets, cornets and flugel-horns.

A. The B♭ Trumpet

The B♭ trumpet is the "common" trumpet which we all see and hear in dance bands, marching bands and concert bands. It is a TRANSPOSING INSTRUMENT.

Range and Transposition of the B♭ Trumpet

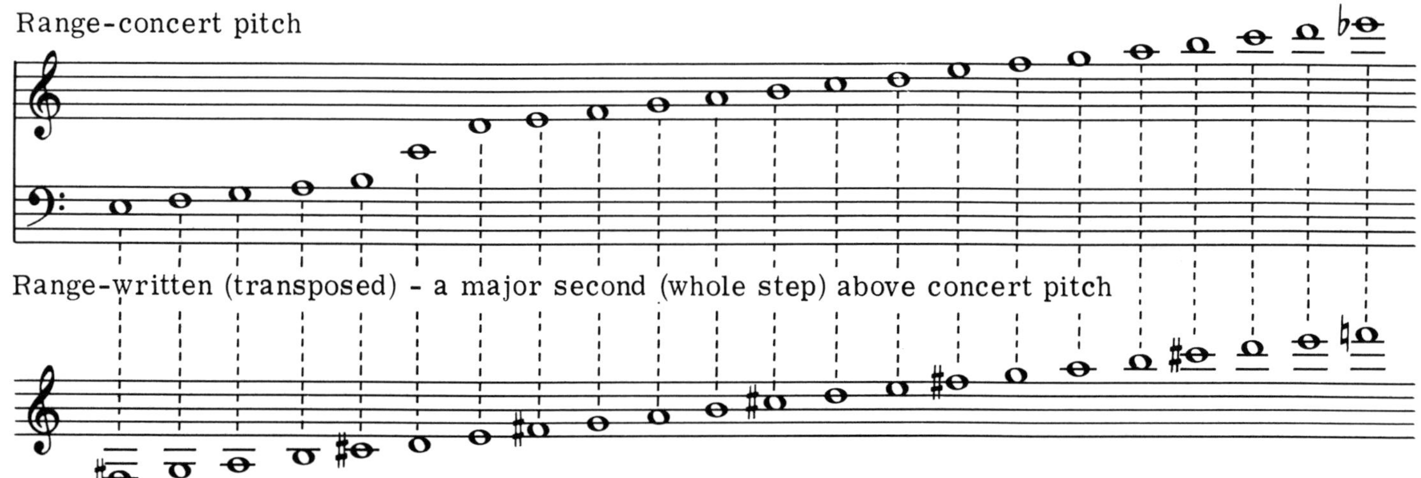

B. The B♭ Piccolo Trumpet

Range and Transposition of the B♭ Piccolo Trumpet

Range-concert pitch

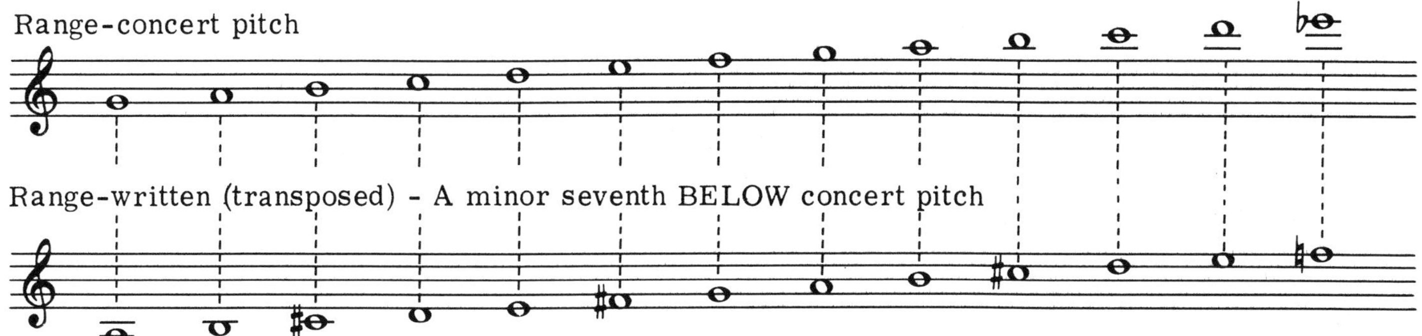

Range-written (transposed) - A minor seventh BELOW concert pitch

C. The D Trumpet

Range and Transposition of the D Trumpet

Range-concert pitch

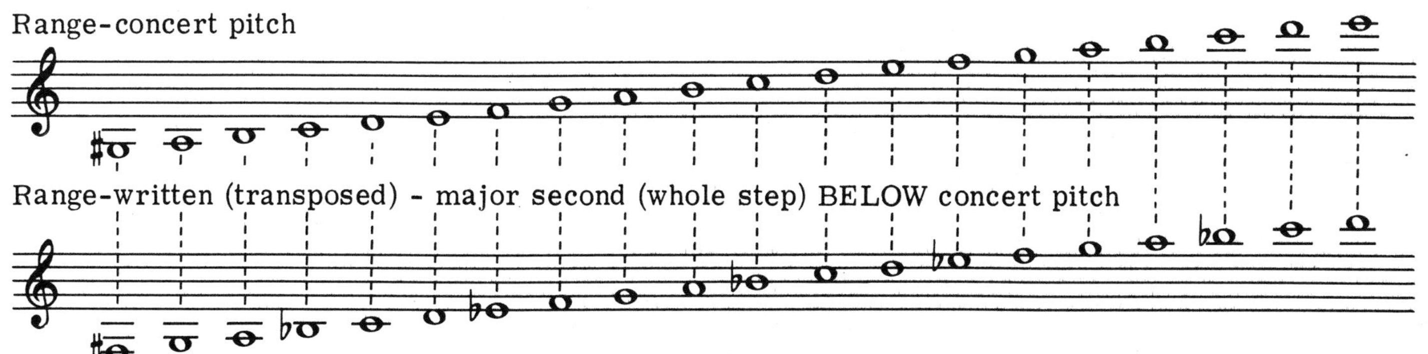

Range-written (transposed) - major second (whole step) BELOW concert pitch

D. The B♭ Cornet

Range and Transposition of the B♭ Cornet

Range-concert pitch

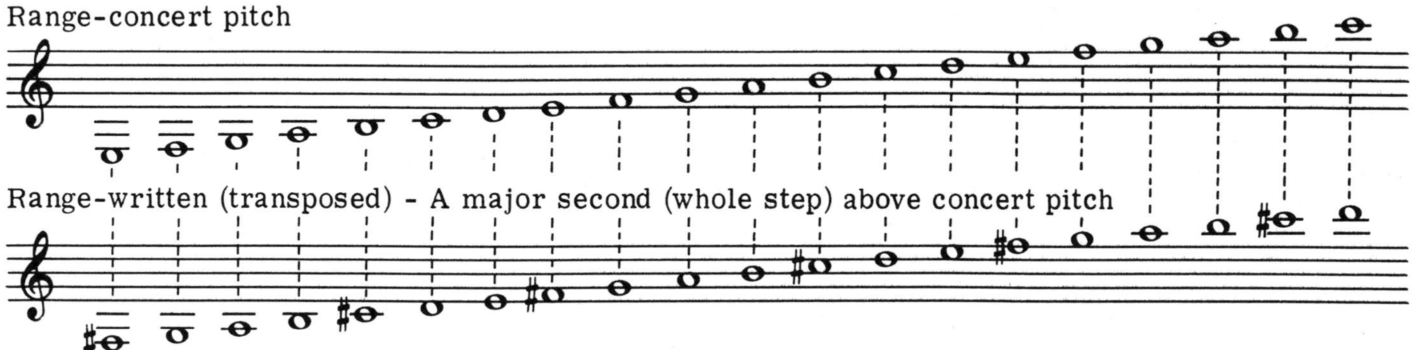

Range-written (transposed) - A major second (whole step) above concert pitch

Range and Transposition of the B♭ Flugelhorn

Range-concert pitch

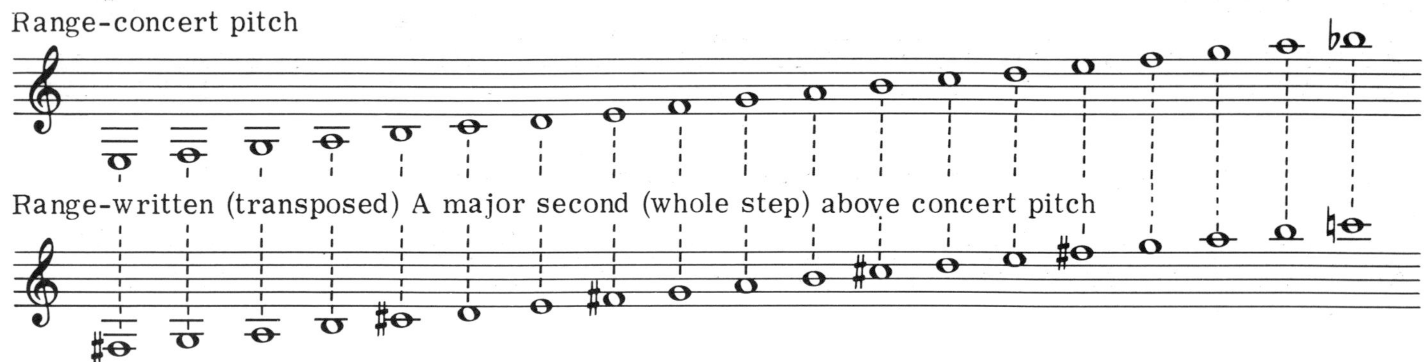

Range and Transposition of the B♭ Slide Trumpet

Range-concert pitch

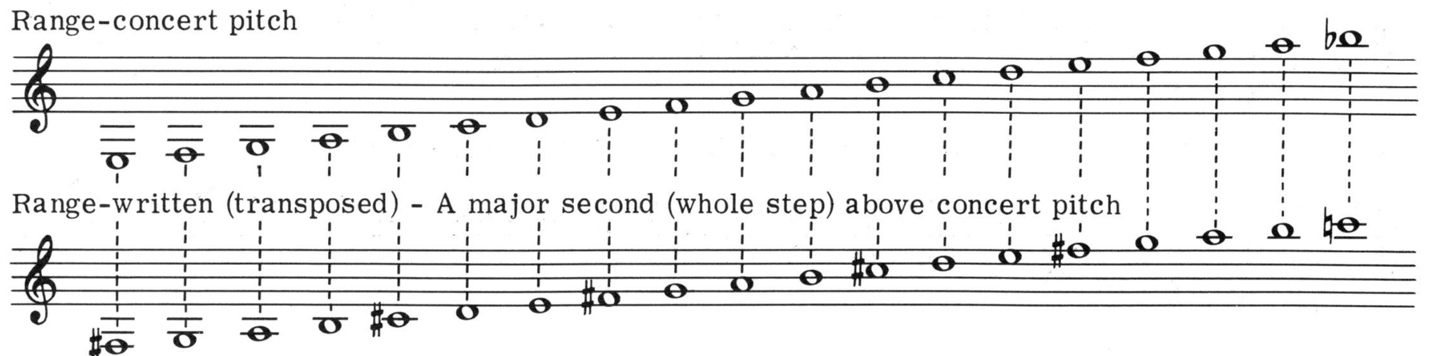

2. Trombones

    A. The Tenor Trombone

       The tenor trombone is the "common" trombone we all see and hear in dance bands, marching bands, concert bands and Dixieland bands. It is written in CONCERT PITCH.

Range (Concert and Written) of the Tenor Trombone

B. The Bass Trombone

The bass trombone is slightly larger than the tenor trombone, contains more
tubing to extend the lower register and has a trigger valve to allow the player to shift
into this extended tubing. It is found in most all dance bands, concert bands and symphony
orchestras. It is written in CONCERT PITCH.

Range (Concert and Written) of the Bass Trombone

C. The Valve Trombone

Range (Concert and Written) of the Valve Trombone

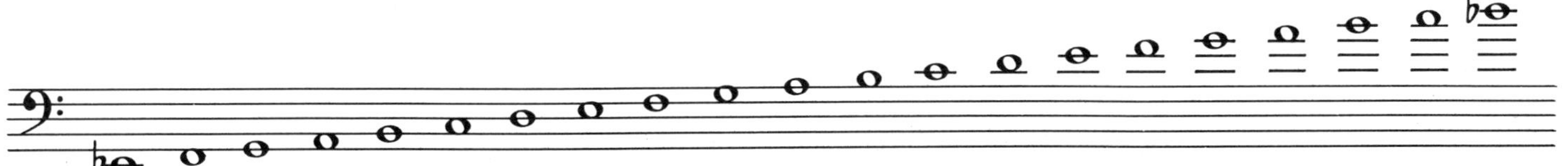

D. The Bass Trumpet

While called a Bass "Trumpet", this instrument is usually played by a trombone
player. If written in the bass clef, it is read in CONCERT PITCH. If written in the treble
clef, it is a TRANSPOSING INSTRUMENT.

Range and Transposition of the Bass Trumpet

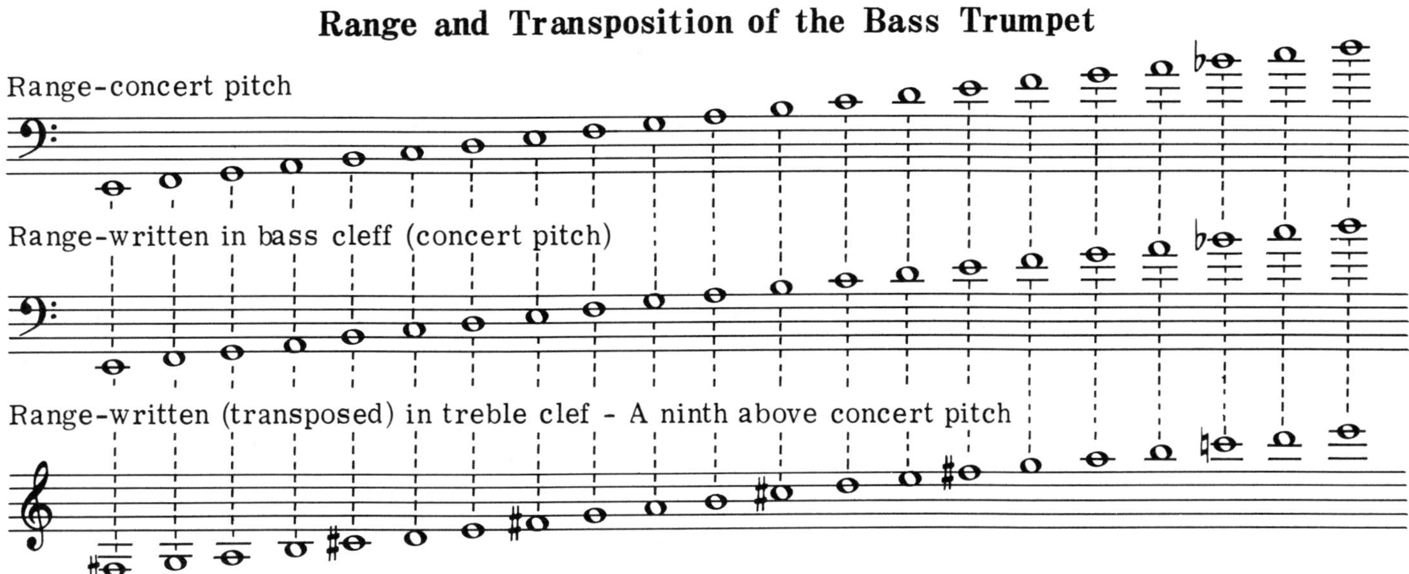

3. The French Horn

The modern day French Horn is a rotary valve instrument which has taken much of

the complication out of writing for the instrument. In years past, there were many French

horns, pitched in many different keys. But today's modern horn is pitched in F (to play C

on the instrument sounds a CONCERT F). Therefore, the French horn is a TRANSPOSING

INSTRUMENT. It should be noted that while most of the music written for French horn is

in treble clef, occasionally, when the bottom part of the register is needed, you will

write parts in the bass clef.

Range and Transposition of the French Horn

Range-concert pitch

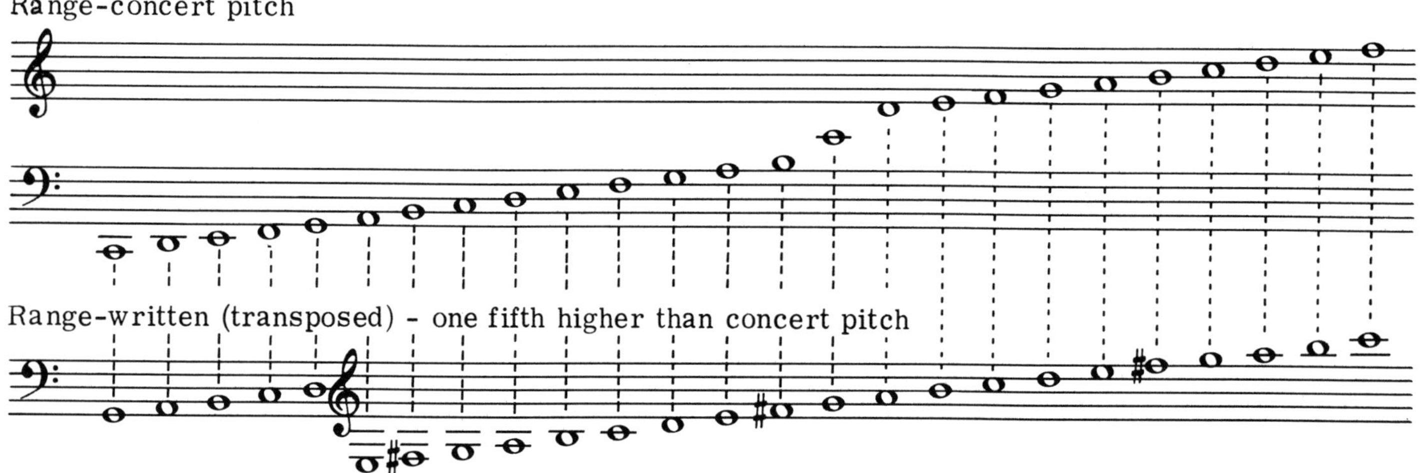

4. The Tuba

It should be noted that the "tuba" is a generic name given to both the Orchestral Tuba

and the Sousaphone. You should be aware that the "Tuba" has its bell pointed up, while

the Sousaphone is a marching band instrument and has its bell pointed forward.

A. The Orchestral Tuba

Range (Written and Concert) for the Double B♭ & Double C Tuba and Sousaphone

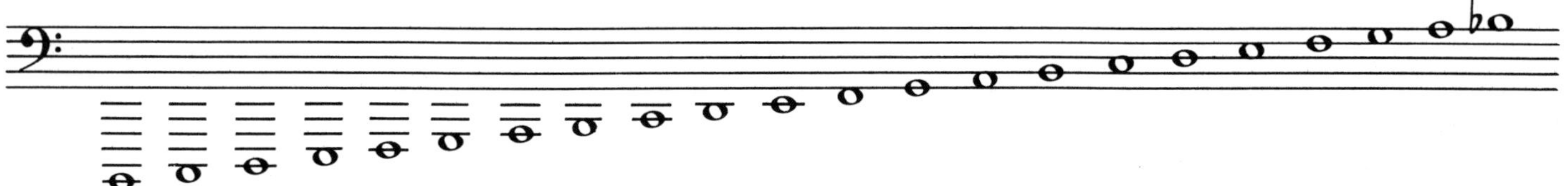

5. Other Brass Instruments

The following are additional brass instruments which you may, from time to time need to write for.

Range and Transposition for the E♭ Piccolo Trumpet

Range-concert pitch

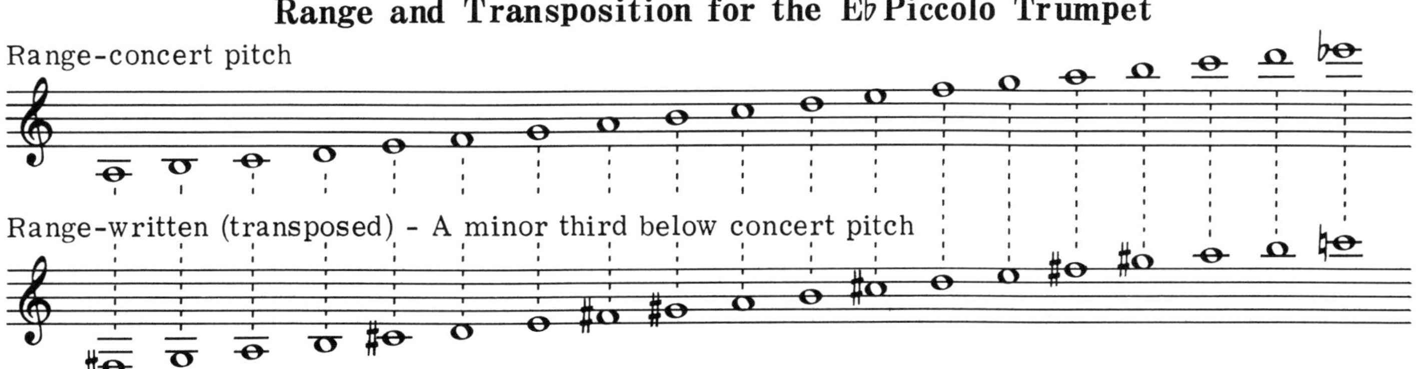

Range and Transposition for Trumpet in F (Alto Trumpet)

Range-concert pitch

Range and Transposition for A Trumpet

Range-concert pitch

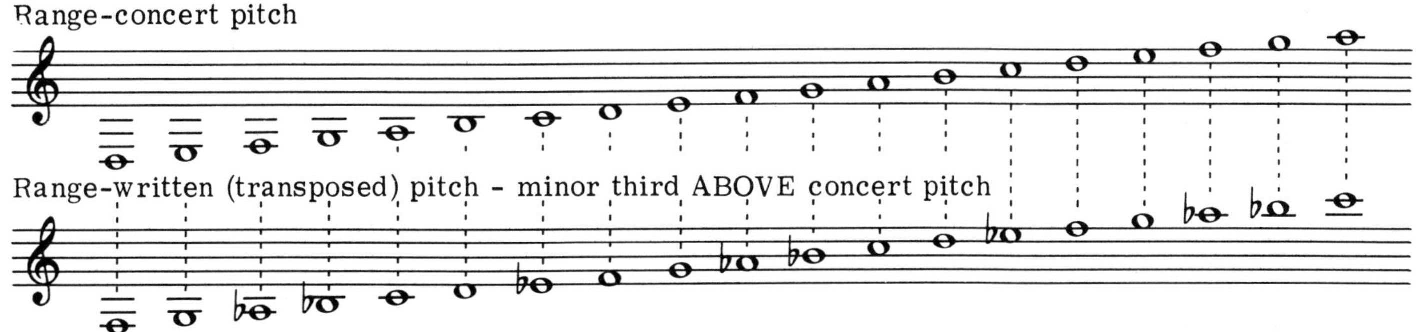

Range and Transposition for E♭ Piccolo Cornet

Range-concert pitch

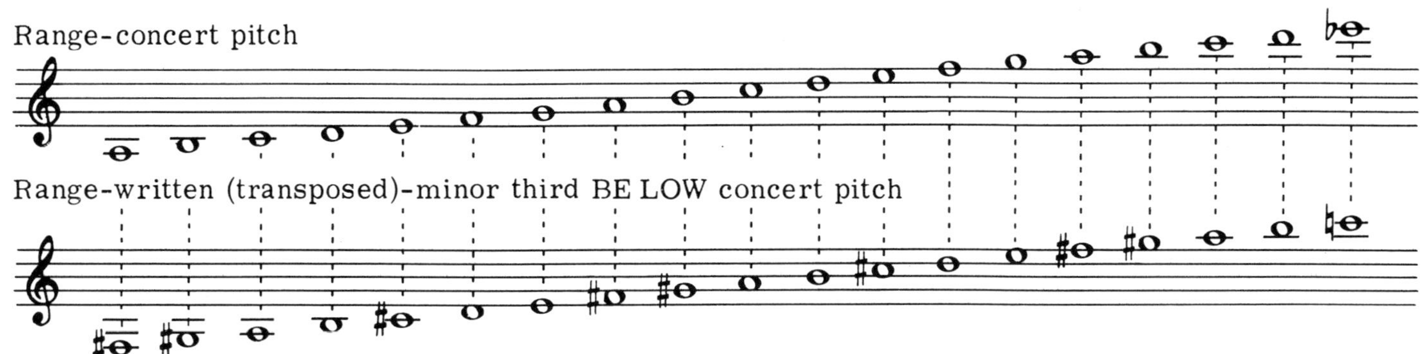

Range and Transposition of Cornet in A

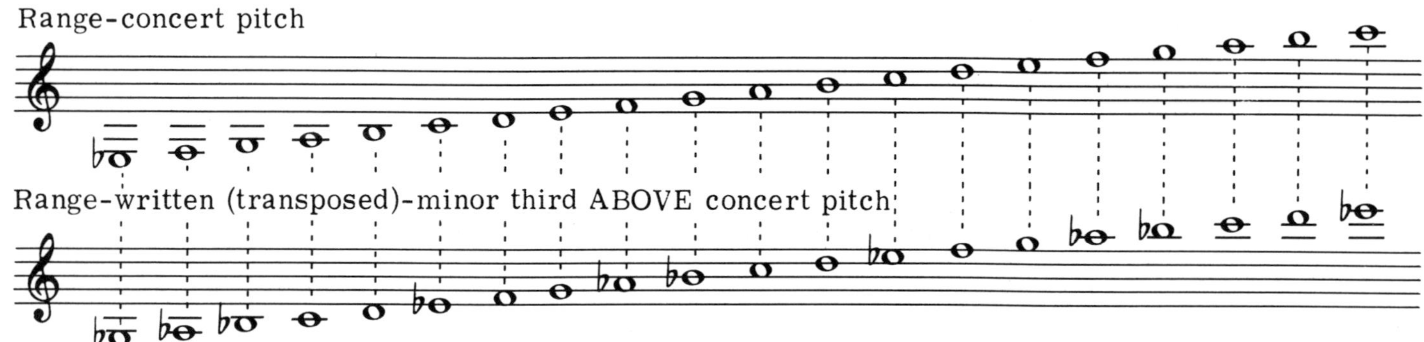

Range and Transposition of Alto Horn in F

Range and Transposition of Alto Horn in E♭

Range and Transposition of E♭ Soprano Flugelhorn

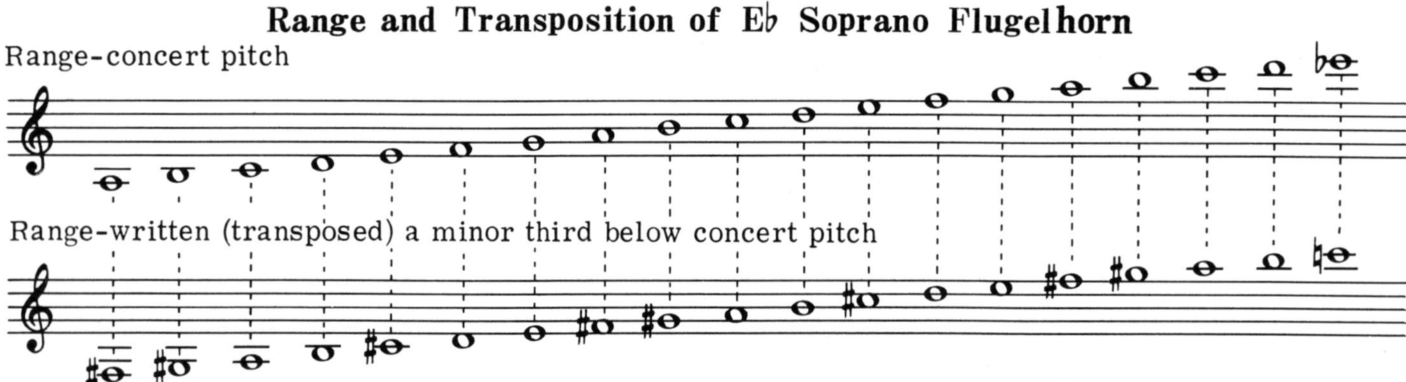

Range and Transposition of the E♭ Alto Flugelhorn

Range-concert pitch

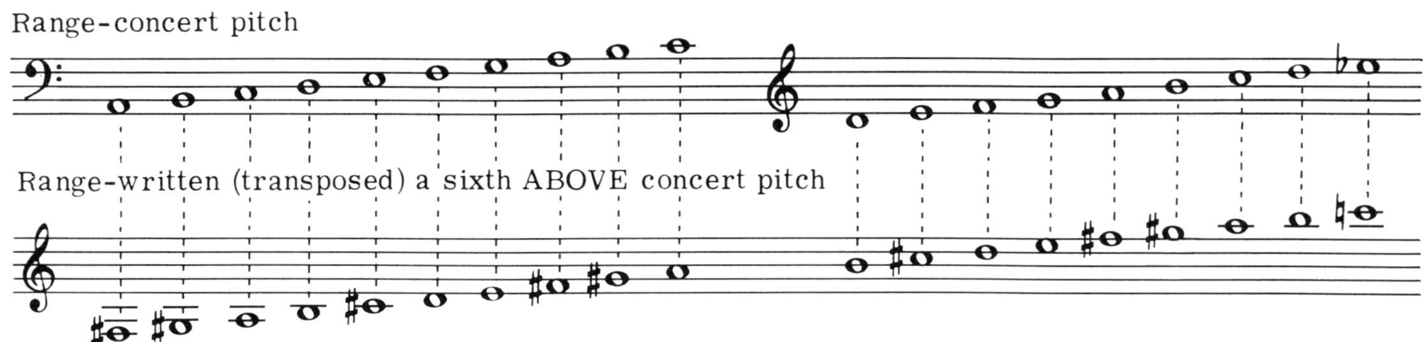

Range-written (transposed) a sixth ABOVE concert pitch

Range and Transposition of B♭ Bugle (non keyed)

Range-concert pitches playable

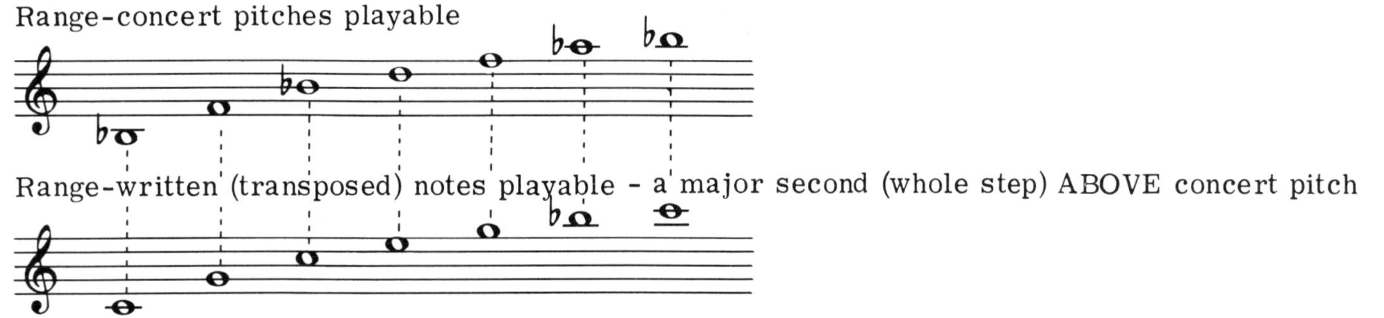

Range-written (transposed) notes playable - a major second (whole step) ABOVE concert pitch

Range and Transposition of G Bugle

Range-concert pitchs playable

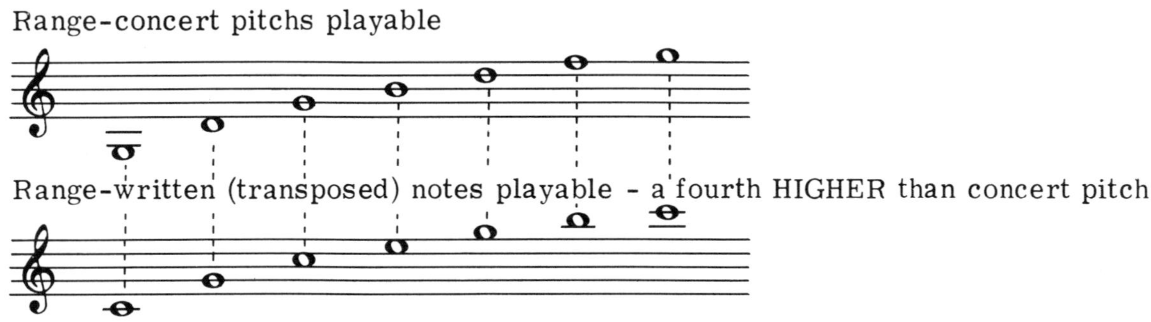

Range-written (transposed) notes playable - a fourth HIGHER than concert pitch

Range and Transposition of Soprano Piston Bugle

Range-concert pitch

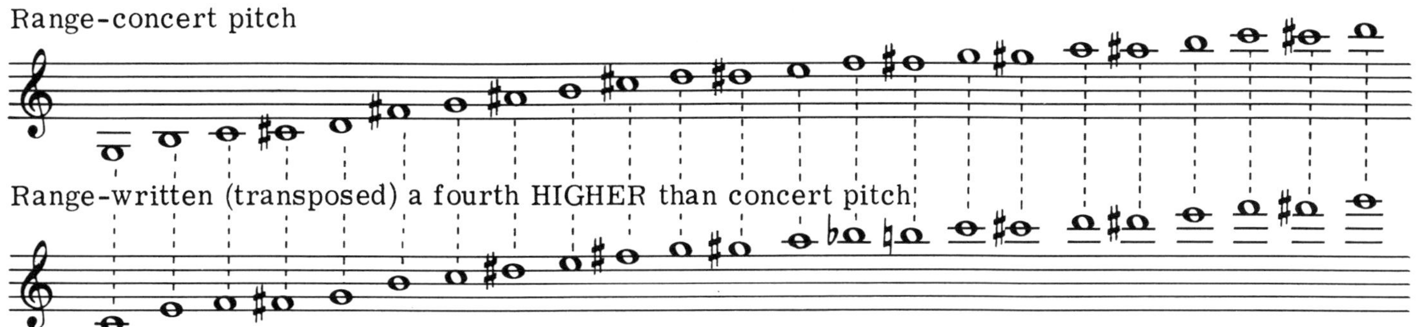

Range-written (transposed) a fourth HIGHER than concert pitch

Range and Transposition of French Horn in B♭

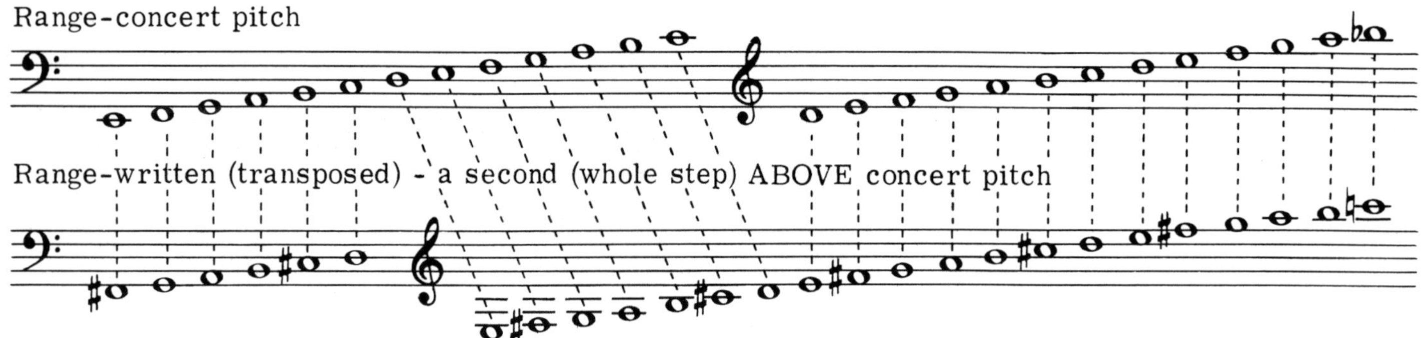

Range and Transposition of the French Horn in E♭

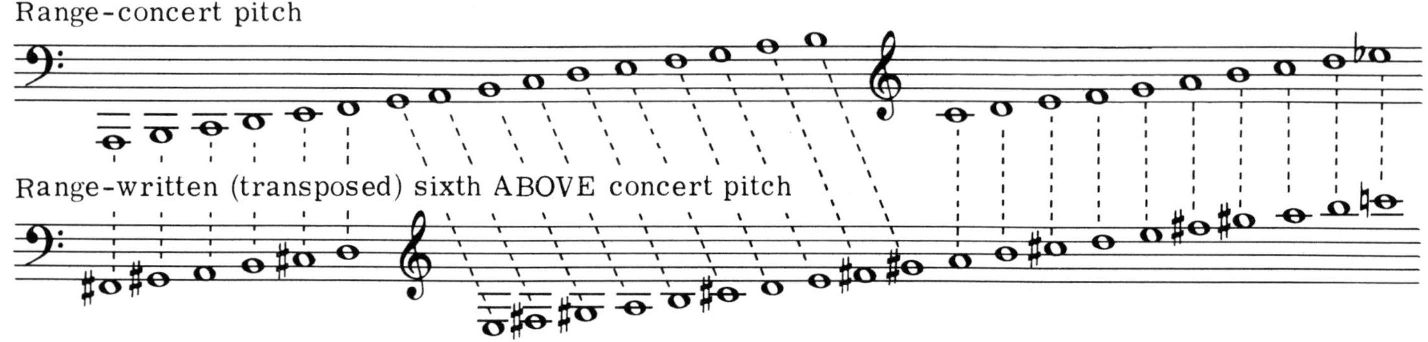

Range and Transposition of Mellophone in E♭

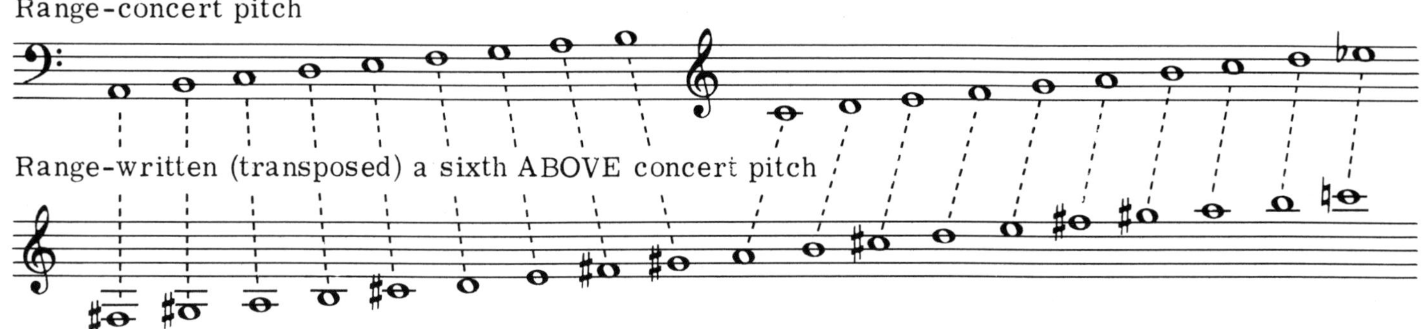

Range and Transposition of the Tuben (Tenor in B♭)

Range (Concert and Written) of Alto Trombone

Range and Transposition of Baritone Horn in B♭ (3 valves)

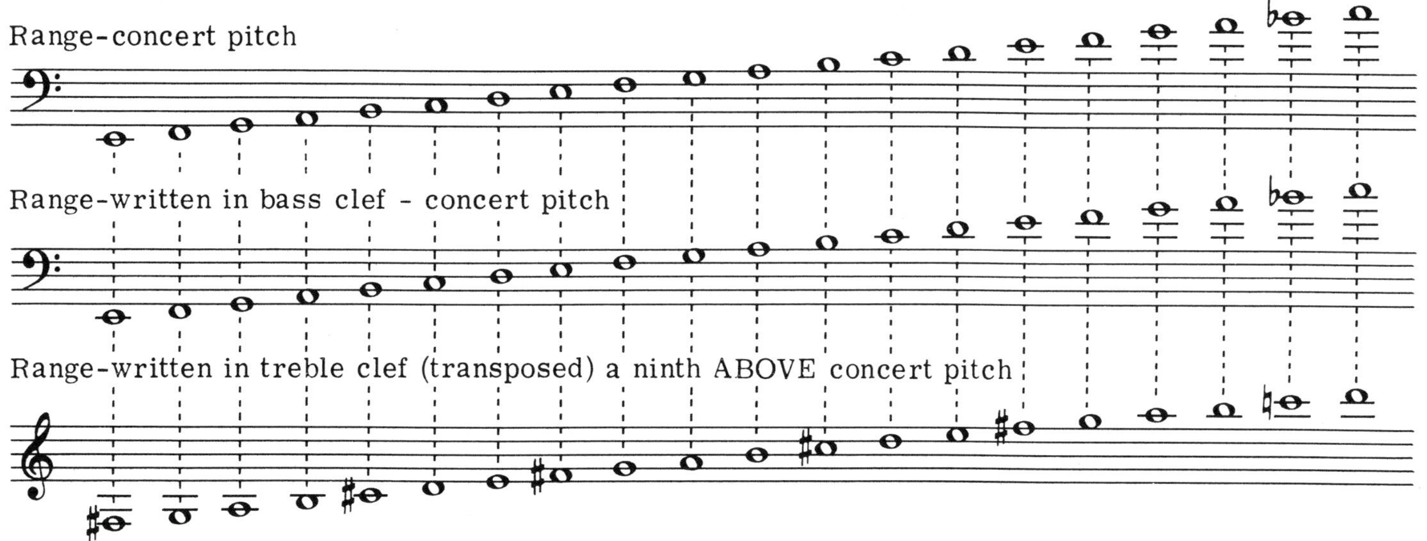

Range and Transposition of Euphonium in B♭ (4 valves)

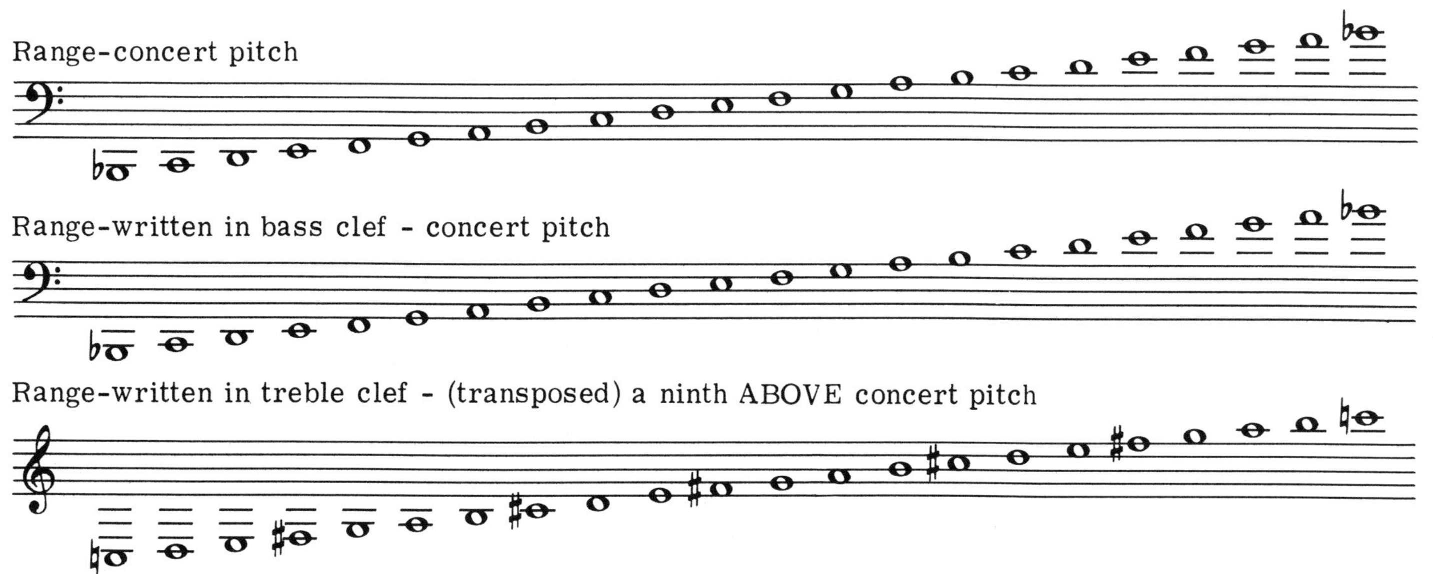

The Strings

When I refer to the group of instruments known as the "Strings", I define that group

as belonging to the instruments which are bowed - violins, violas, cellos and string basses

(as opposed to guitar, mandolin, banjo, etc. which are stringed instruments but are NOT

bowed).

1. The Violin

The violin is a CONCERT PITCH instrument, as you write it exactly where it sounds on the Grand Staff.

Range (Concert and Written) of the Violin

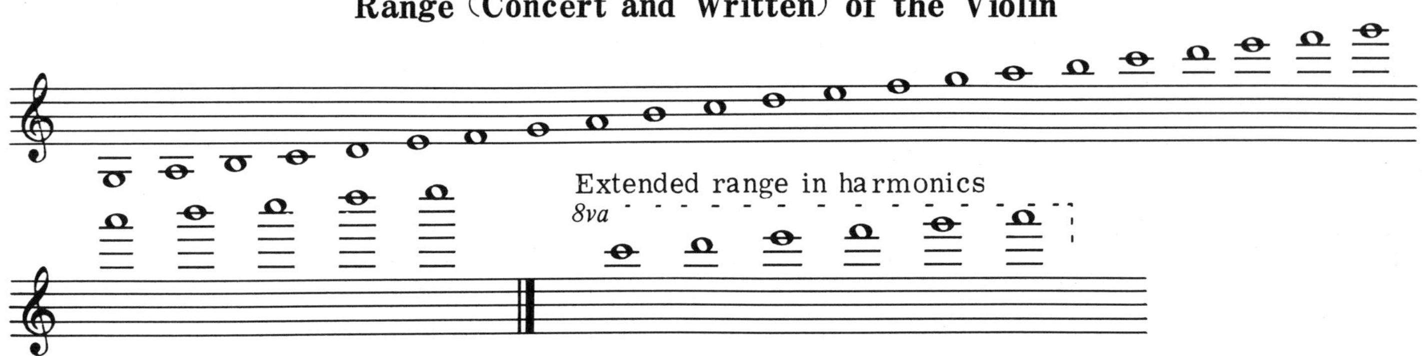

2. The Viola

The viola is written entirely in the ALTO CLEF. Below, you will see the violas register illustrated on the Grand Staff (in concert pitch) as well as where it is written (in the alto clef) which is also in CONCERT PITCH.

Range (Concert and Written) of the Viola

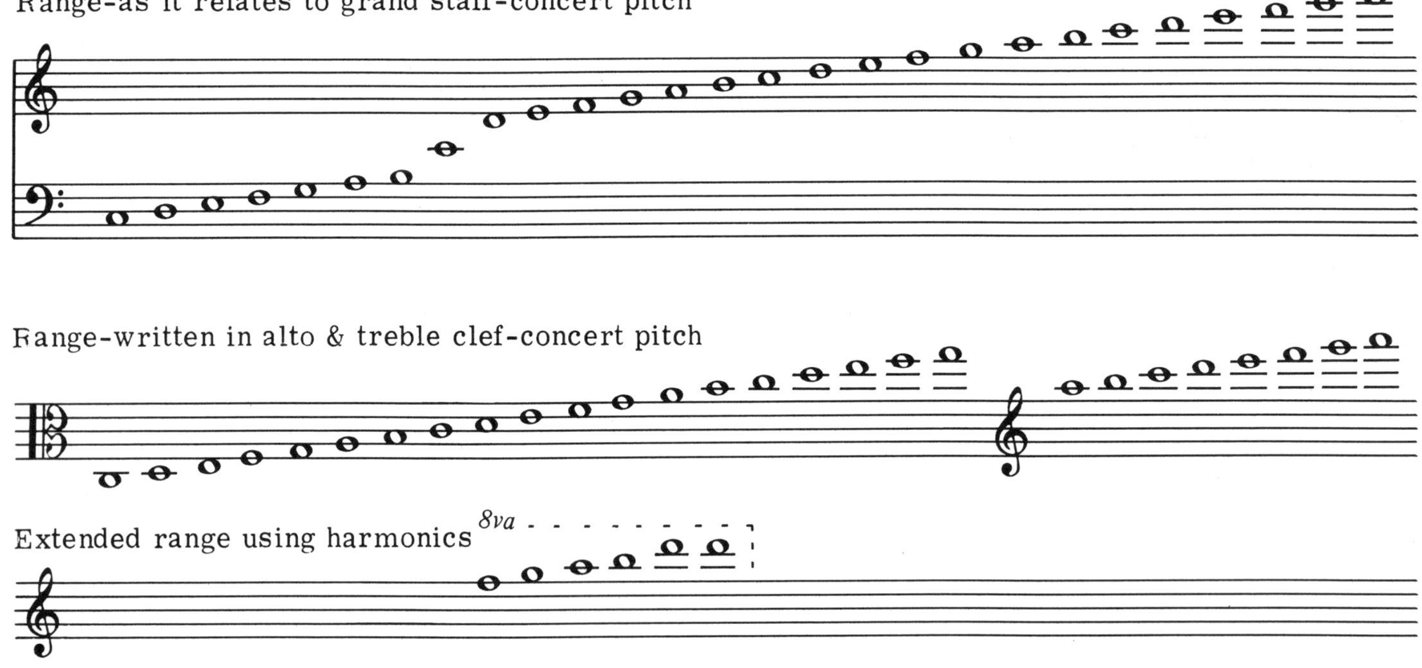

3. The Cello

The cello is usually written in the bass clef, but on occasion you will see it written in tenor and even treble clefs. It is a CONCERT PITCH instrument, so you write it as it sounds on the Grand Staff. For illustration of the cello's range, I will only use bass and tenor clef (although treble clef is used frequently too).

Range (Concert and Written) of the Cello

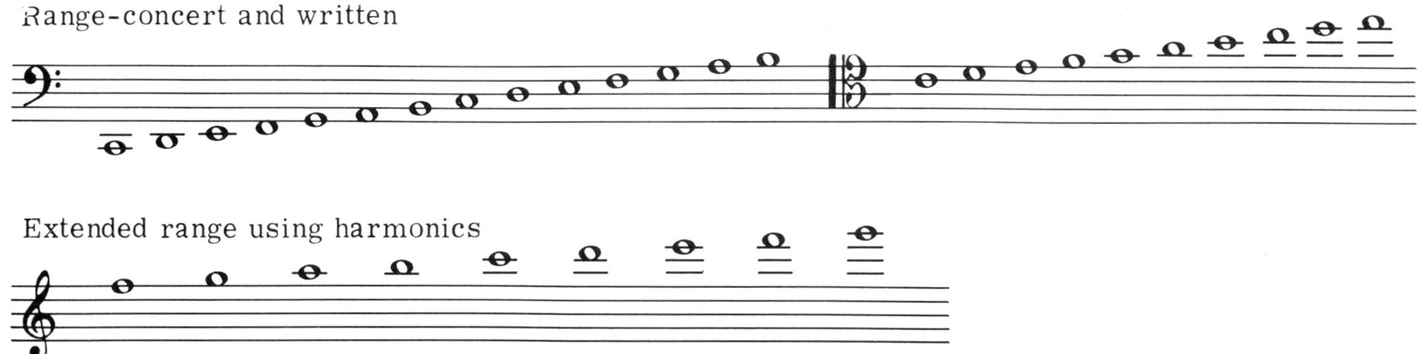

4. The String Bass (Double Bass)

The string bass is a TRANSPOSING INSTRUMENT, as it sounds one octave lower than it is written. Illustrated below is the Grand Staff (concert) range of the string bass and the written (transposed) range of the instrument as well.

Range and Transposition of the String Bass

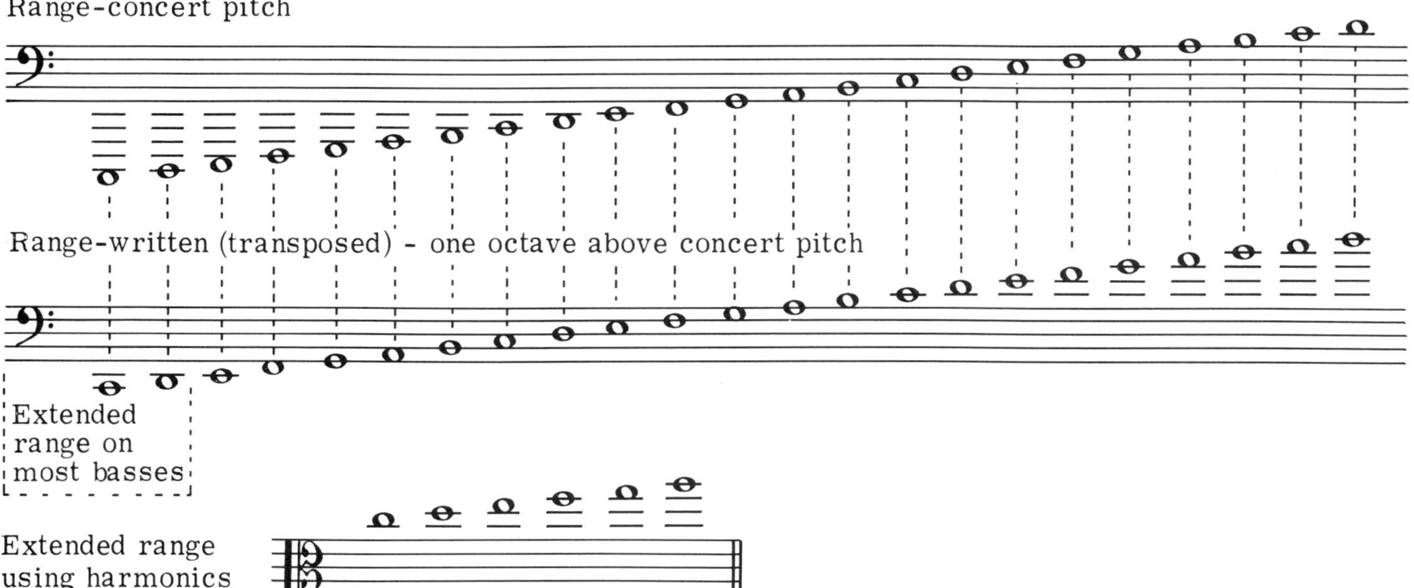

Please notice by the above examples that the string bass is "primarily" written in bass clef, although tenor clef is used in extreme high registers. Also, most modern day "orchestral" string basses use an extension to facilitate their going down to a low C. Jazz and dance band string basses normally only go down to the low E.

Keyboard Instruments

Instruments in the Keyboard group are piano, celesta, accordion, concertina, electric piano, harpsichord, clavichord, calliope, clavietta and synthesizers. Since synthesizers are such a specialized study, they will be omitted.

1. The Piano

Since the piano was illustrated by the Grand Staff early in the book, we will now use an abbreviated illustration of its tremendous range. Of course, the piano is a CONCERT PITCH INSTRUMENT.

Range (Concert and Written) for the Piano

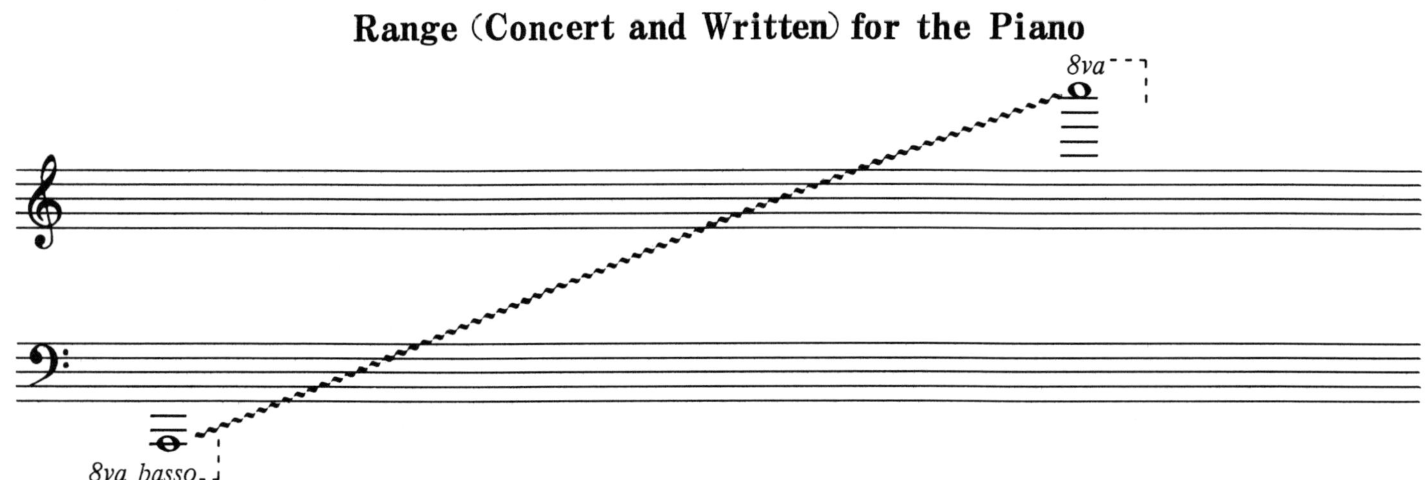

2. The Celesta

The celesta is a keyboard instrument, sometimes considered part of the percussion
family, and uses metal bars to produce its sound. It is played on a keyboard which in
turn strikes the metal bars, sounding much like orchestra bells played with a soft mallet.
It is a TRANSPOSING INSTRUMENT.

Range and Transposition for the Celesta

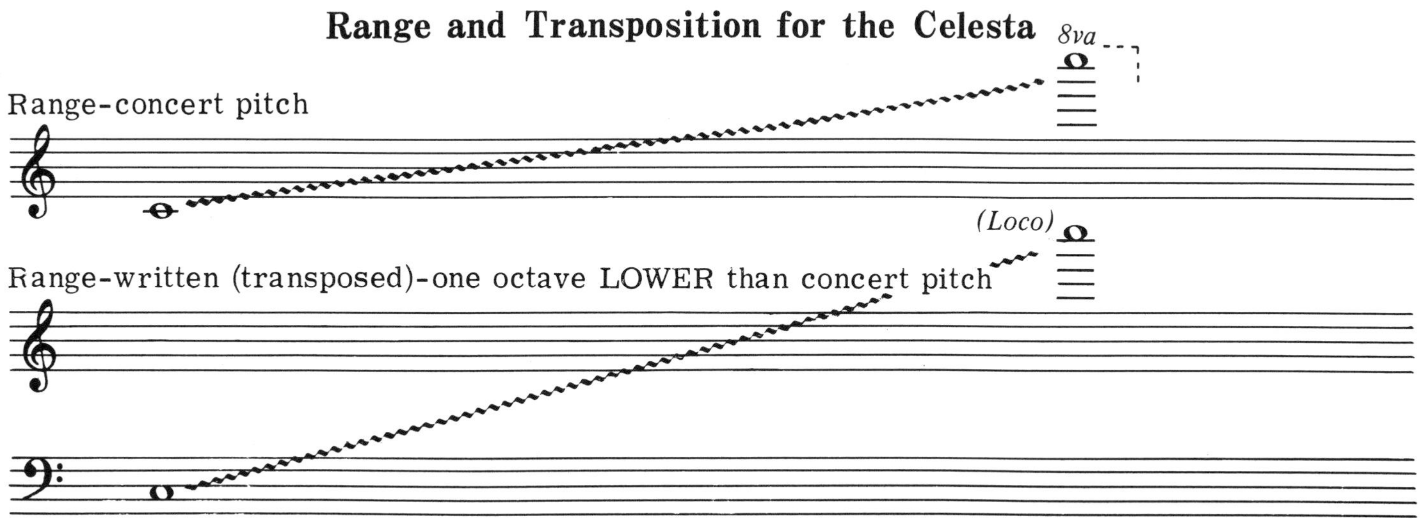

3. The Accordion

Played by squeezing a diaphragm and forcing air through reeds, this keyboard
instrument is written in CONCERT PITCH.

Range (Concert and Written) for the Accordion

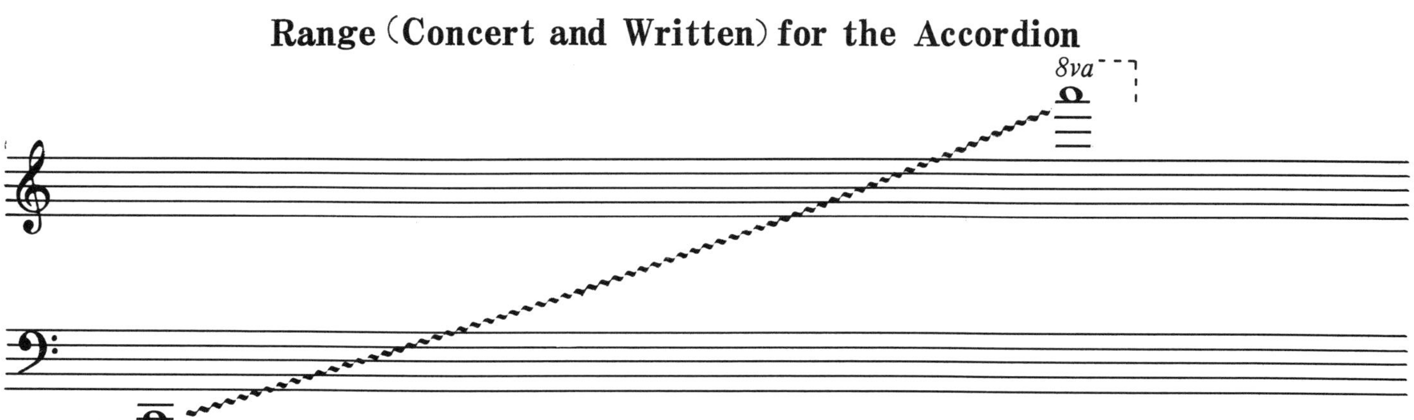

4. The Concertina

A variation of an accordion, the concertina is quite smaller in size. It is written in
CONCERT PITCH.

Range (Concert and Written) of the Concertina

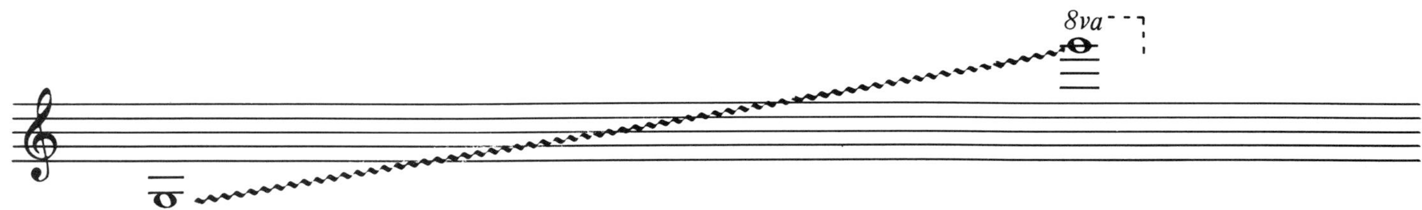

5. The Electric Piano

The electric piano "generally" has a somewhat narrower range than the standard
eighth-eight key piano, although there are some eighty-eight key electric pianos available.
Of course, this is a CONCERT PITCH INSTRUMENT.

Range (Concert and Written) of the Electric Piano
Non-Eighty-Eight Key Variety

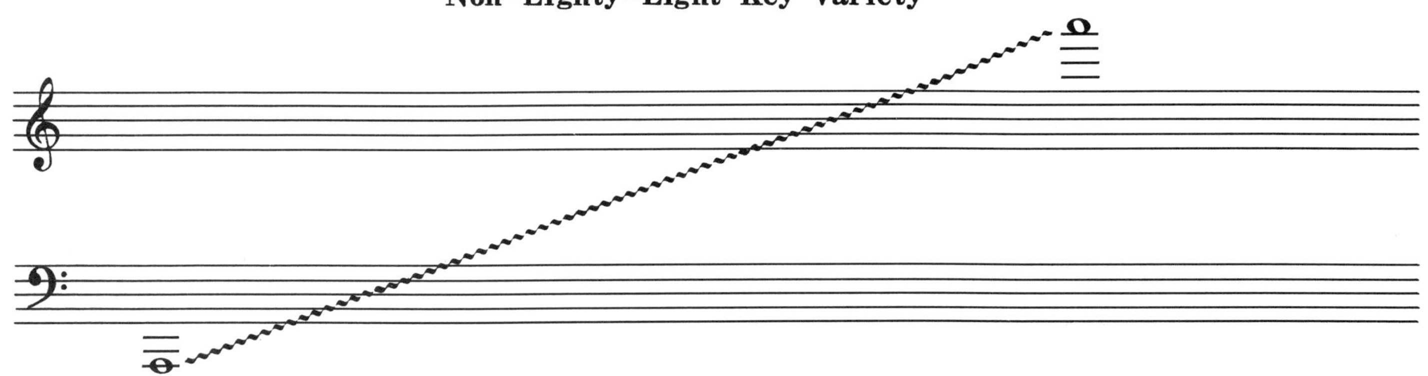

6. The Harpsichord (double and single keyboards) - CONCERT PITCH INSTRUMENT.

Range (Concert and Written) of the Harpsichord
(Double Keyboard) Employing 16', 8'   4' Stops

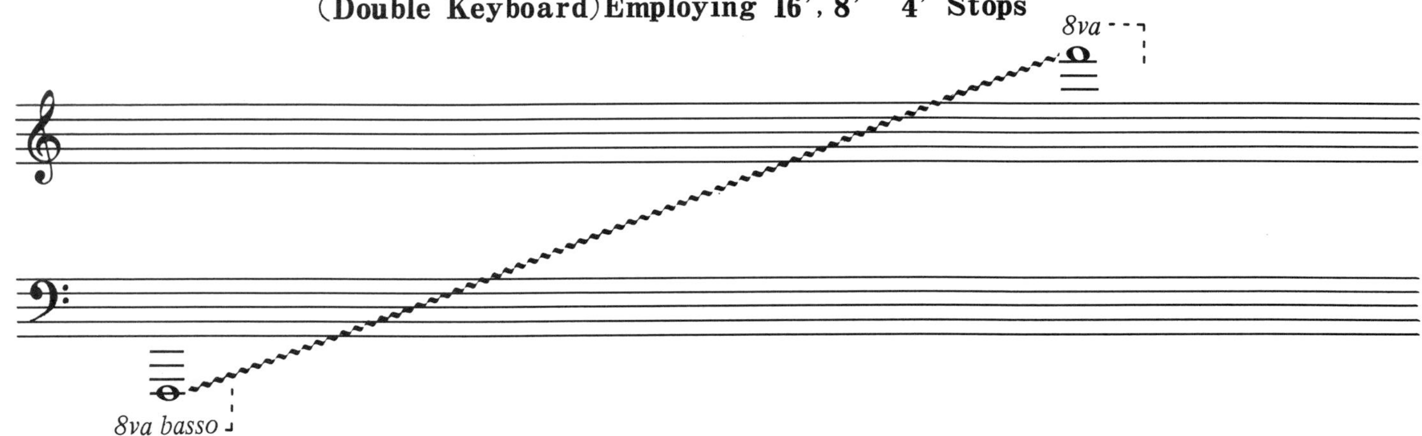

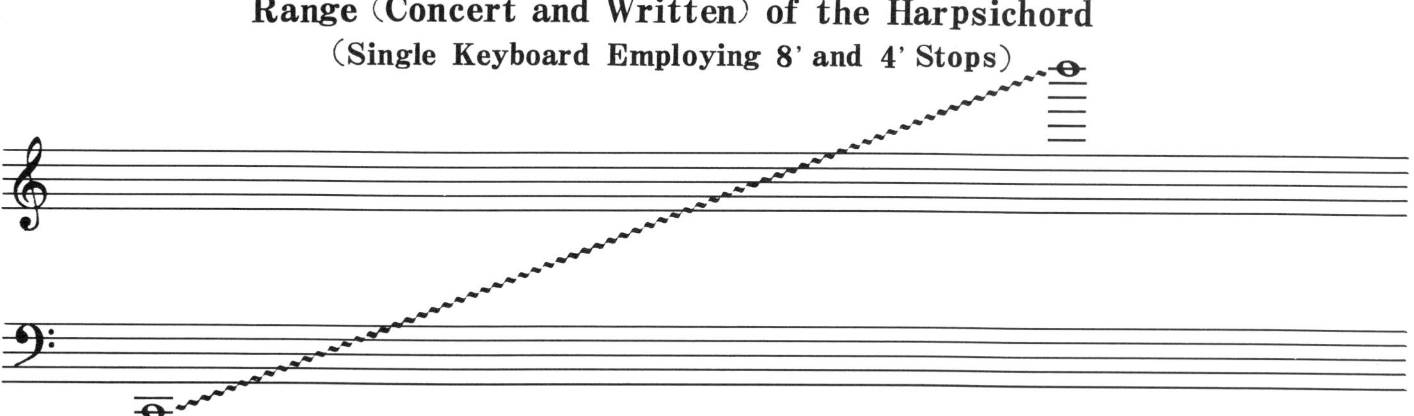

7. The Clavichord - CONCERT PITCH INSTRUMENT

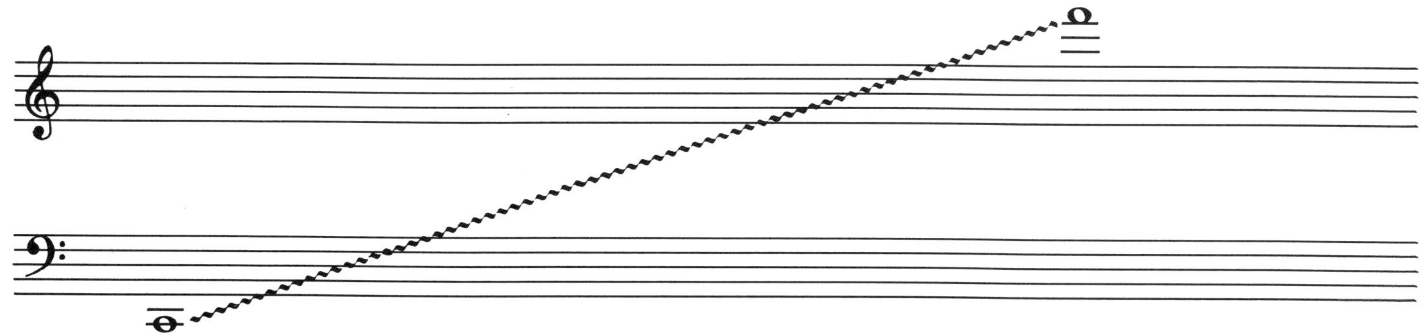

8. The Calliope

Since the calliope is such an individulaized instrument (so many different types were made over the last 150 years), it is best to know exactly what instrument you are writing a part for BEFORE you write it.

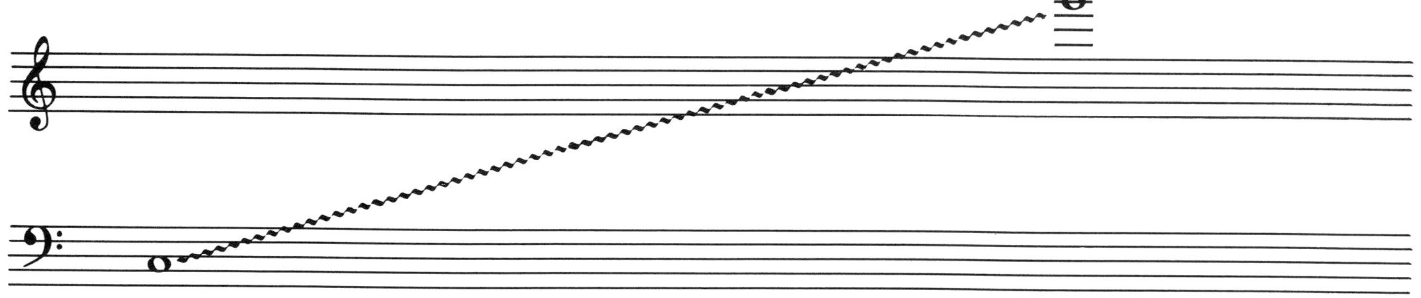

9. The Clavietta

The clavietta is a small "wind" instrument that has a mouthpiece and a keyboard
which resembles a piano.

Range (Concert and Written) of the Clavietta

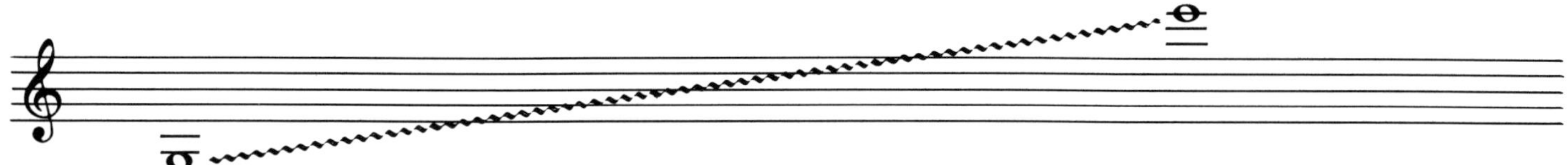

Fretted Instrument Family

1. Guitars

A. The Electric or Acoustic Guitar

The guitar is a TRANSPOSING INSTRUMENT, sounding one octave below where
it is written.

Range and Transposition of the Electric or Acoustic Guitars

Range-concert pitch

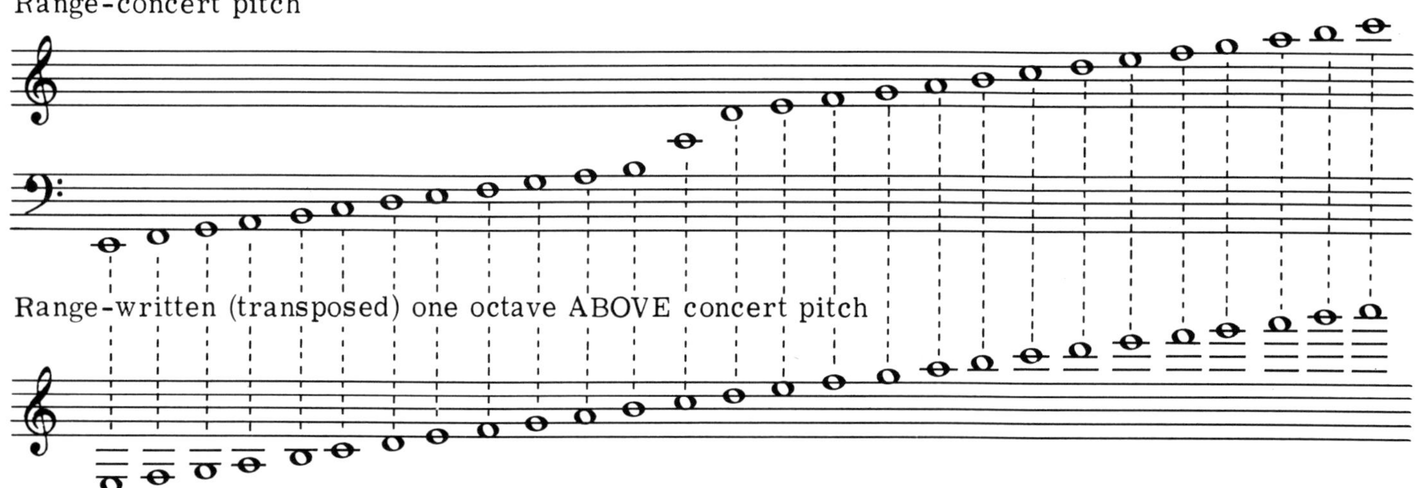

B. The Twelve String Guitar

The twelve string guitar is unique, as four of its strings are tuned in octaves.
You notate ONLY the bottom octave note when writing a twelve string guitar part. Study
the following illustration to grasp this concept. The first two strings are double strings
of the same pitch.

Range and Transposition of the Twelve String Guitar

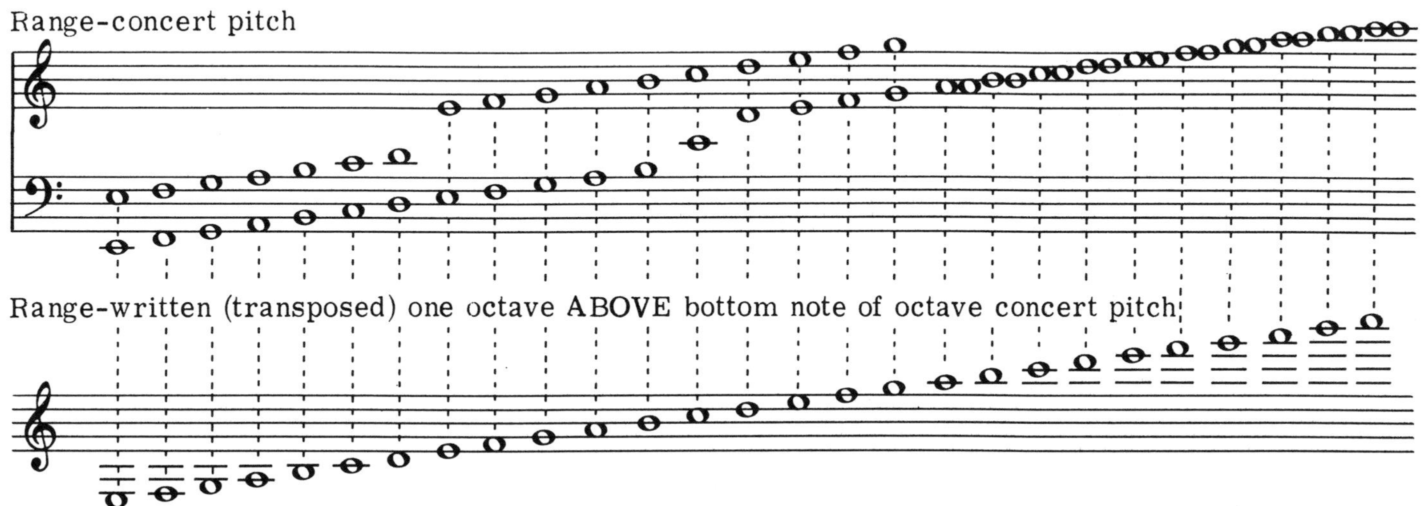

C. The "Classical" (Gut String) Guitar

Strung with nylon string, the "Classical" guitar is used in the true classical
style as well as in folk, flamingo, Mexican and "mood" music. It's range is slightly less
than the electric guitar in the top register, because of its construction.

Range and Transposition of the Classical Guitar (Gut String)

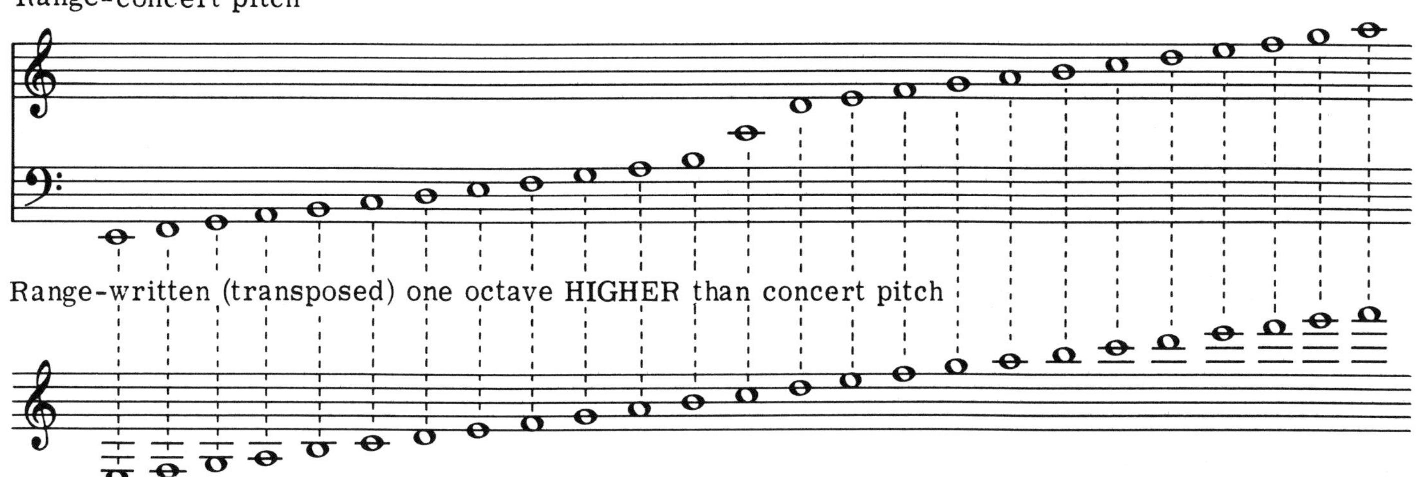

Range and Transposition of the Alto Guitar in F
(The Mexican Riquinta)

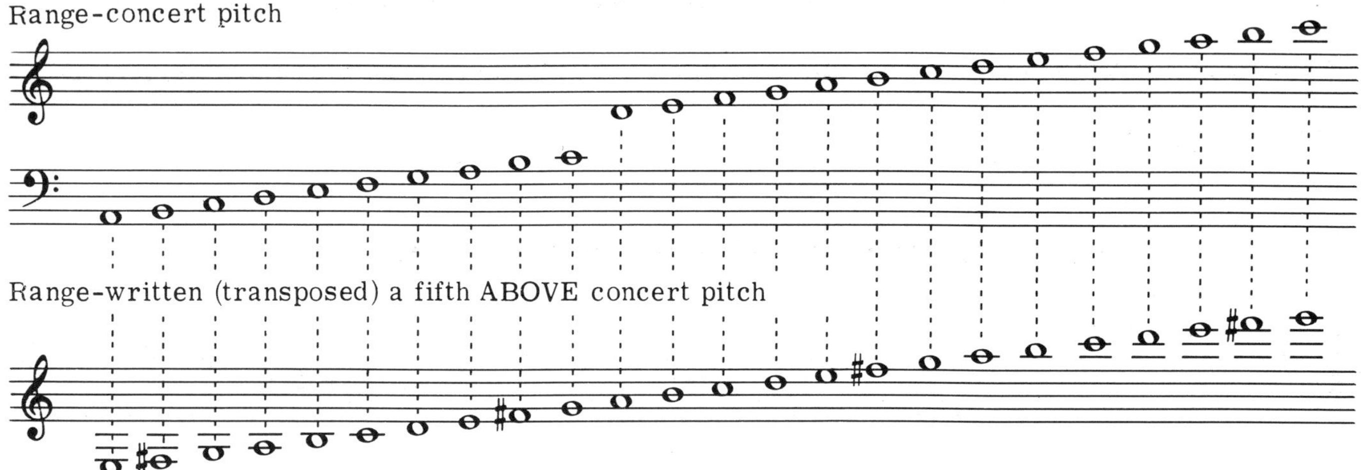

E. The Six String Bass Guitar

This instrument is almost always played by guitarists and is written entirely in the TREBLE CLEF.

Range and Transposition of the Six String Bass Guitar

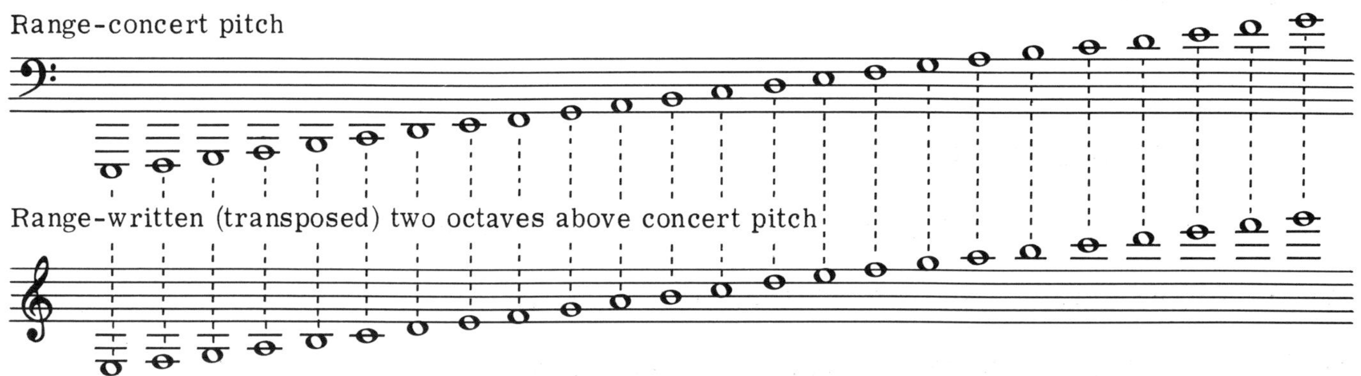

F. The Bass Guitar (4 String) - also known as the "Fender" Bass

The bass guitar (Fender Bass) is almost always played by "bass players" and is written entirely in the Bass Clef.

Range and Transposition of the Bass Guitar
(4 String "Fender" Bass)

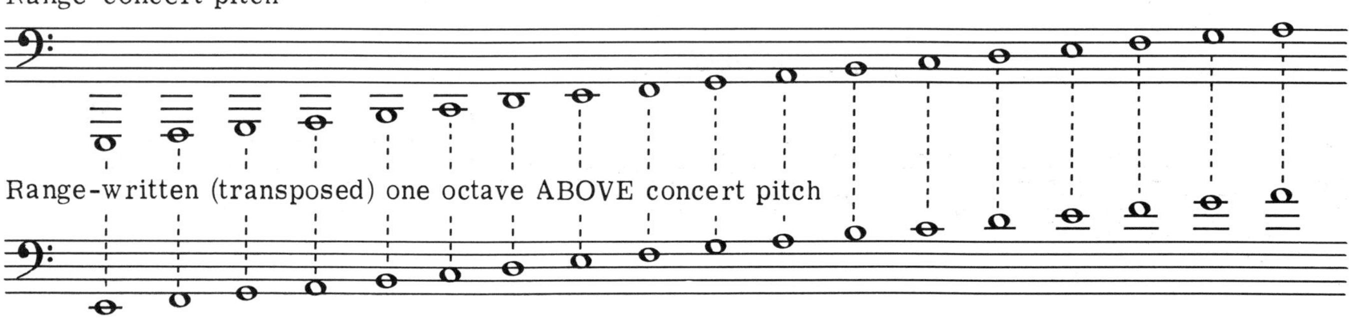

G. Guitarron (Mexican bass guitar)

Range and Transposition of the Guitarron
(Mexican Bass Guitar)

Range-concert pitch

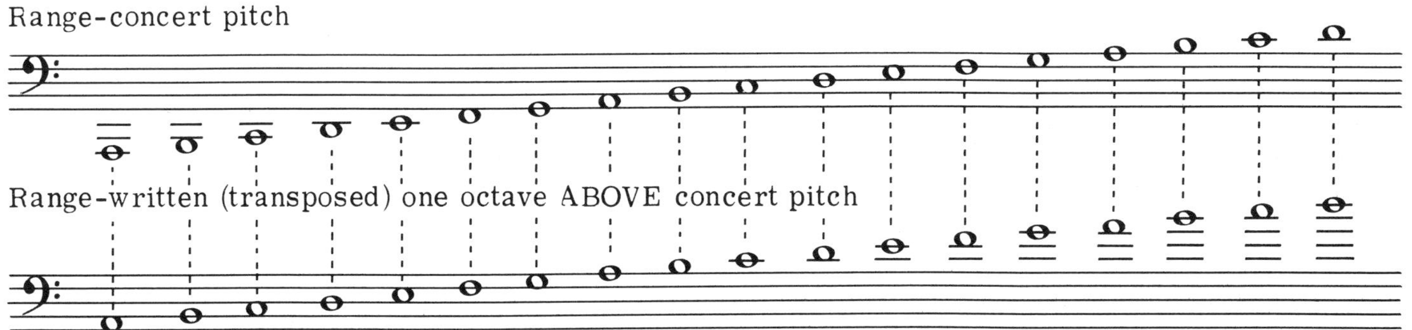

2. The Banjo

The banjo is a "guitarlike" fretted instrument with a resonating drum head type of sound chamber (as opposed to a carved wood acoustical chamber of most guitars).

A. The Tenor Banjo

Range and Transposition of the Tenor Banjo

Range-concert pitch

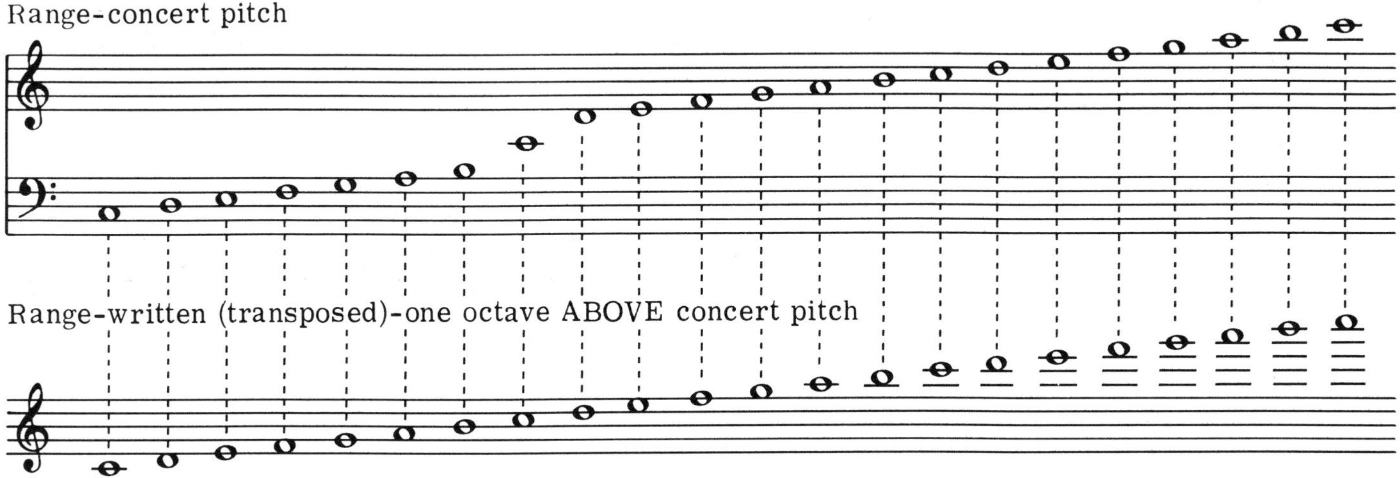

B. The Plectrum Banjo

Range and Transposition of the Plectrum Banjo

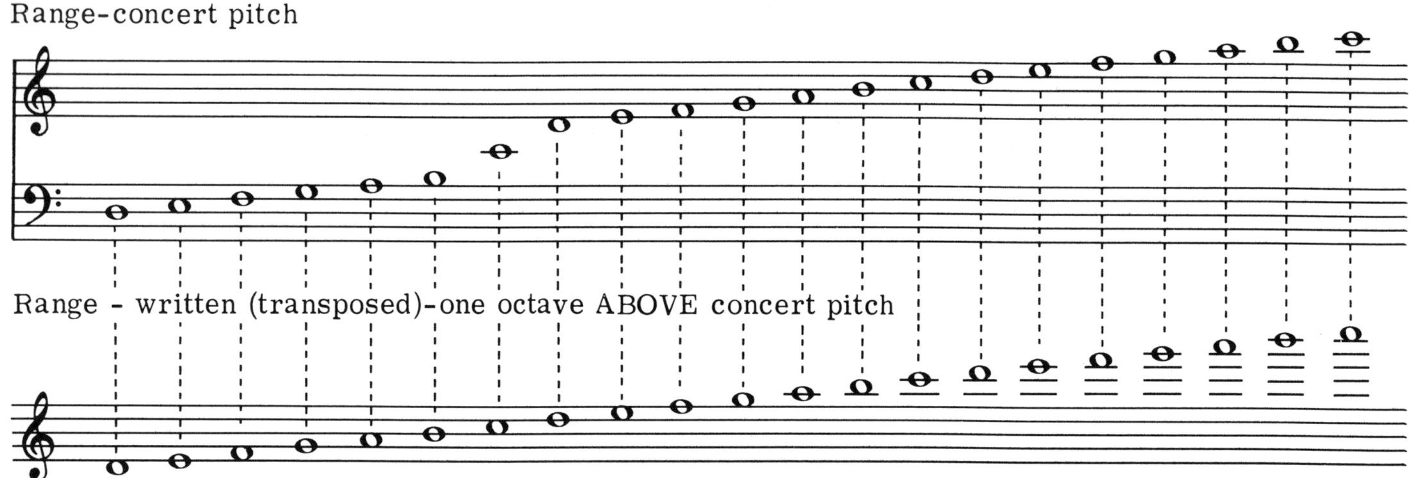

C. The 5 String Banjo

Since there are many varied tunings of the 5 string banjo, the following is just a "general" register for the instrument.

Range and Transposition of the 5 String Banjo

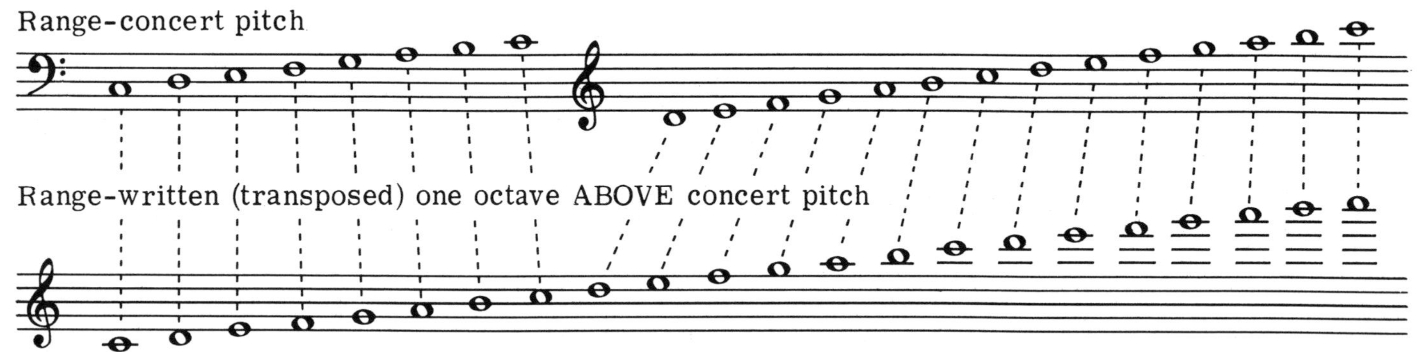

3. The Mandolins

A. The Mandolin

Range (Concert and Written) of the Mandolin

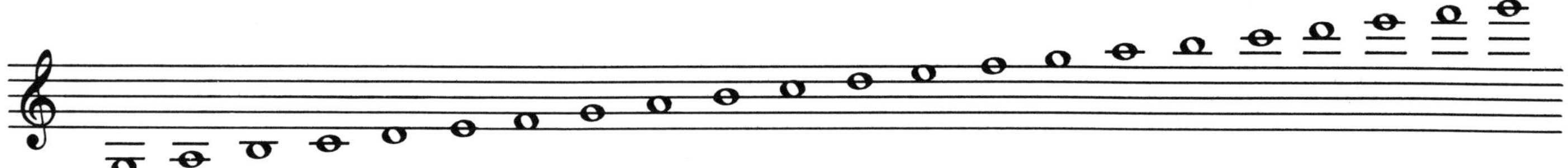

B. The Mandola

Range and Transposition of the Mandola

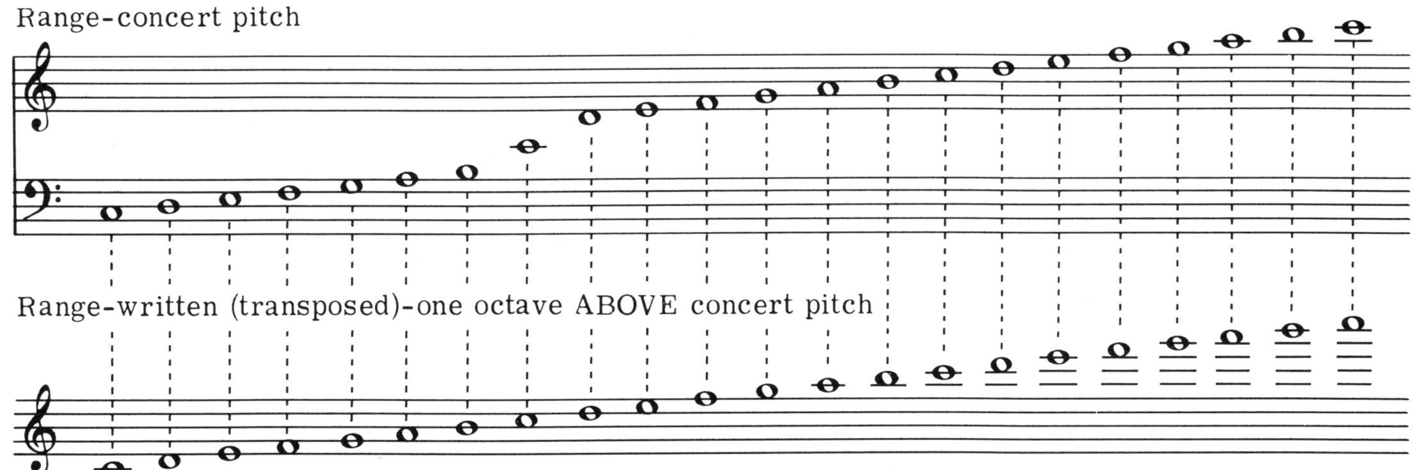

C. The Mandocello

Range and Transposition of the Mandocello

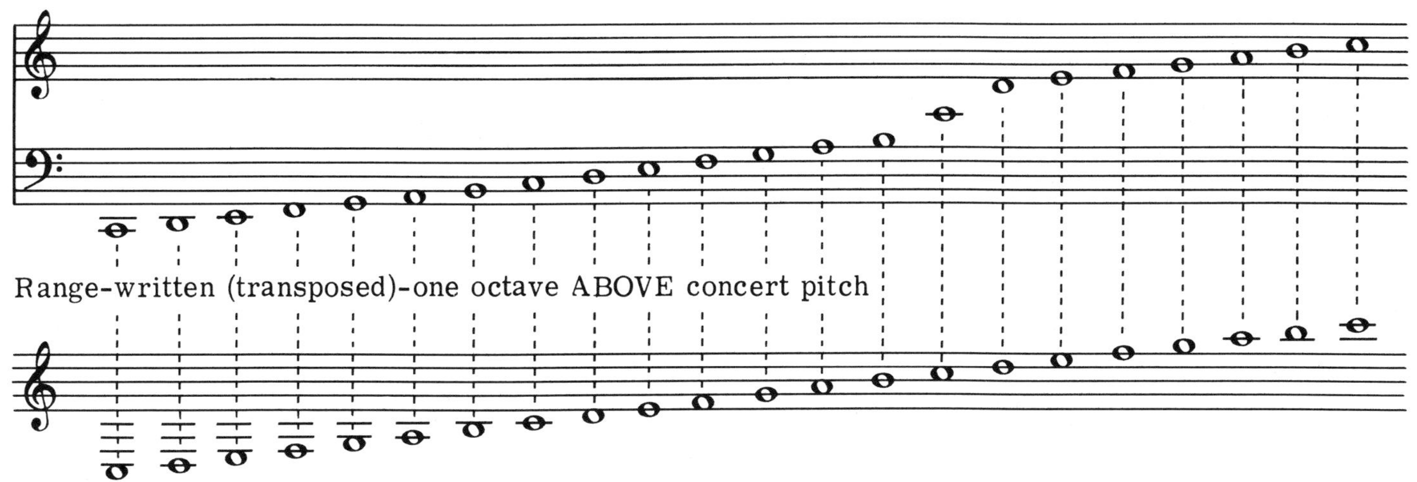

4. The Ukuleles

A. The Soprano Ukulele

Range and Transposition of the Soprano Ukulele

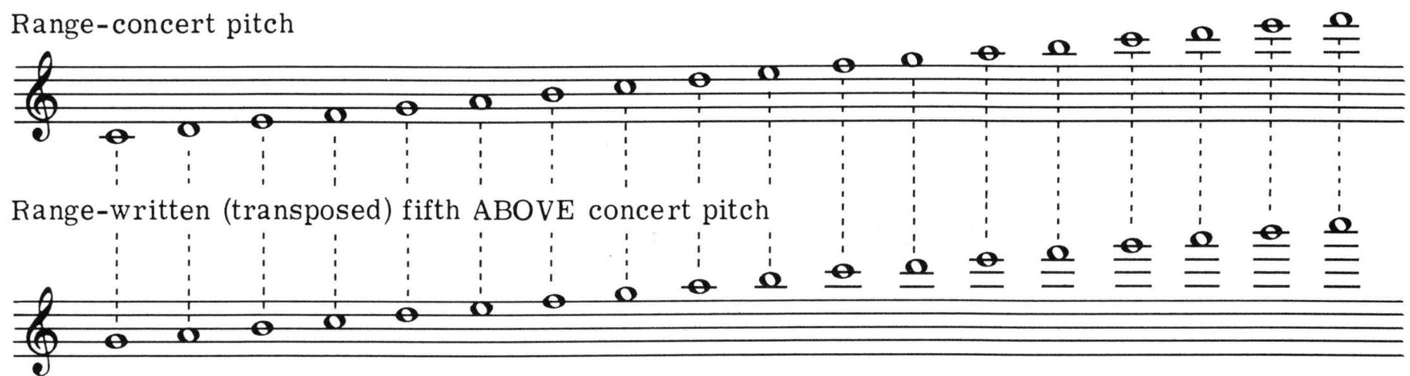

B. The Tenor Ukulele

Range and Transposition of the Tenor Uke

Range-concert pitch

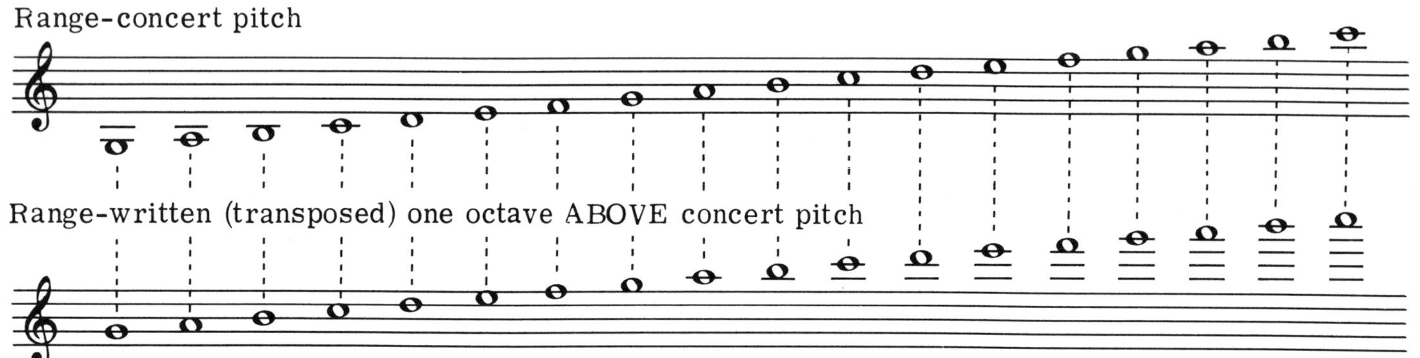

C. The Baritone Ukulele

Range and Transposition of the Baritone Uke

Range-concert pitch

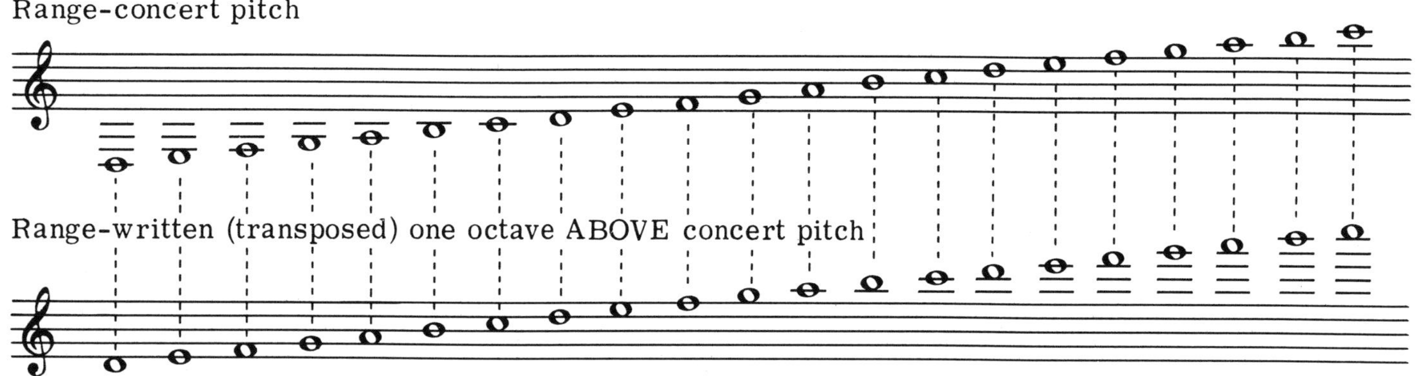

5. The Balalaikas

A. The standard Balalaika

Range (Concert and Written) of the Balalika

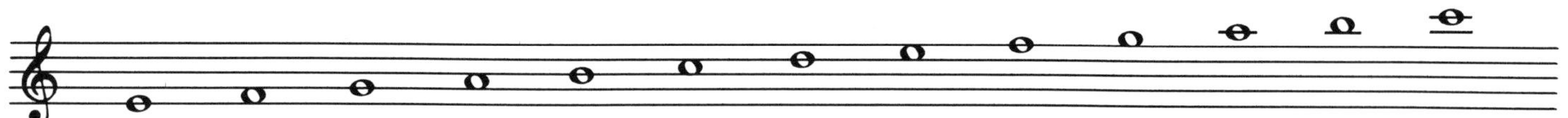

B. The Alto Balalaika

Range and Transposition of the Alto Balalika

Range-concert pitch

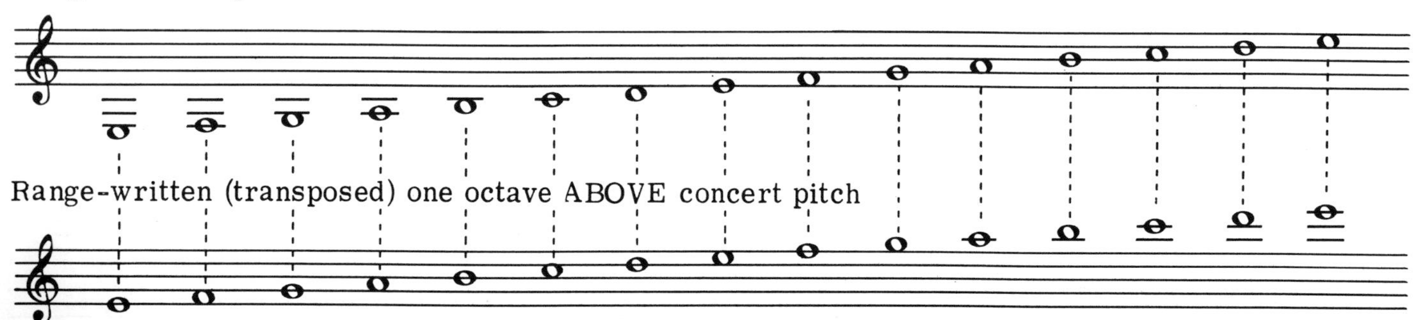

C. The Bass Balalaika

Range (Concert and Written) of Bass Balalika

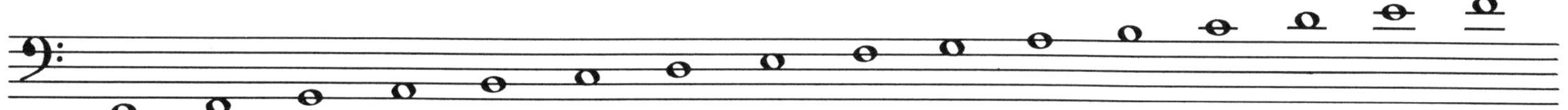

6. Other Fretted Instruments

   A. The Electric Sitar

Range and Transposition of the Electric Sitar

Range-concert pitch

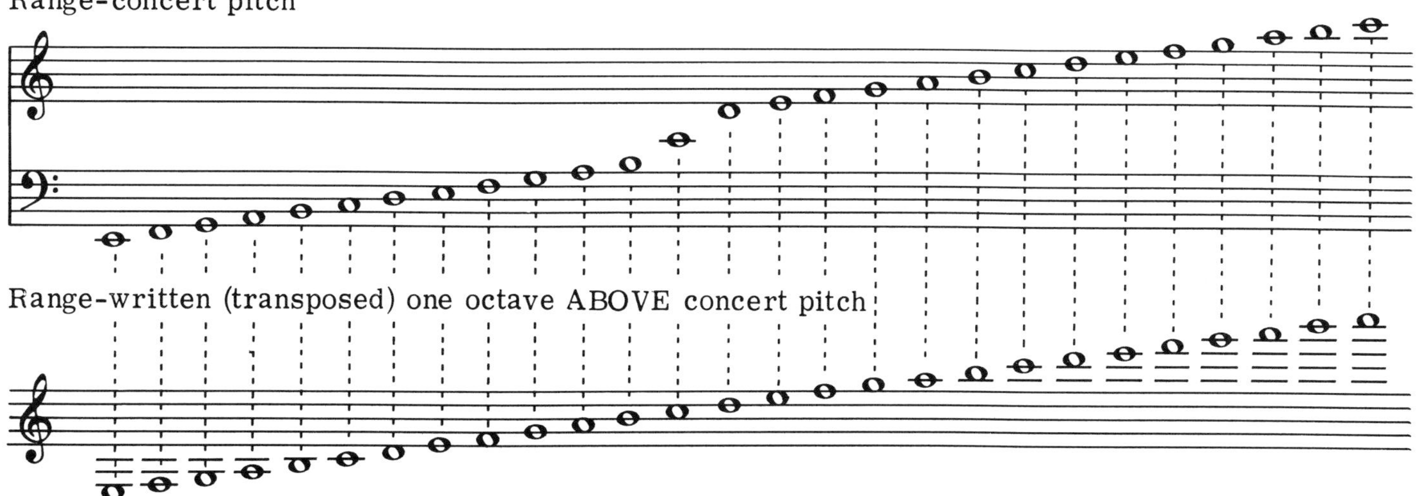

   B. The Dobro

Range and Transposition of the Dobro

Range-concert pitch

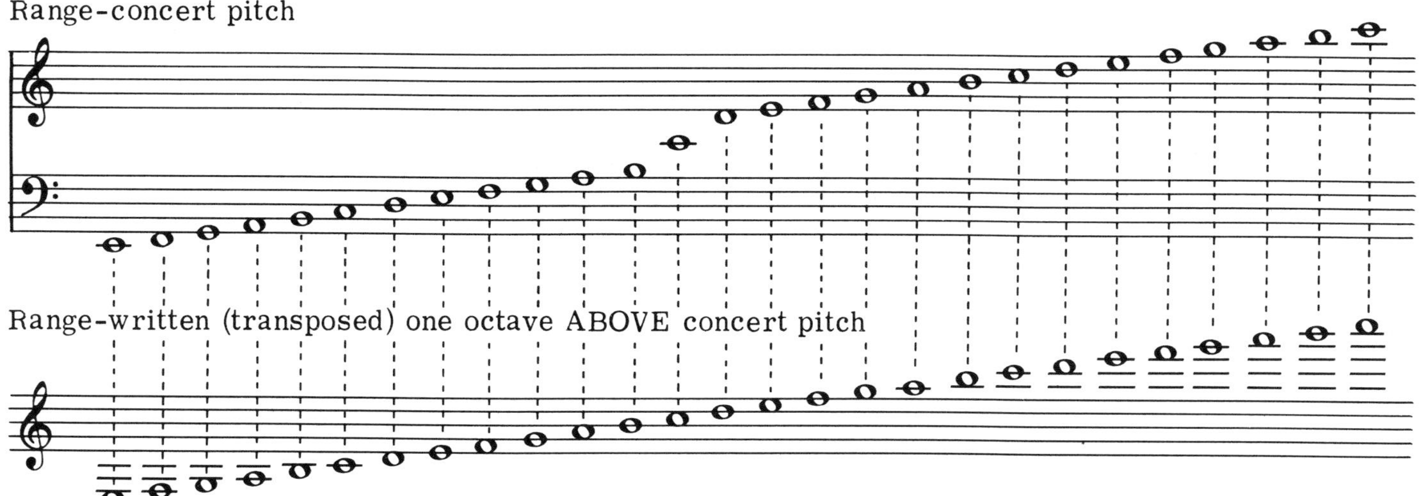

Range and Transposition of the Tiple

Range-concert pitch

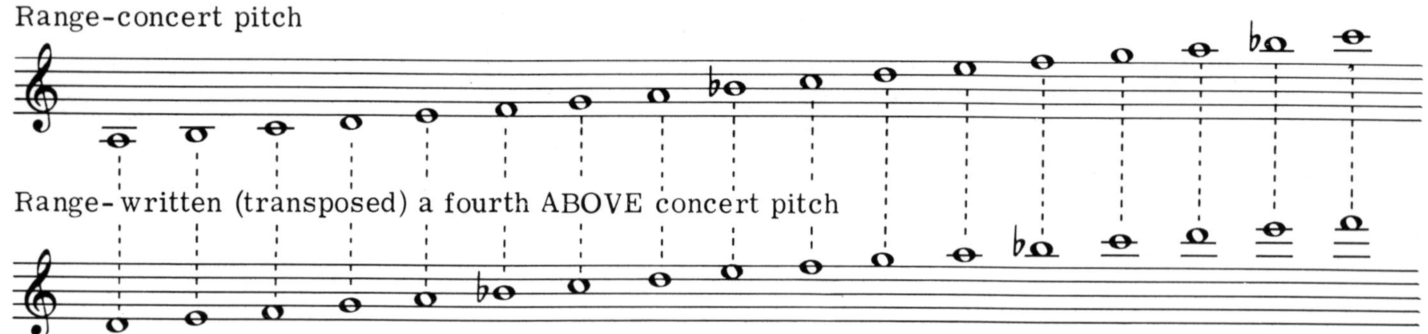

D. The Bouzouki

Range and Transposition of the Bouzouki

Range-concert pitch

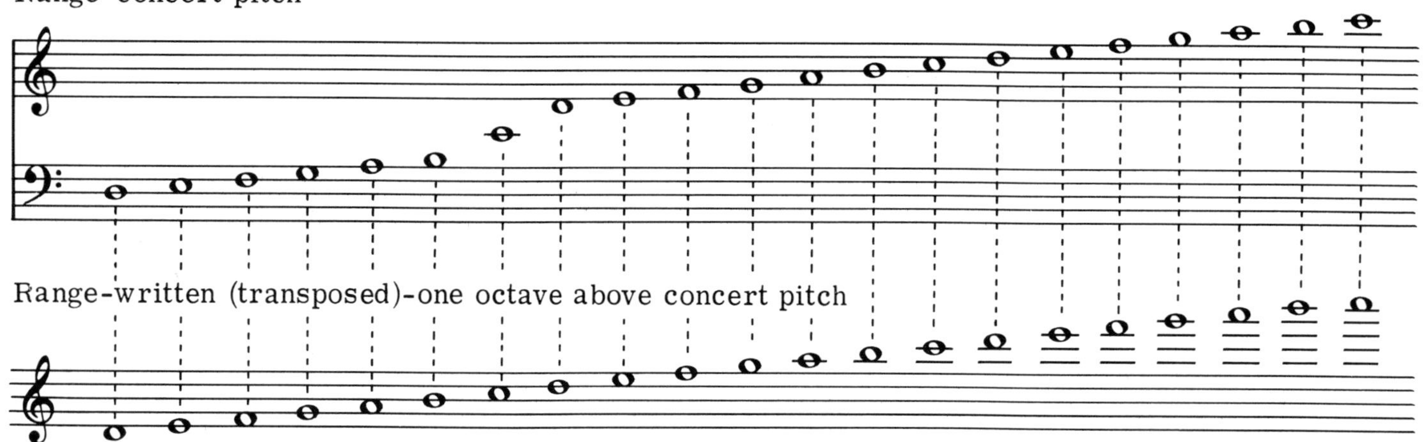

Percussion Instruments

1. Definite Pitch Instruments

    A. Orchestra Bells

Range and Transposition of the Orchestra Bells

Range-concert pitch

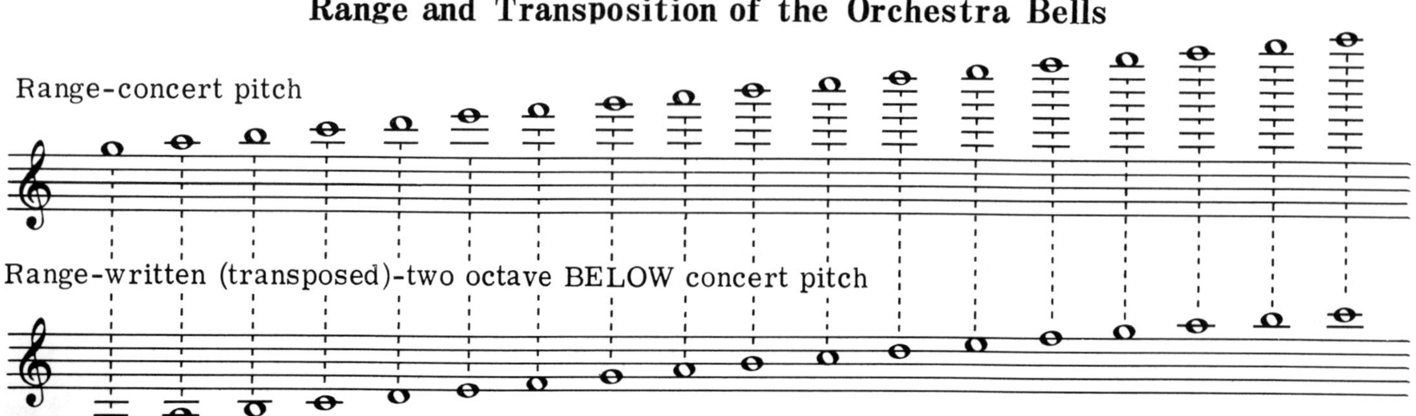

B. Glockenspiel (Bell lyra for marching bands)

Range and Transposition of the Glockenspiel Bell Lypa

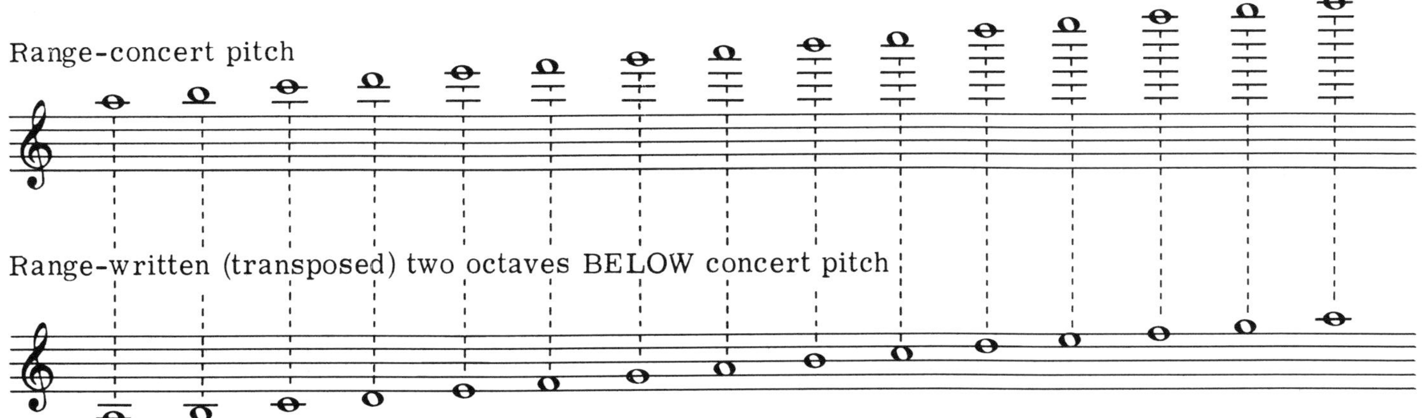

C. Xylophone

Range and Transposition of the Xylophone

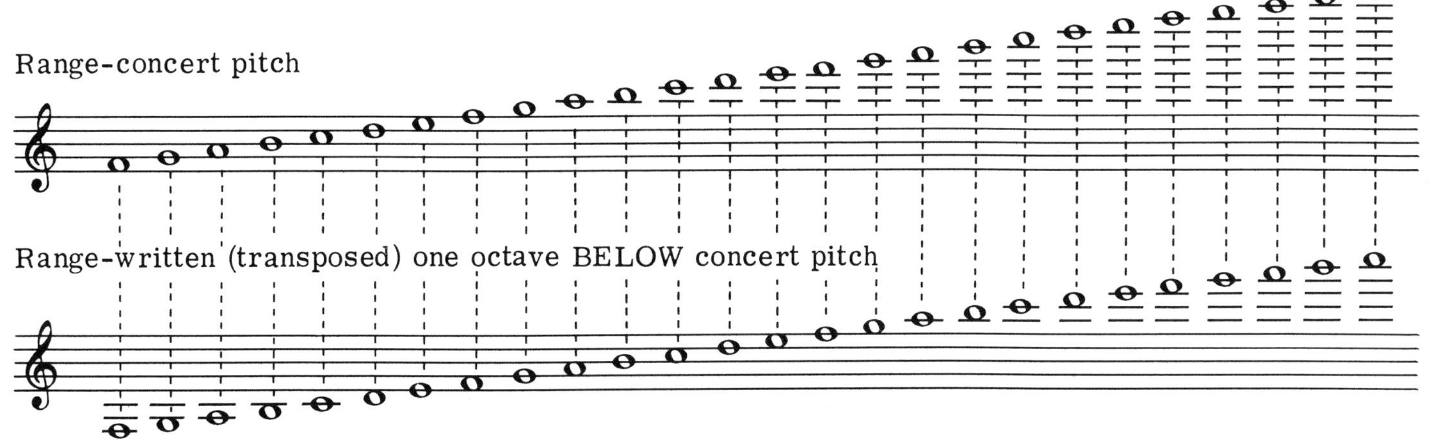

D. Marimba

Range (Concert and Written) of the Marimba

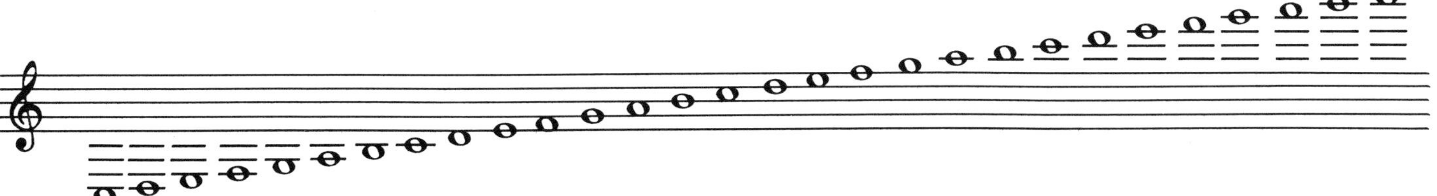

E. Bass Marimba

Range and Transposition of the Bass Marimba

Range-concert pitch

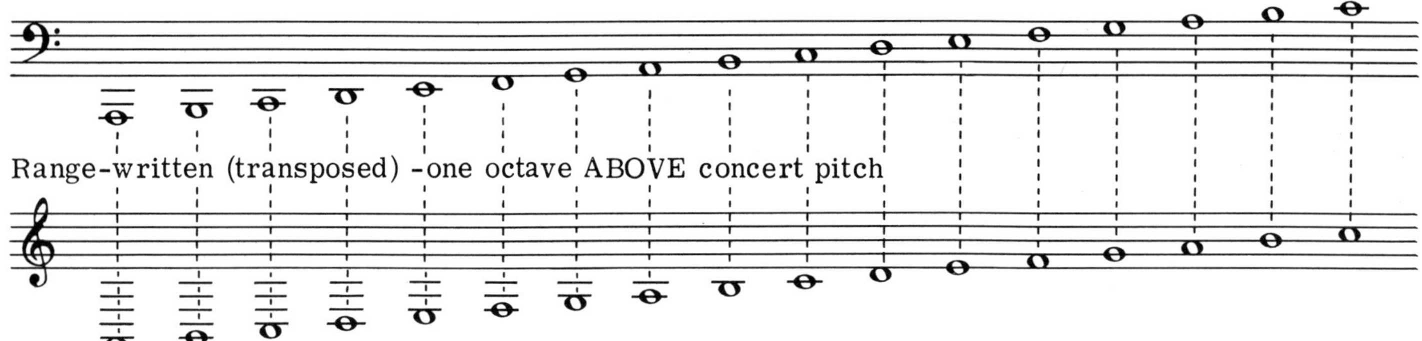

Range-written (transposed) -one octave ABOVE concert pitch

F. Vibraphone

Range (Concert and Written) of the Vibraphone

G. Chimes

Range (Concert and Written) of the Chimes

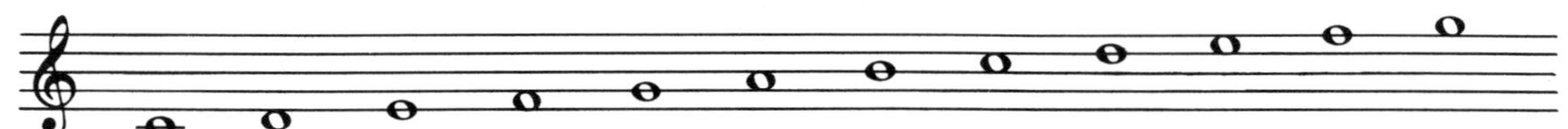

H. Boobams (tuned bongo drums)

Range (Concert and Written) of the Boobams

I. Timpani

Range (Concert and Written) of the Timpani

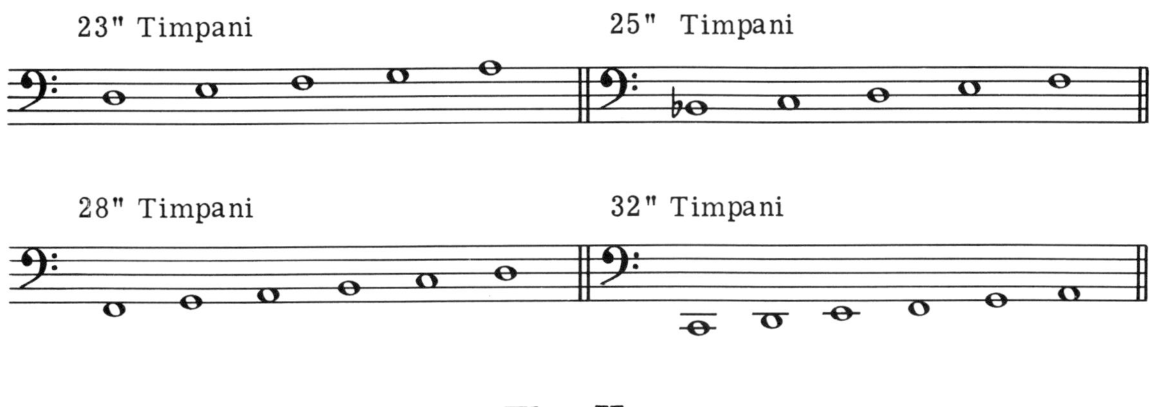

The Harp

The range of a Harp is almost as great as that of a piano. While writing for it can
sometimes be complex (we will delve into this later), its range should be noted.

Range (Concert and Written) of the Harp

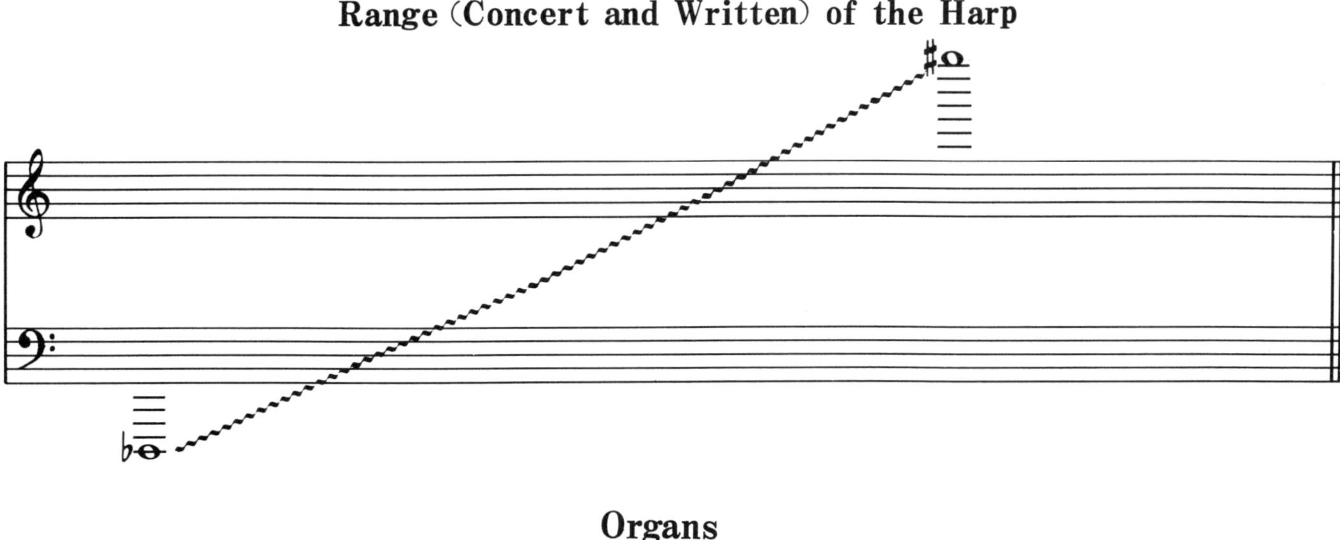

Organs

1. The Pipe Organ

Range (Concert and Written) of the Pipe Organ

2. Electronic Organ (Church and Concert Models)

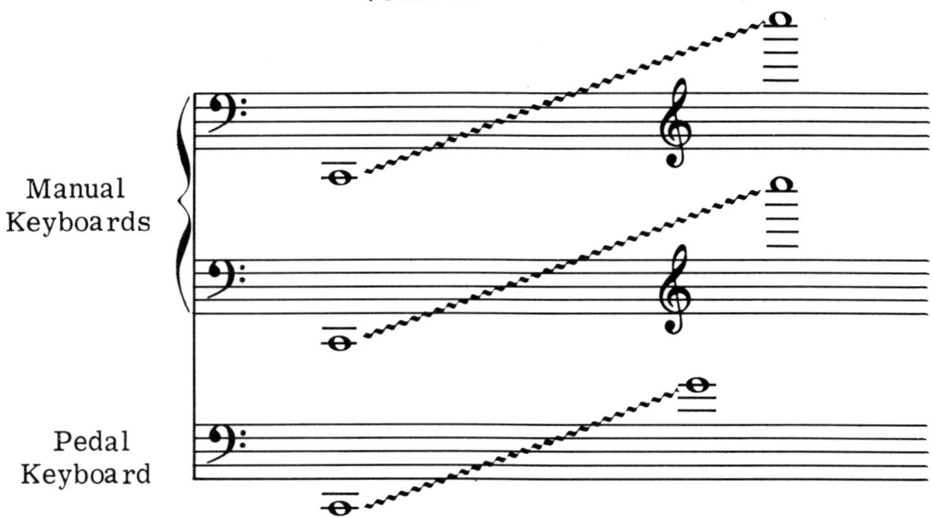

3. Electronic Organ (Home-type Spinet Models)

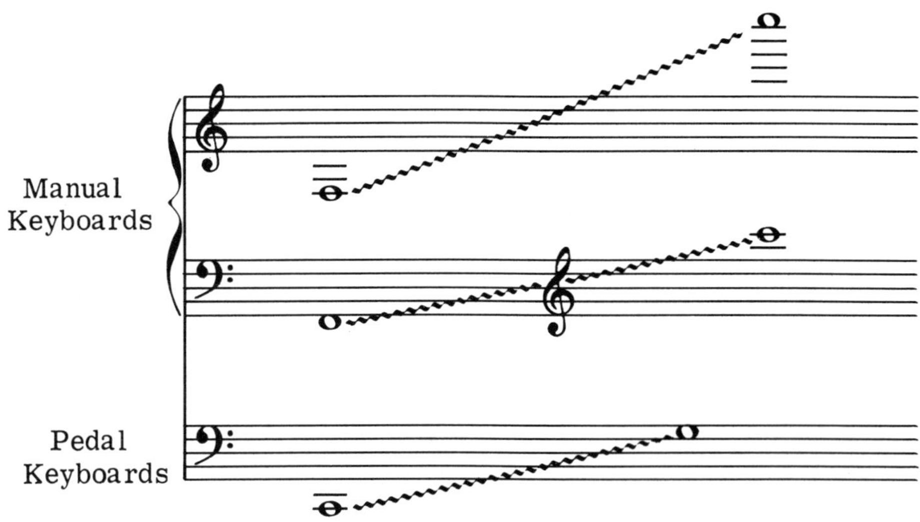

Harmonicas

1. The "Standard" Chromatic Harmonica

2. The 4 octave Chromatic Harmonica

Range (Written and Concert) of the 4 Octave Chromatic Harmonica

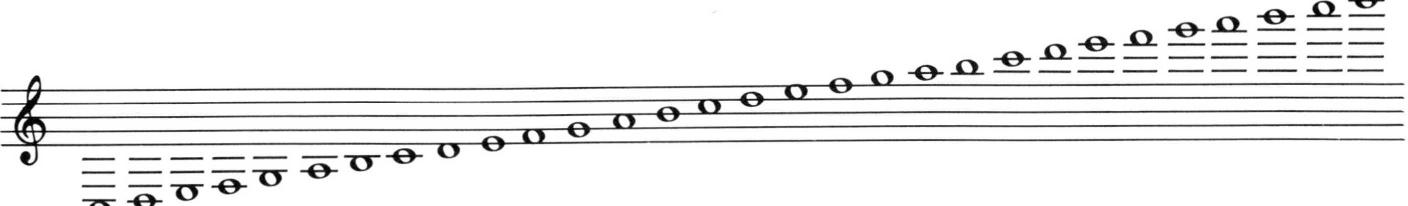

3. The Bass Harmonica

Range and Transposition of the Bass Harmonica

Range-concert pitch-sounds in octaves

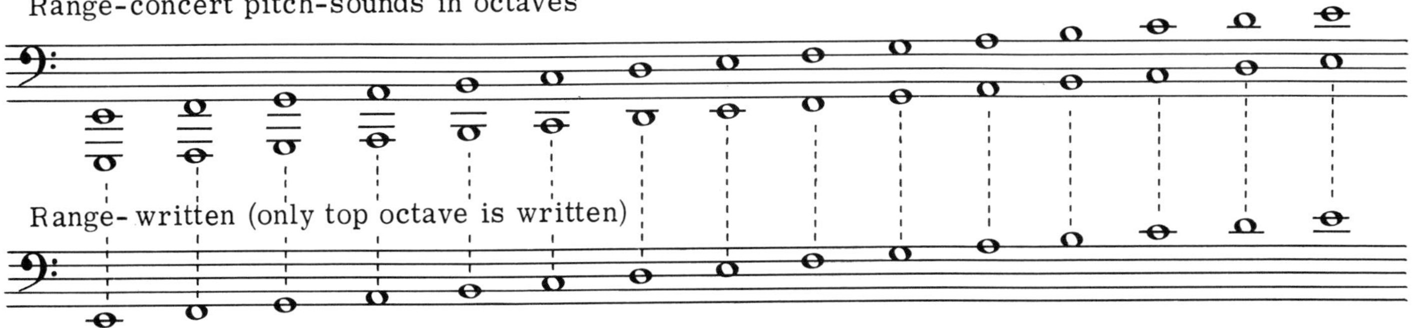

PART V

PRACTICAL EXERCISES IN TRANSPOSITION

Now that we have been exposed to the ranges and transpositions of the various

instruments, it is time to put to use these transpositions of different instruments

and groups of instruments. Again I must emphasize how vitally important

it is to a composer/arranger/orchestrator to COMPLETELY KNOW both HOW

to transpose and the TRANSPOSITIONS (commited to memory) of the more common

instruments.

Complete all the assigned exercises in this chapter, then check them in the

appendix to see if you have done them correctly. WRITE THE APPROPRIATE

TRANSPOSED PARTS SO THAT UNISON OCCURS.

Exercise #25

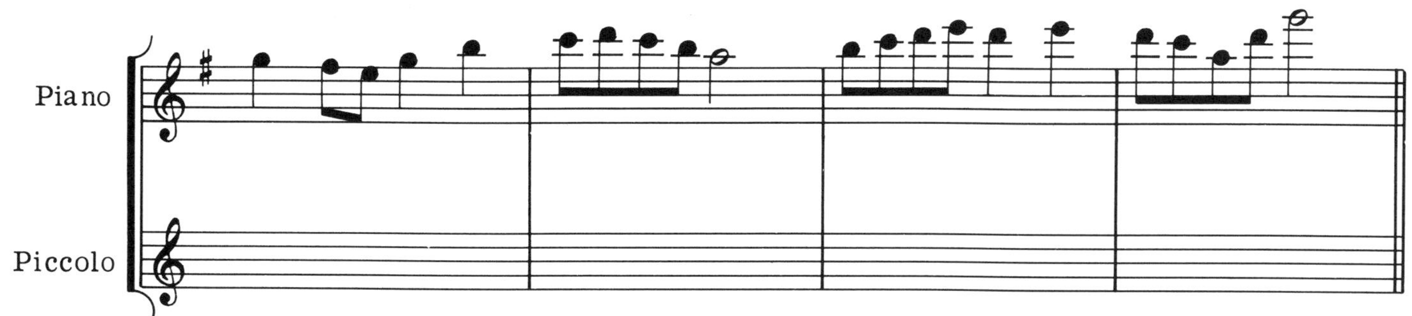

Exercise #26

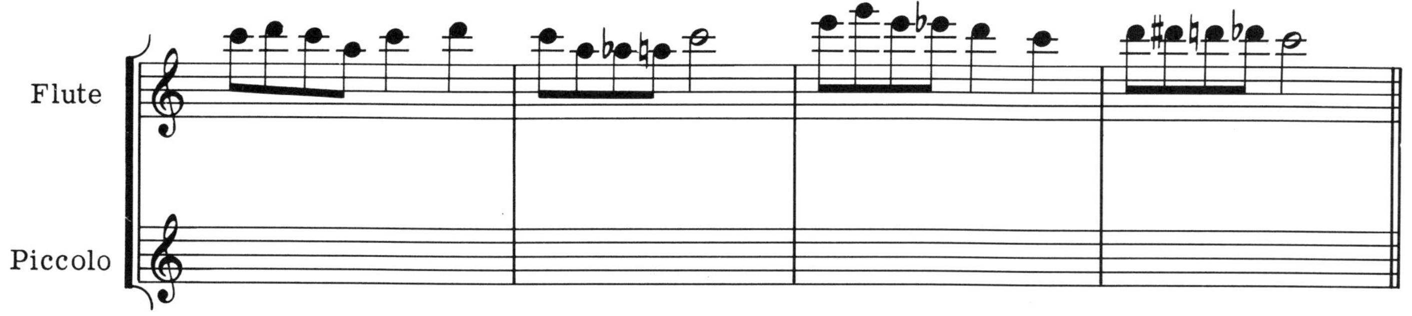

Exercise #27

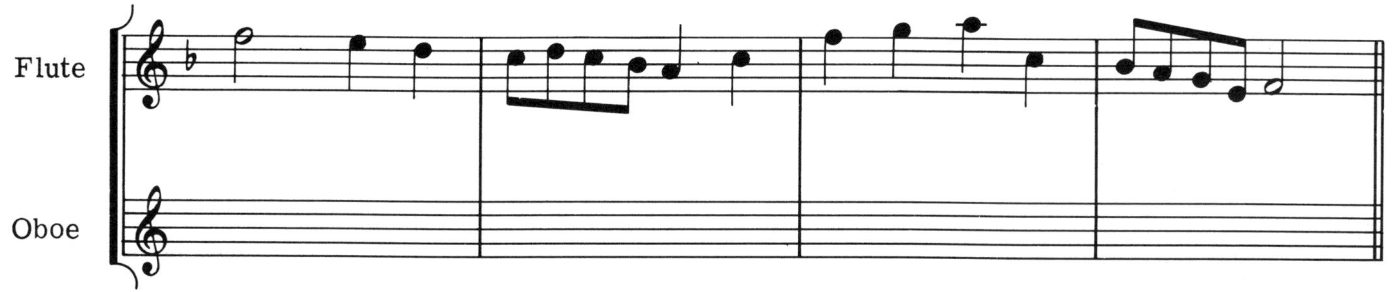

Exercise #28

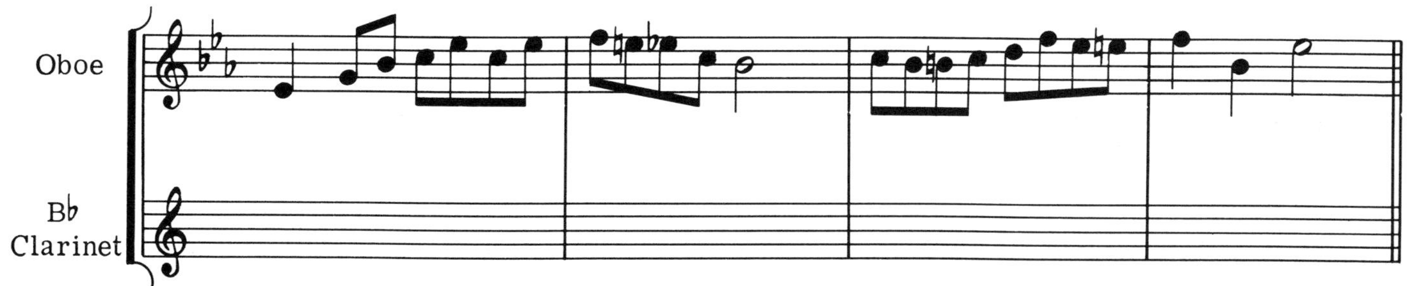

Exercise #29

Exercise #29
Bb Clarinet
Flute
Exercise #30
Piccolo
Bb Clarinet
Exercise #31
Piano
Alto Flute
Exercise #32
Bb Clarinet
Alto Flute
Exercise #33
Piano
Bass Flute

Exercise #34

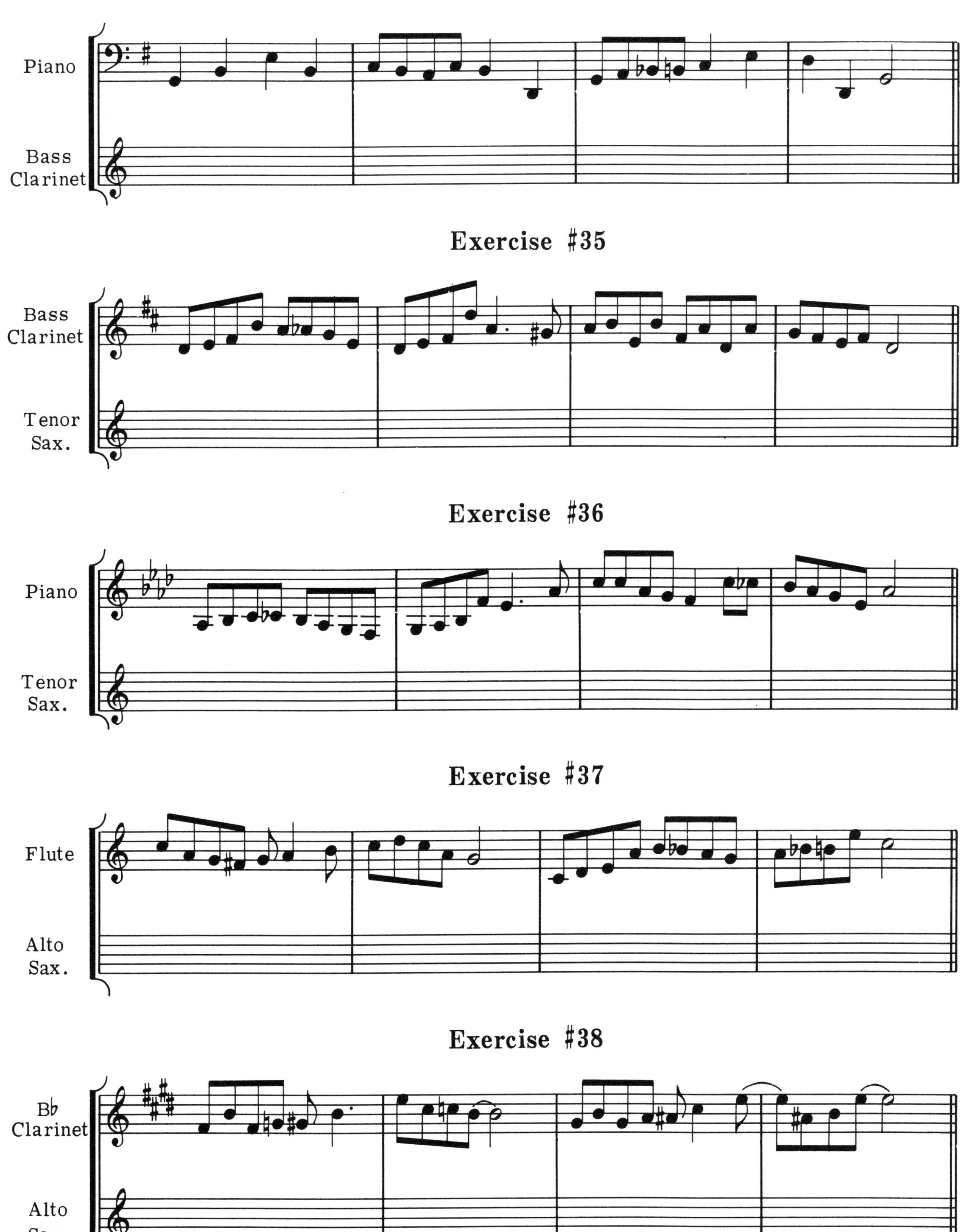

Exercise #35

Exercise #36

Exercise #37

Exercise #38

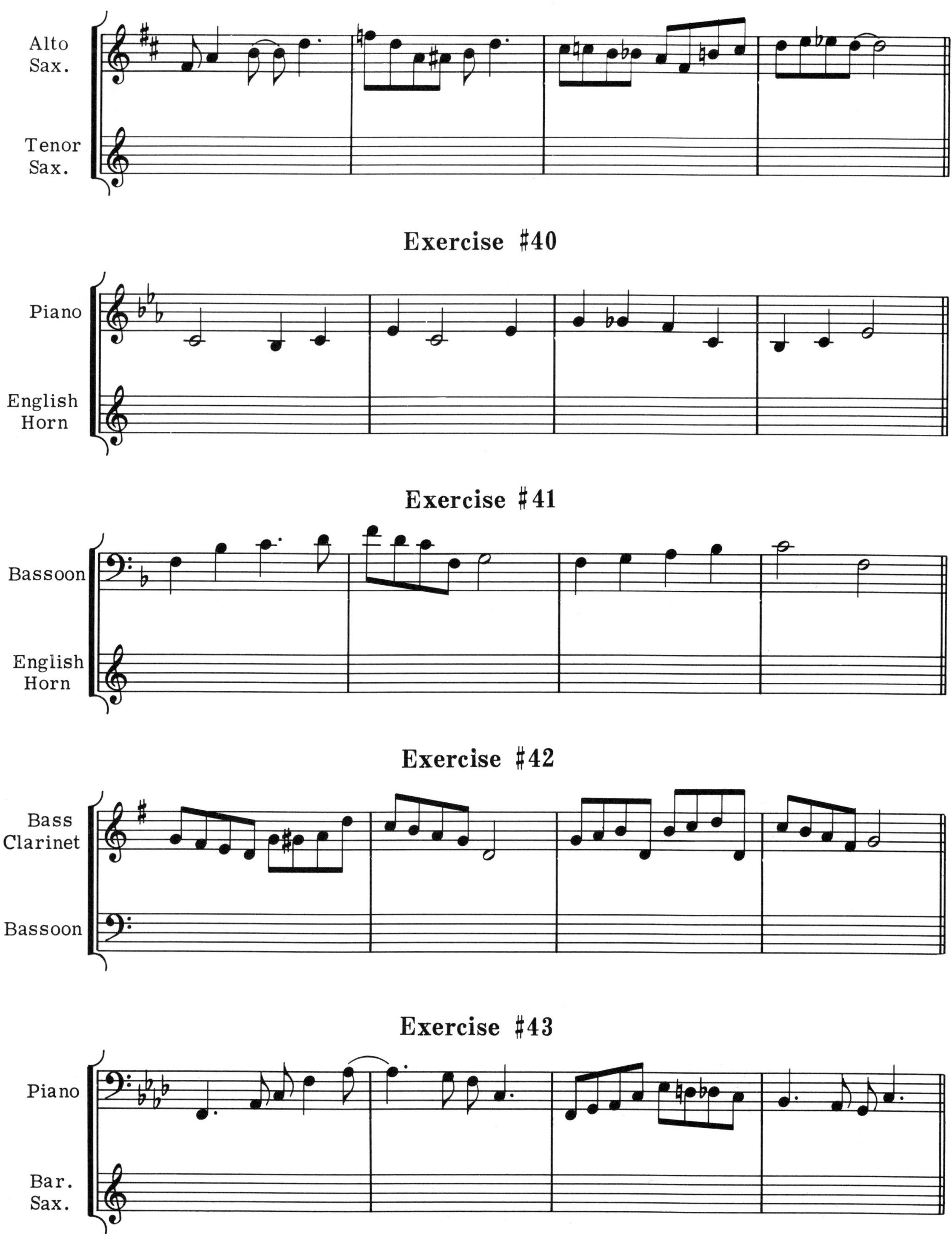
Exercise #39
Alto Sax.
Tenor Sax.
Exercise #40
Piano
English Horn
Exercise #41
Bassoon
English Horn
Exercise #42
Bass Clarinet
Bassoon
Exercise #43
Piano
Bar. Sax.

Exercise ♯44

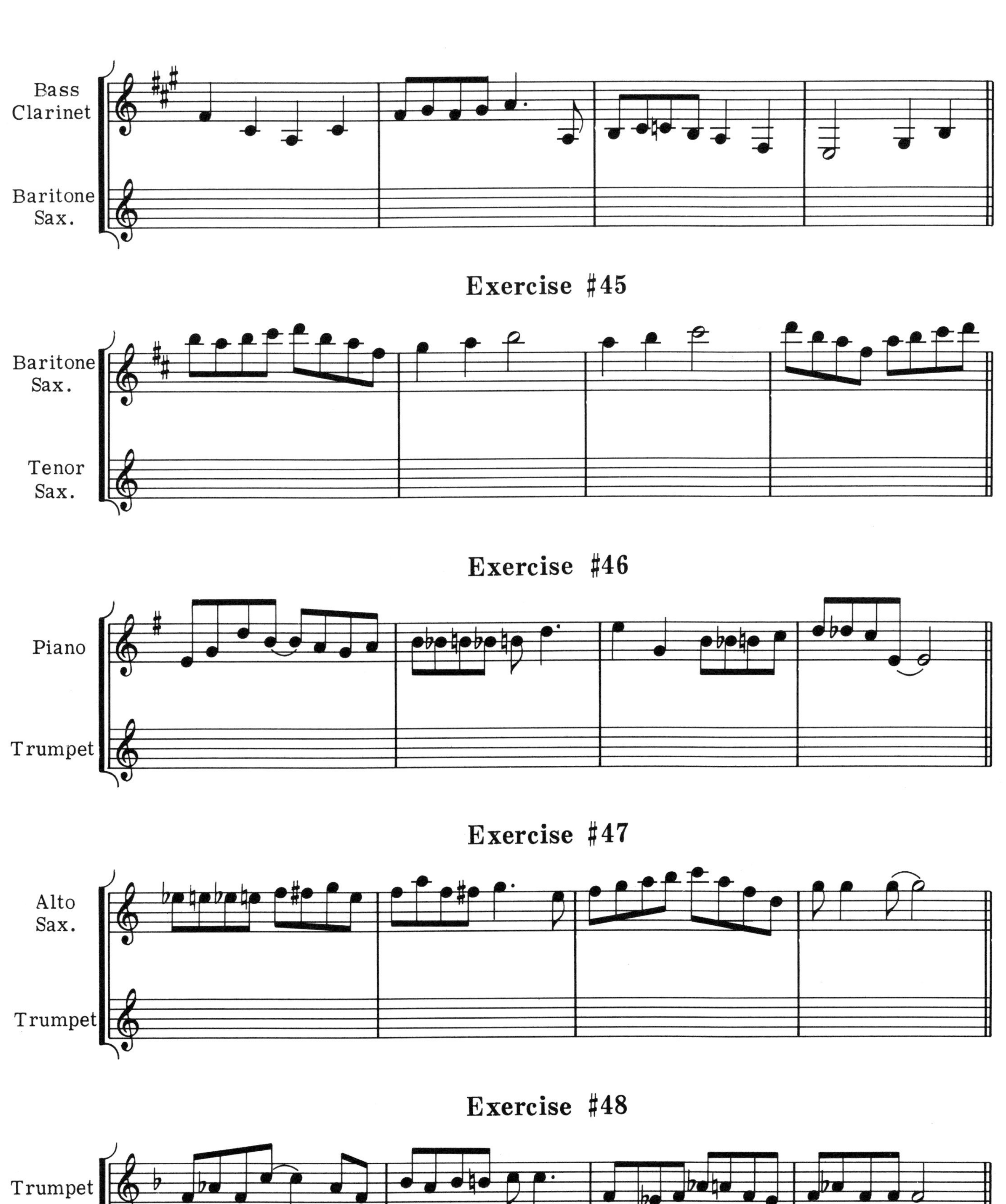

Exercise ♯45

Exercise ♯46

Exercise ♯47

Exercise ♯48

Exercise #49
Clarinet
Tenor Sax.
Exercise #50
Piano
Trombone
Exercise #51
Trombone
Tenor Sax.
Exercise #52
Trombone
Alto Sax.
Exercise #53
Trumpet
Flute

Exercise #54

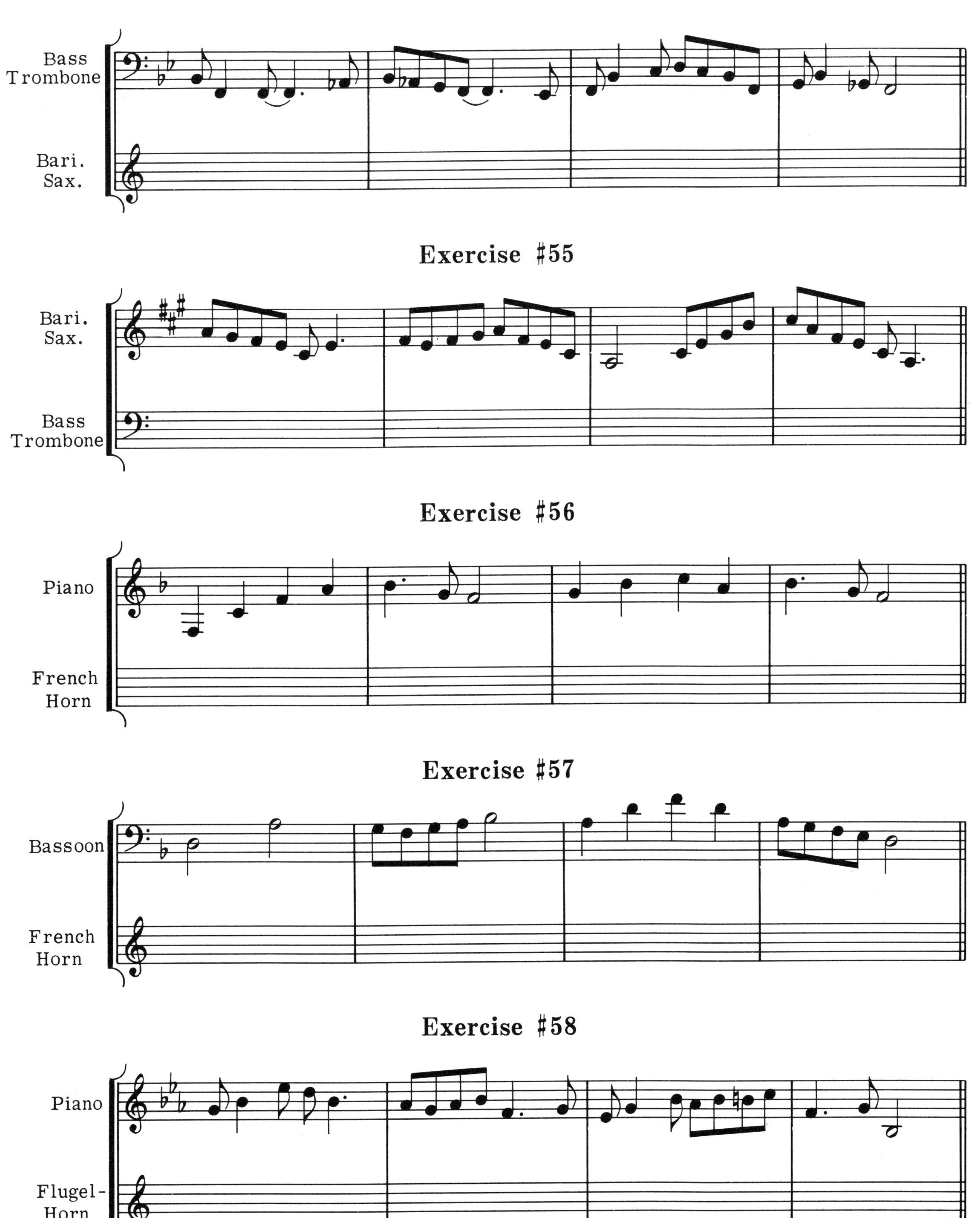

Exercise #55

Exercise #56

Exercise #57

Exercise #58

Exercise #59

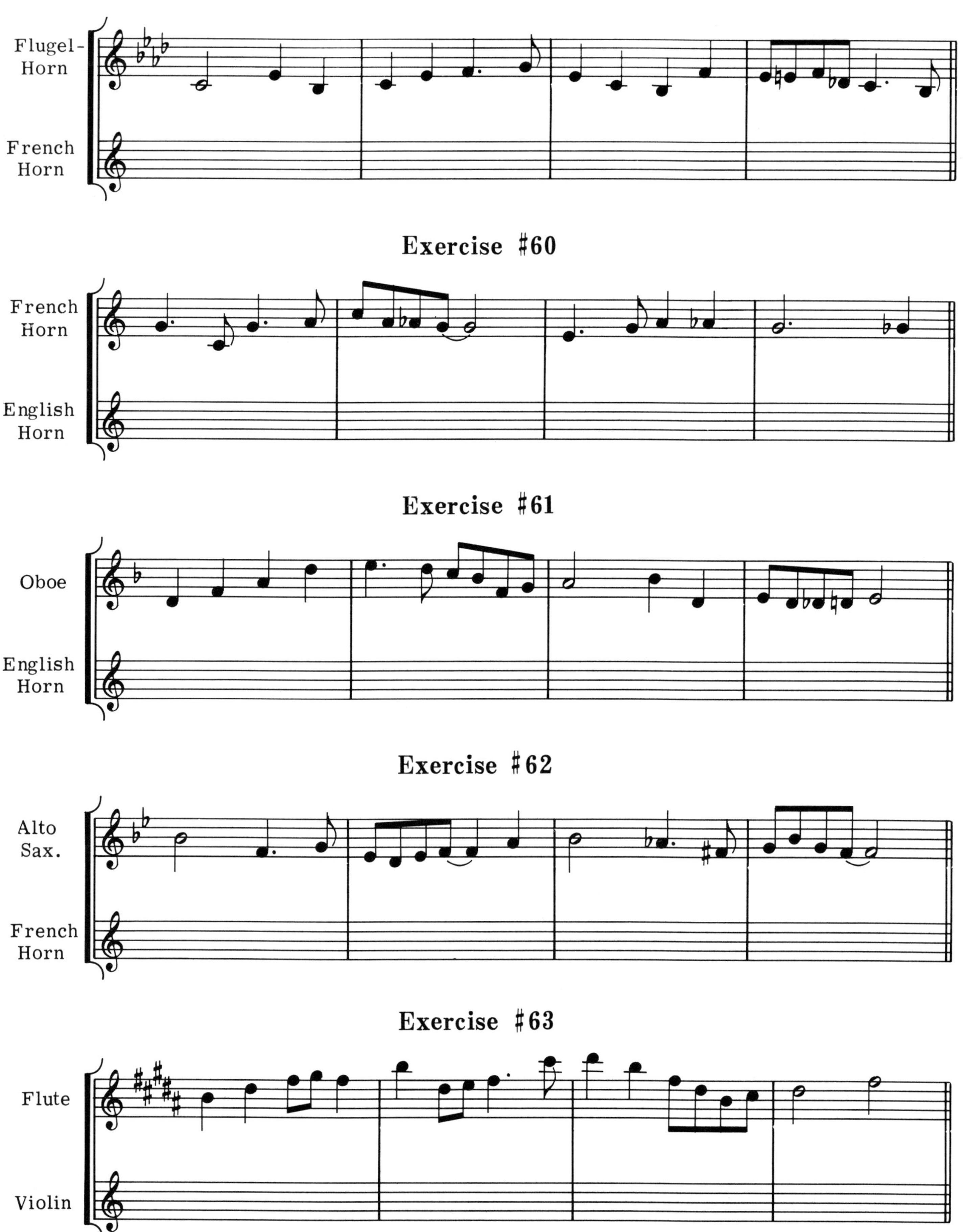

Exercise #60

Exercise #61

Exercise #62

Exercise #63

Exercise ♯64

Exercise ♯65

Exercise ♯66

Exercise ♯67

Exercise ♯68

Exercise #69

Exercise #70

Exercise #71

Exercise #72

Exercise #73

Exercise #74

Exercise #75

Exercise #76

Exercise #77

Exercise #78

<h1 style="text-align:center">Exercise #79</h1>

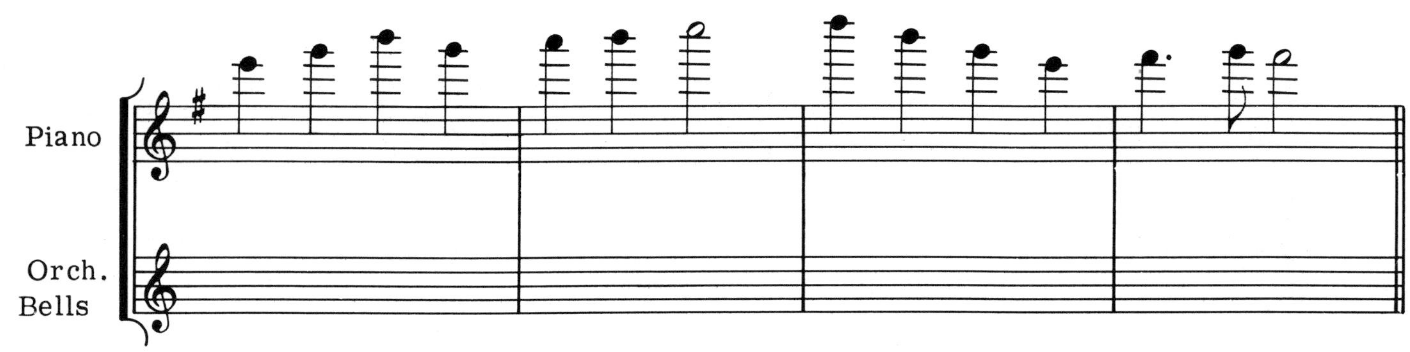

<h1 style="text-align:center">Exercise #80</h1>

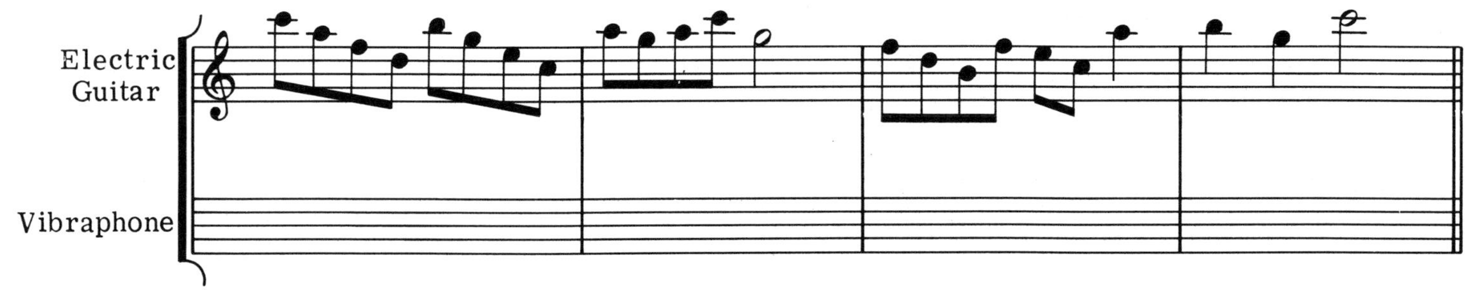

<h1 style="text-align:center">Exercise #81</h1>

<h1 style="text-align:center">Exercise #82</h1>

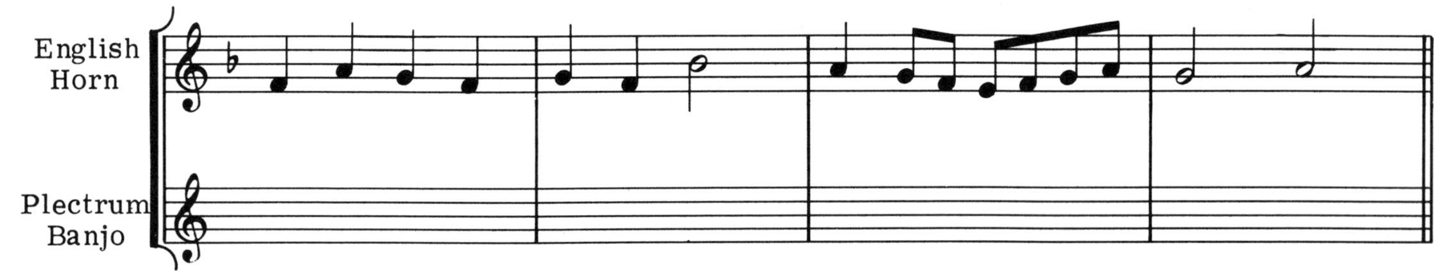

<h1 style="text-align:center">Exercise #83</h1>

PART VI

INSTRUMENTAL POTENTIALS & LIMITATIONS

The purpose of this chapter is to begin a basic introduction to the possibilities and limitations which instruments have. It will be very fundamental and "general" as more detail will be afforded each instrument and instrument group in the Intermediate and Advanced books.

1. The Woodwinds

Generally, the larger an instrument is, the more "awkward" it is in terms of execution. Conversely, the smaller an instrument is, the more agile it usually is in terms of execution. For example, in the woodwind instrument family, the piccolo is a very "fluid" and "agile" instrument, able to play extremely fast and complicated passages with relative ease. The contra bass clarinet in B$\flat$, on the other hand, is a rather awkward instrument to play "fast" notes on or in a "virtuoso" manner. This general concept holds true in most of the woodwind instruments simply because the larger instruments take longer streams of air and thus more "wind" to blow through the longer tubing PLUS larger and more awkward keys to control this stream of air. As we delve further into our study of orchestration in later chapters of the Intermediate and Advanced books, we will study specific characteristics and idiosyncrasies of each of the instruments.

2. The Brass

The valved brass instruments (trumpets, horns, baritone, euphonium and tuba) are all rather agile instruments in terms of "fingering" execution. The limitations come by the nature of the embouchure. By pressing the lips to the mouthpiece, certain physical strains are put upon the muscles in the face and lips in order to produce tone (various notes) on the instruments. Thus, overcoming embouchure limitations (especially in the higher register where the overtones become very close together) is the foremost obstacle a brass player has to conquer. Physical endurance is an inherent problem in playing a brass instrument.

You just can not write the long, continuous passages of unrelenting notes for brass instruments as you can for strings, keyboards or even woodwinds.

As a beginning student of orchestration, you should "under-write" brass parts until you get a feel for both the range and endurance of the performers as well as the nature of the individual instruments.

3. The Strings

By and large, the string instruments (especially violin and viola) are the most agile and "fluid" instruments you will have to write for. Even though the flute, piccolo and to some extent the clarinet are as agile, they can not play the long, seemingly endless phrases of notes which the string instruments can play.

The general concept of the smaller instruments being more agile than the larger instruments is appropriate for the strings as well. The deep, beautiful tone of the string bass will roar thunderously across the symphony hall when a section of eight basses is playing a tutti section. But the somewhat technically ponderous bass fiddle is no match for the violin in terms of virtuoso execution of rapid passages and flurries of notes.

Bowings are a staple of the string players diet that you, as an orchestrator will have to learn to write and deal with. The very way you mark bowings over a particular musical phrase will determine the precise articulation of the string section playing as a unit. Here again, we will delve into the problem of bowings and how to notate them a little later. Just be aware that string players draw the bow across the strings of their instruments to create a tone whereas wind players "blow" into their instruments to create their tone. Both have advantages and disadvantages. You as an orchestrator will soon learn the fine points of dealing with each, for knowing the potentials and limitations of the instruments which you write for is the most basic and probably most IMPORTANT aspect of being an arranger/orchestrator.

PART VII

LEARNING HOW TO THINK IN TERMS
OF INSTRUMENTAL COLORS

Thus far, this book has dealt with the academic knowledge and techniques involved in preparing yourself to begin to arrange and orchestrate music. Now, it is time to introduce you to the mental "inductive" techniques you will need as an arranger/orchestrator. You see, academic knowledge is necessary and beneficial as a prerequisite to your beginning on the road to learning how to be a good orchestrator. But, you must possess MORE than just academic knowledge about music. You must be able to learn how to PROJECT sounds and colors of instruments in your mind AS YOU WRITE an arrangement. You must know what the parts are going to sound like as you put them down on your score! This must be INHERENT! And to further complicate matters, you must be able to project what COMBINATIONS of instrumental colors will sound like, either played in unison, in counterpoint or in harmony with each other. INDUCTIVE THINKING and MENTAL PROJECTION then become very real and important techniques which you will have to learn how to use.

THE PRIMARY REGISTERS

The most common mistake which new students of arranging and orchestrating make on their first orchestration is putting instruments in the wrong registers. This probably happens for several reasons:

1. Not completely understanding transposition, thus transposing a specific instrument wrong.

2. Not understanding (and thus not mentally projecting) what a specific instrument even sounds like.

3. Not grasping which registers on a given instrument best typify the SOUND of that instrument.

A. Understanding Transposition

If you are not COMPLETELY sure of your ability to TRANSPOSE CORRECTLY any part for any instrument, you should review the segments of this book which deals with transposition.

B. The Sounds of Various Instruments

In order for you to begin to "hear" the sounds of the various instruments in your mind, I will ask you to do 3 things:

1. Buy a record of Benjamin Britten's <u>Young Person's Guide To The Orchestra</u>. This work will serve as a basic orientation to instruments colors and instrumental sections' sounds within a symphony orchestra. HEARING what a specific instrument sounds like is worth a million words trying to describe what it sounds like.

2. Have your friends play their instruments for you. If you are into music, surely you have friends who play instruments other than the one you play. If not, seek out high school or college music students to demonstrate instrumental colors for you. Have them play in their low, middle and high registers so that you will mentally be able to begin to associate what these registers sound like relating to the Grand Staff. Play a few notes melodically on the piano, then have that same series of notes played on these different instruments. Once again, HEARING an instrument is worth a book of written descriptions!

3. Pick a note on the Grand Staff (for purposes of illustration, lets use middle C). Find a quiet place where you can totally concentrate (where there are no audio or visual distractions). Now, concentrate on the pitch (concert middle C). Soon, you will begin to HEAR that pitch in your mind (by thinking about it, not playing it). After you can HEAR this pitch from the Grand Staff, concentrate on what a B♭ clarinet would sound like PLAYING THIS PITCH. Concentrate long and hard until you actually begin to HEAR (in your mind) what the B♭ clarinet SOUNDS like playing this pitch. Then, move the pitch to several other places on the Grand Staff, each time concentrating intently until you HEAR (in your mind) the B♭ clarinet sounding that pitch.

Next, do this exercise with a trumpet. Then an alto saxophone, flute, trombone, bassoon, violin, cello, guitar, oboe, etc. until, through this mental exercise, you can HEAR any instrument playing any pitch within your mind. Obviously, this will take a great deal of effort and time. But it WILL work. It will get you to HEAR the instruments before you write for them - an absolute must for orchestrators and arrangers.

C. Specific Registers Which Typify Instruments - Primary Registers

Every instrument has a specific register which typifies the SOUND of that instrument. When you hear an instrument being played in this register (I call it the Primary Register) there is no question in your mind WHAT that instrument is.

To define what an instrument's Primary Register is (at least for this study) we will say that it is that "meaty" part of an instrument's register which lies from a 5th above its lowest note to a 6th below its highest note. For an example, here would be the Primary Register of some common instruments.

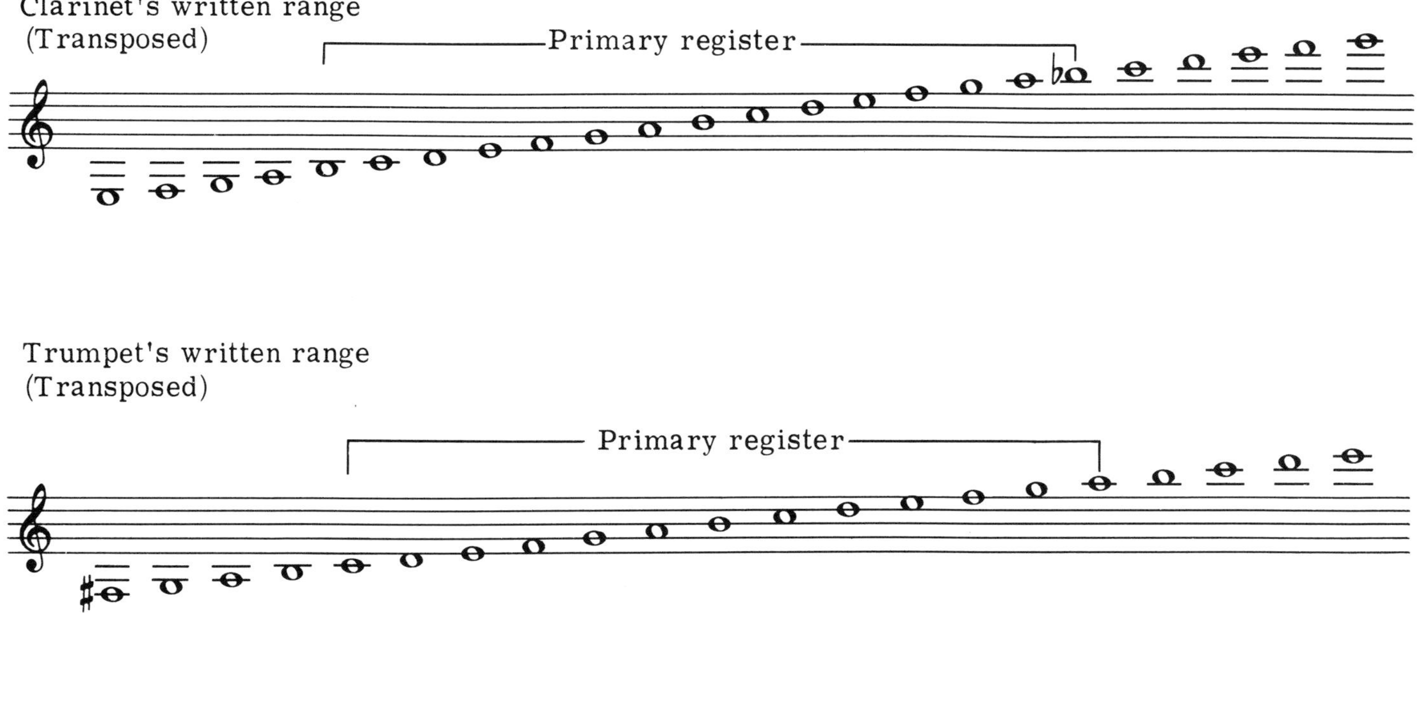

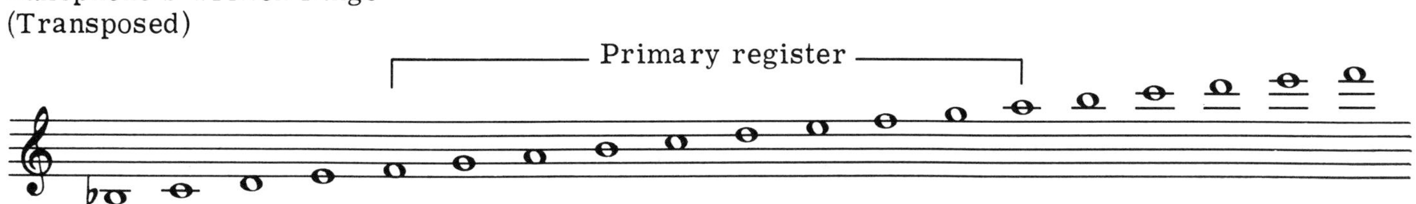

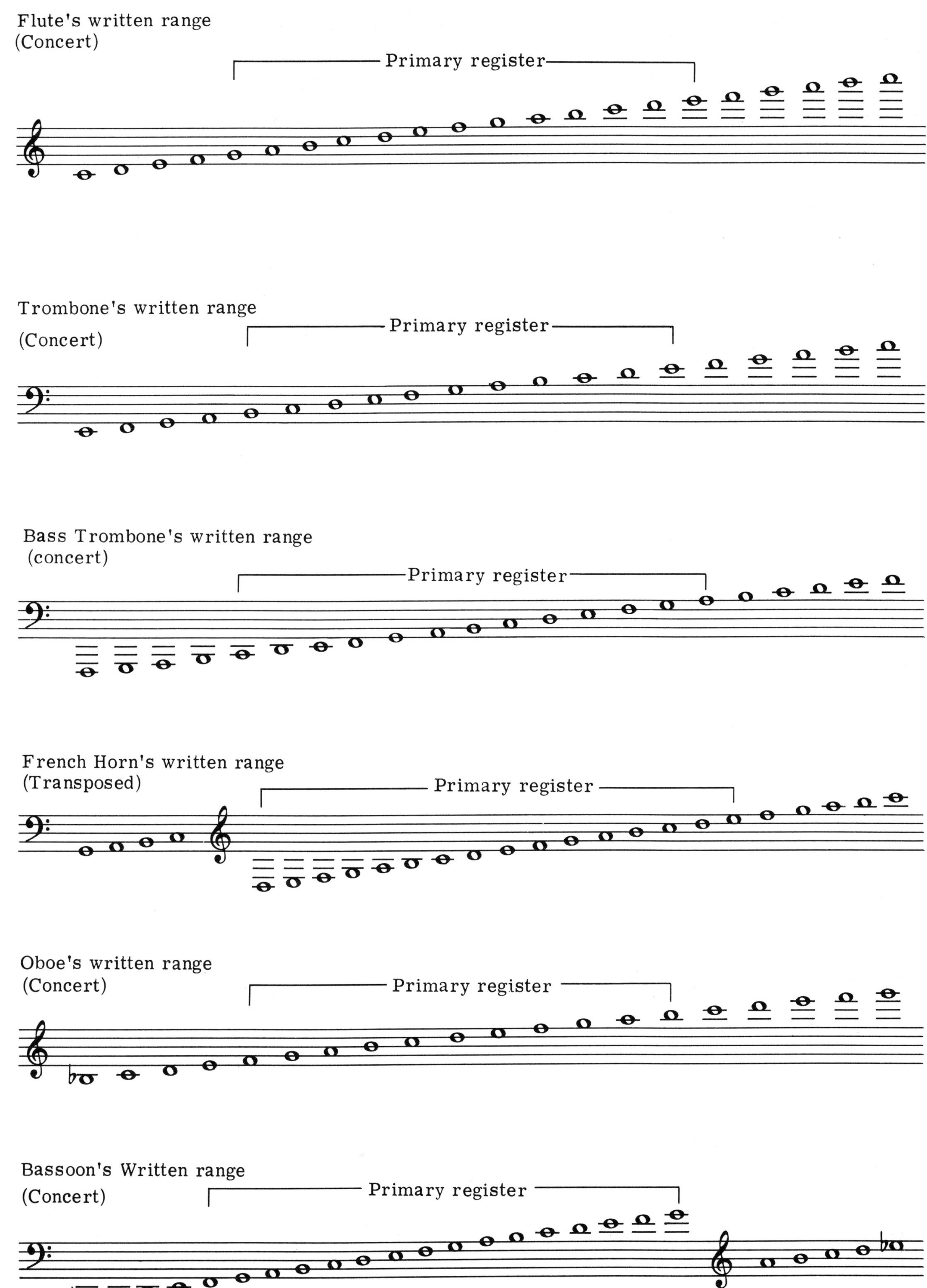

Flute's written range
(Concert)
Primary register
Trombone's written range
(Concert)
Primary register
Bass Trombone's written range
(concert)
Primary register
French Horn's written range
(Transposed)
Primary register
Oboe's written range
(Concert)
Primary register
Bassoon's Written range
(Concert)
Primary register

English Horn's written range
(Transposed)

The Tuba's wirtten range
(Concert)

The Violin's written range
(Concert)

The Viola's written range
(Concert)

The Cello's written range
(Written)

The String Bass' written range
(Transposed)

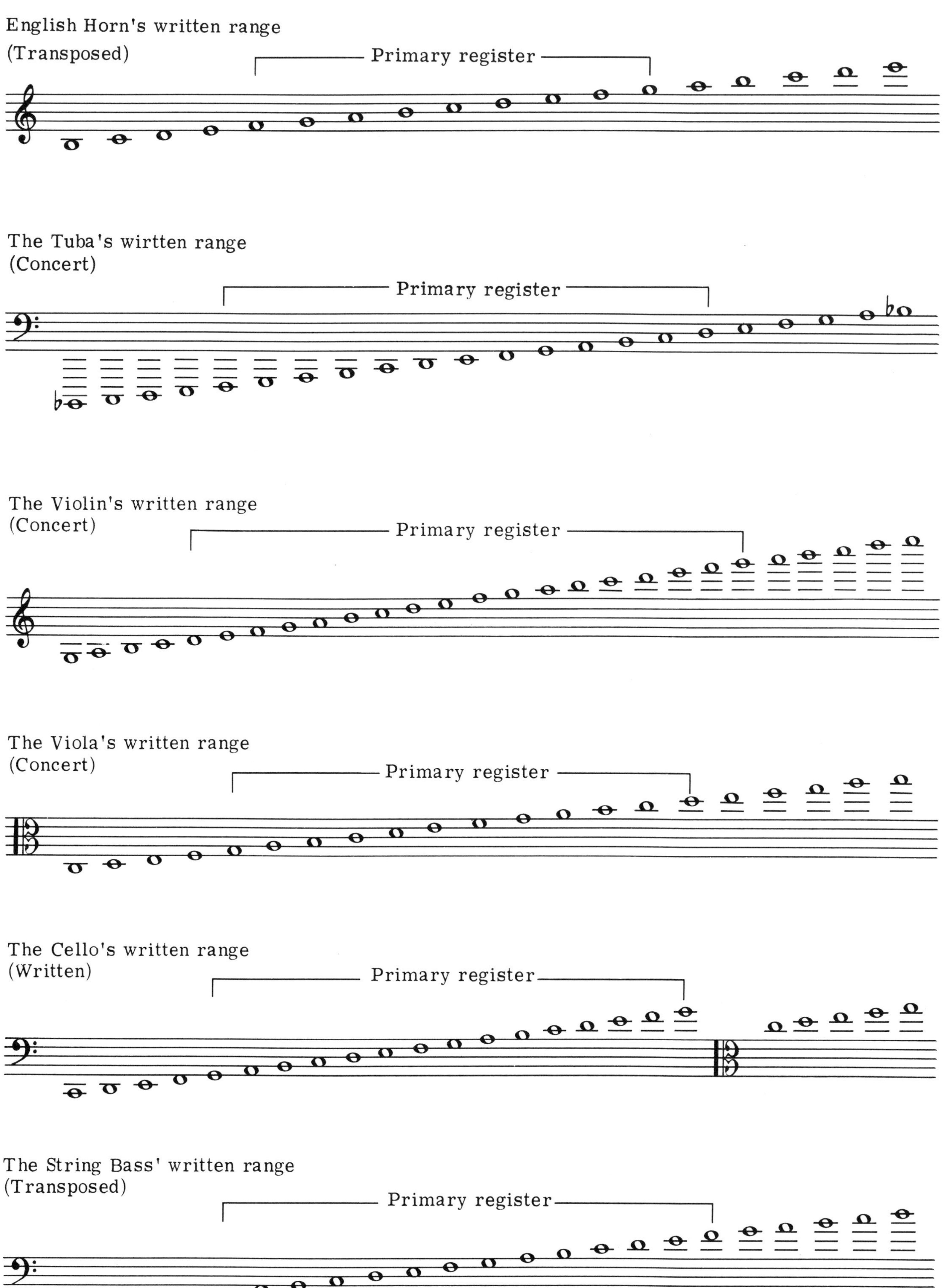

The Guitar's written range
(Transposed)

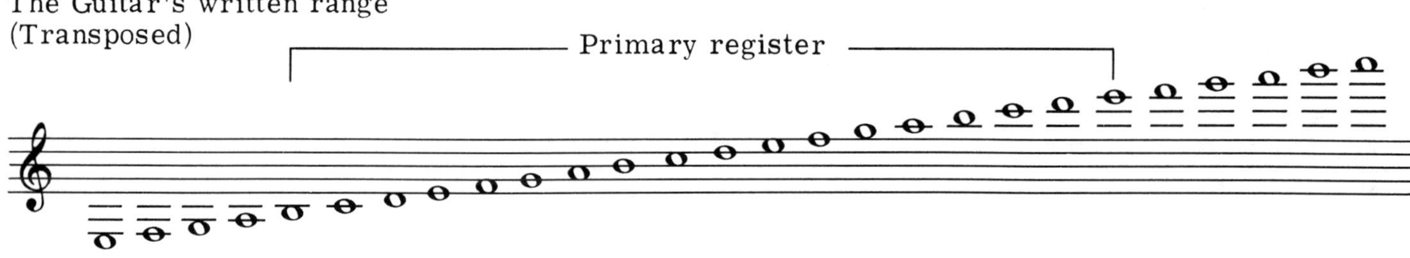

The Bass Guitar (Fender Bass) written range
(Trnasposed)

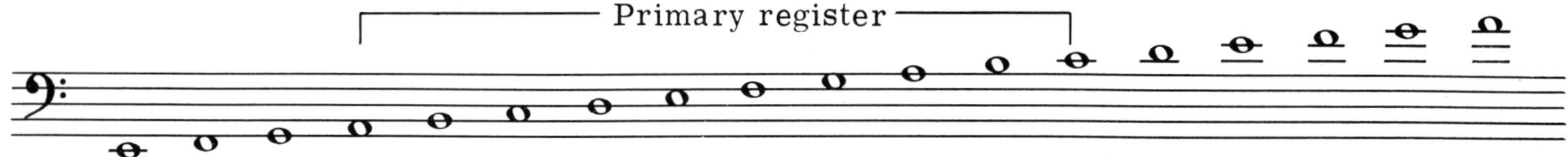

As a beginner in the world of music orchestration, it is advisable to stay within the Primary Registers of the instruments you initially write for because of these reasons.

1. Notes from the primary registers of instruments almost always typify the "sound" of that instrument and will generally sound good, either by themselves OR blended within a mixed voicing of other instruments.

2. Notes from the Primary Register are generally "easier" to play on the various instruments and therefore you are less likely to write a passage of music which might present a great deal of difficulty for the instrumentalist to perform.

As you gain more and more experience writing for the different instruments and inherently begin to know ALL of their register colors as well as their potentials AND limitations within their overall range, you will be able to expand the registers in which you can proficiently write. But until that time comes (possibly at some point in the study of the Intermediate book of this series), you should generally limit your writing to the Primary Registers.

Exercise #84

Transpose the following melody to within the primary register of the instruments listed.

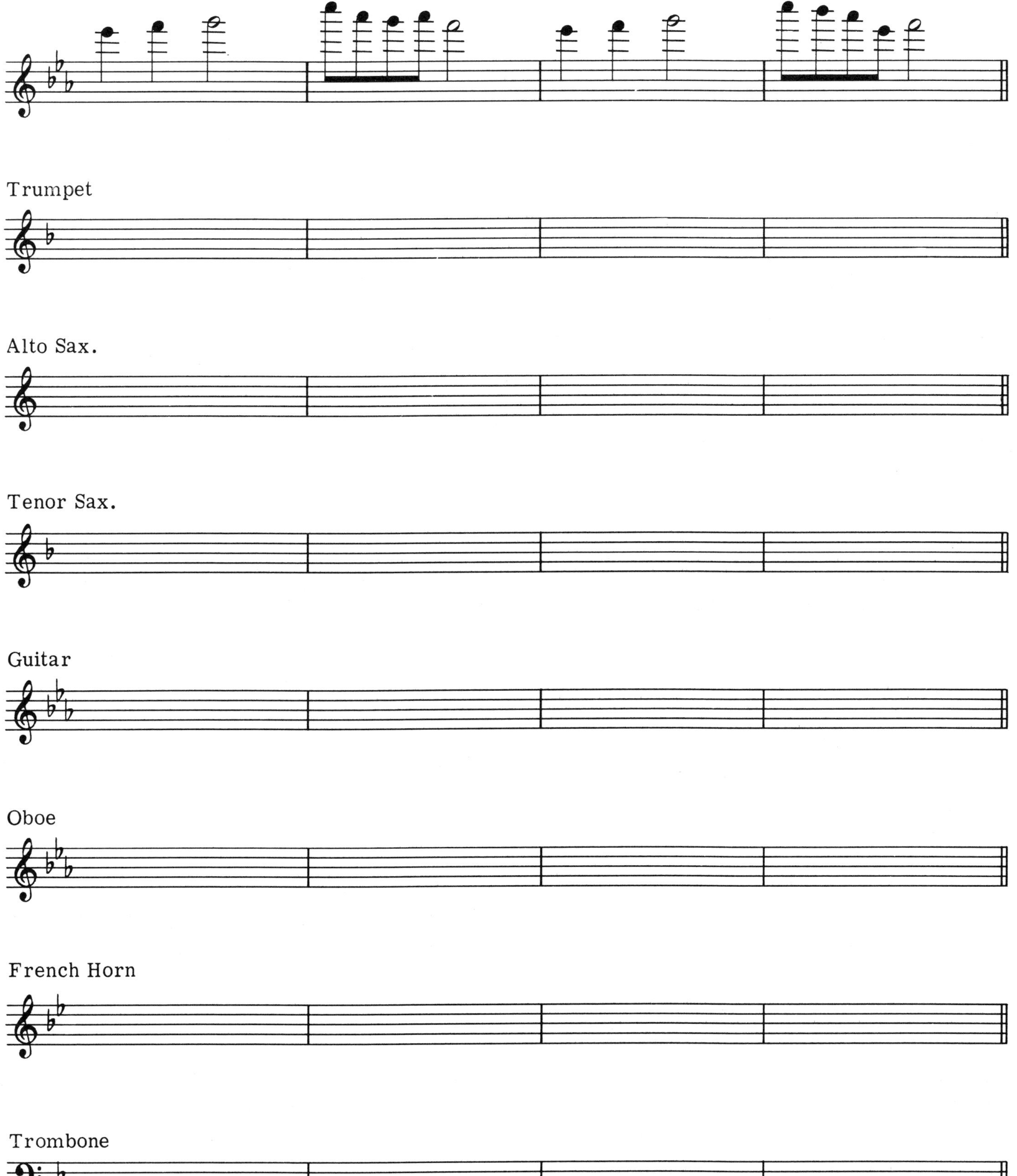

Tuba

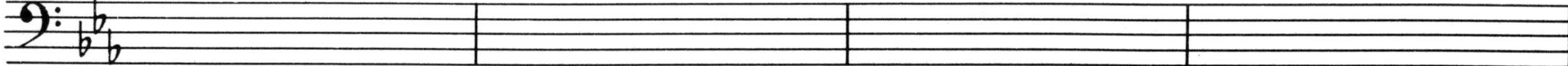

Flute

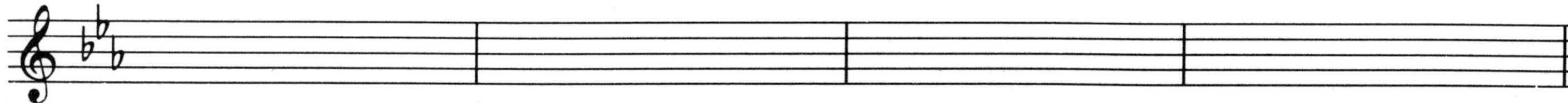

Violin

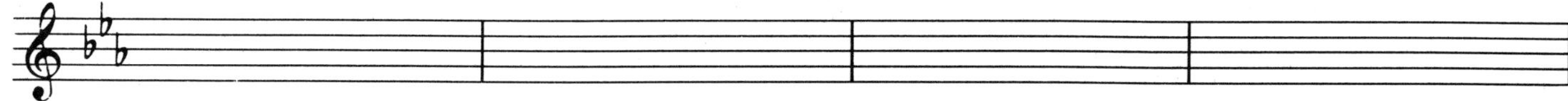

Viola

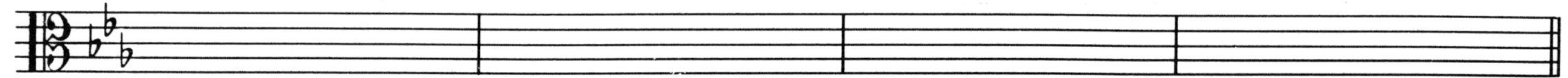

Cello

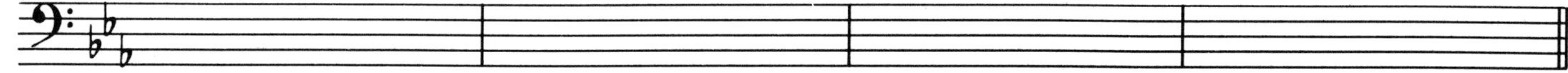

Bass Guitar

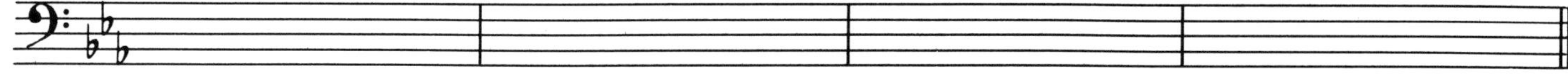

Clarinet in B♭

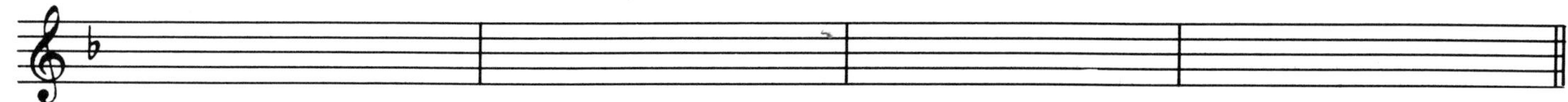

Bassoon

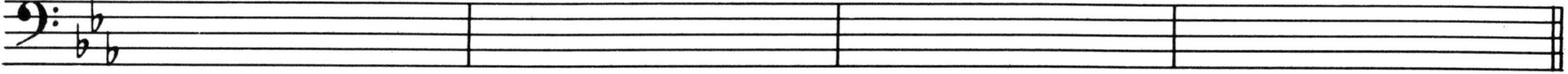

PART VIII
FUNDAMENTAL HARMONIC VOICE LEADING

In earlier parts of this book we briefly touched upon the subject of good voice leading. We learned that a melody should be "comfortable" in terms of execution (scale-wise without consecutive large interval skips) and should sound good by itself.

When writing parts for instruments to play within harmonic voicings, the same principles of voice leading would apply.

For instance, in this I, V, vi, V, I progression, if we wrote the parts as illustrated we would NOT have good voice leading.

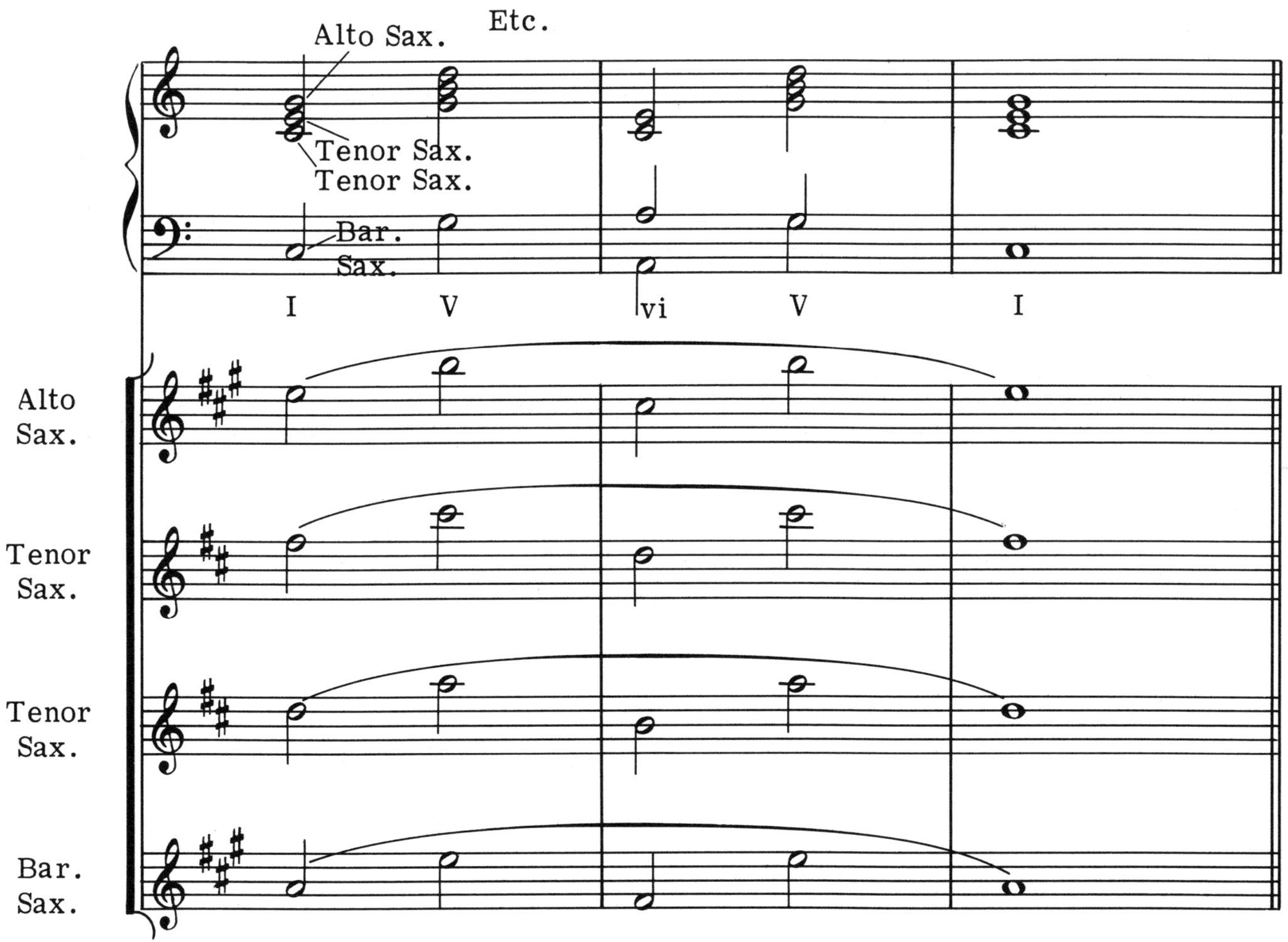

Study the preceeding example and you will notice that when we wrote parts for the
saxophone section (taken from the progression as it is voiced) we ended up with "disjointed"
sounding melodies which are neither smooth (scale-wise) OR sound good on their own.

Below is an example of preferable voice leading. Notice by re-arranging the notes
in the chords (using inversions) we are able to create smoother voice leading in the
individual saxophone parts.

Study the concepts outlined in the preceeding 2 examples. Next play both examples
on the piano, paying particular attention to the way the different saxophone parts sound in
each.

The concept of good voice leading remains the same when we add extensions to triads
in a given progression. Below is an example of a 5 voice harmonic progression where
good voice leading is NOT a consideration.

Play the above progression on the piano and notice how disjointed and "unmusical"
the voicings sound one to the other.

Write and transpose 5 saxophone parts using the preceeding example's voice leading.
Notice how erratic and disjointed the individual parts are.

Exercise #85

125

As you can see, after writing out the individual sax parts, each "melody" which is created is rather disjointed sounding.

A better progression of the preceeding voicings would thus be:

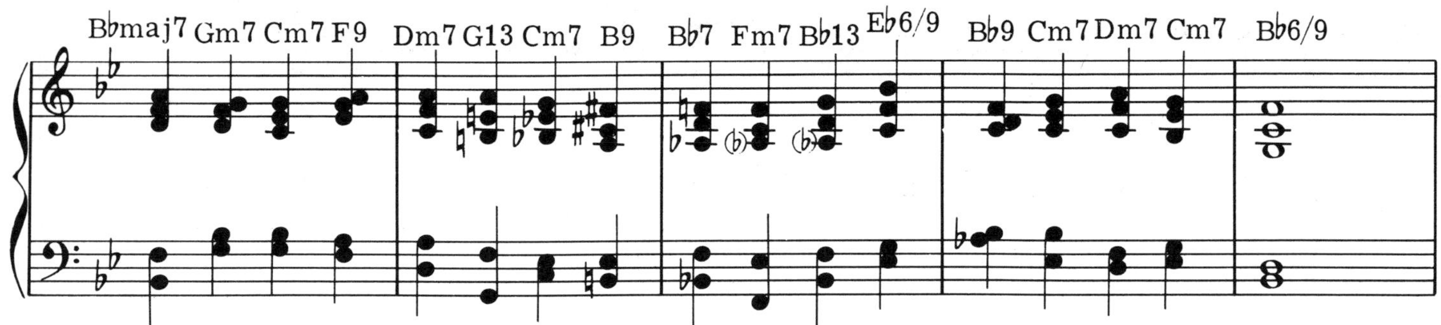

Now, write out (and properly transpose) the preceeding progression of voicings for 5 saxophones, using the top note of each voicing for Alto I, the 2nd note for Alto II, the 3rd note for Tenor I, the 4th note for Tenor II and the bottom note for Bari.

Exercise #86

You should notice how much better the voice leading for the individual parts are after completing the above exercise. The melodies which each saxophone plays is much more scale-wise and large, awkward interval skips have been avoided. Play the progression on the piano and note how much smoother it sounds. Next, play each individual sax part to check how much smoother each sounds.

Write out 5 part progressions of good voice leading for the following exercises. Then, write out each progression (and properly transpose) for each group of instruments noted. Melody notes are provided for the top note of each voicing.

Because of the chromatic nature of the following exercises (many accidentals and key modulations), good voice leading may be a little more difficult to achieve. Try to make each "part" as scale-wise as possible and avoid awkward interval skips. Intervals of seconds and thirds are preferable. Intervals of fourths and fifths are acceptable too, as long as they are followed by scale-wise movement. Try to avoid the interval of the augmented 4th (although sometimes it is nearly impossible in inner voices).

Exercise #87

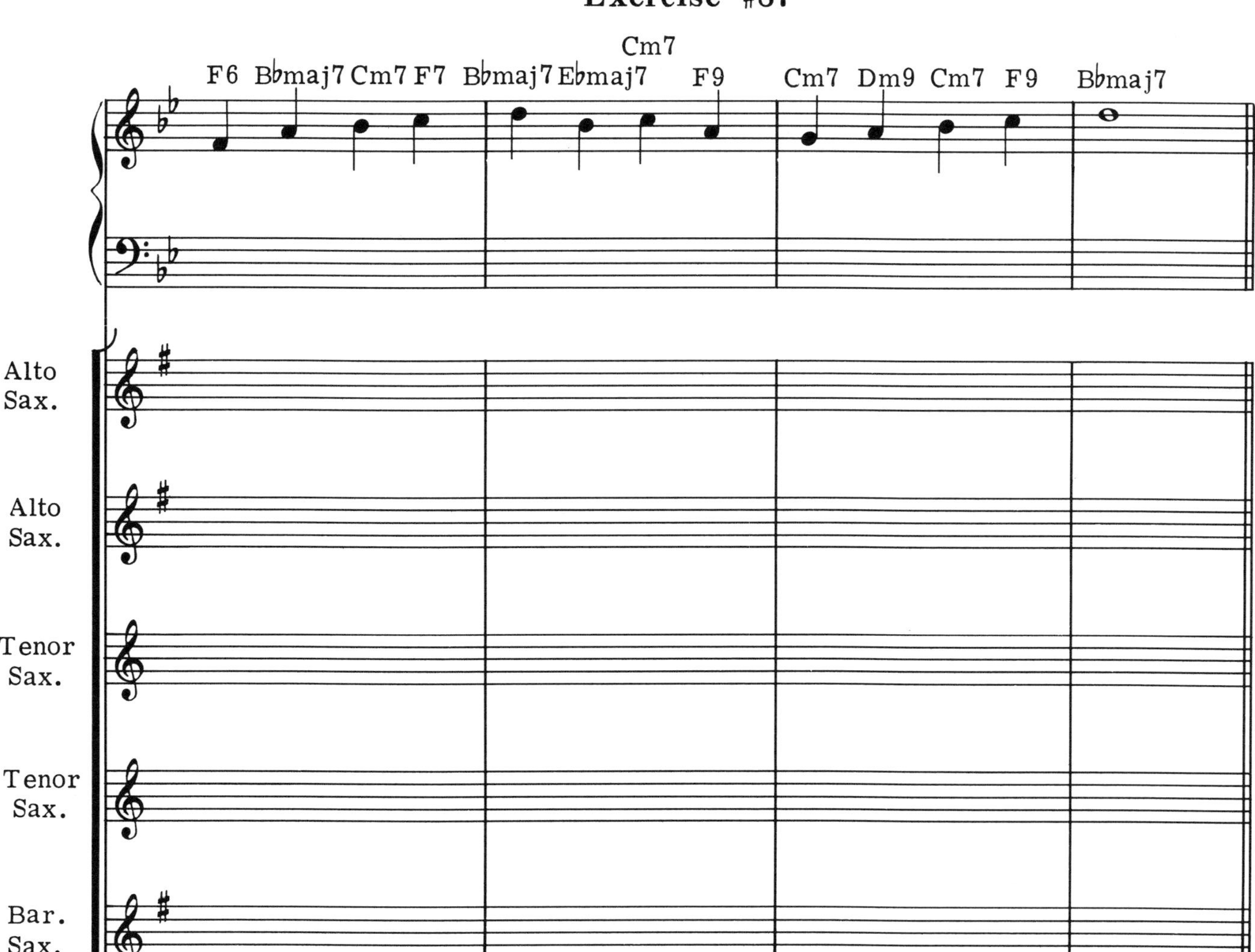

Exercise #88

Exercise #89

Fm7 Bbm7 Eb7 Abmaj9 Dm7 G7 Cmaj7 C6/9 Cm7 Fm7 Bb13   Ebmaj9   Am7 D7b9 Gmaj7
Alto Sax.
Alto Sax.
Tenor Sax.
Tenor Sax.
Bar. Sax.

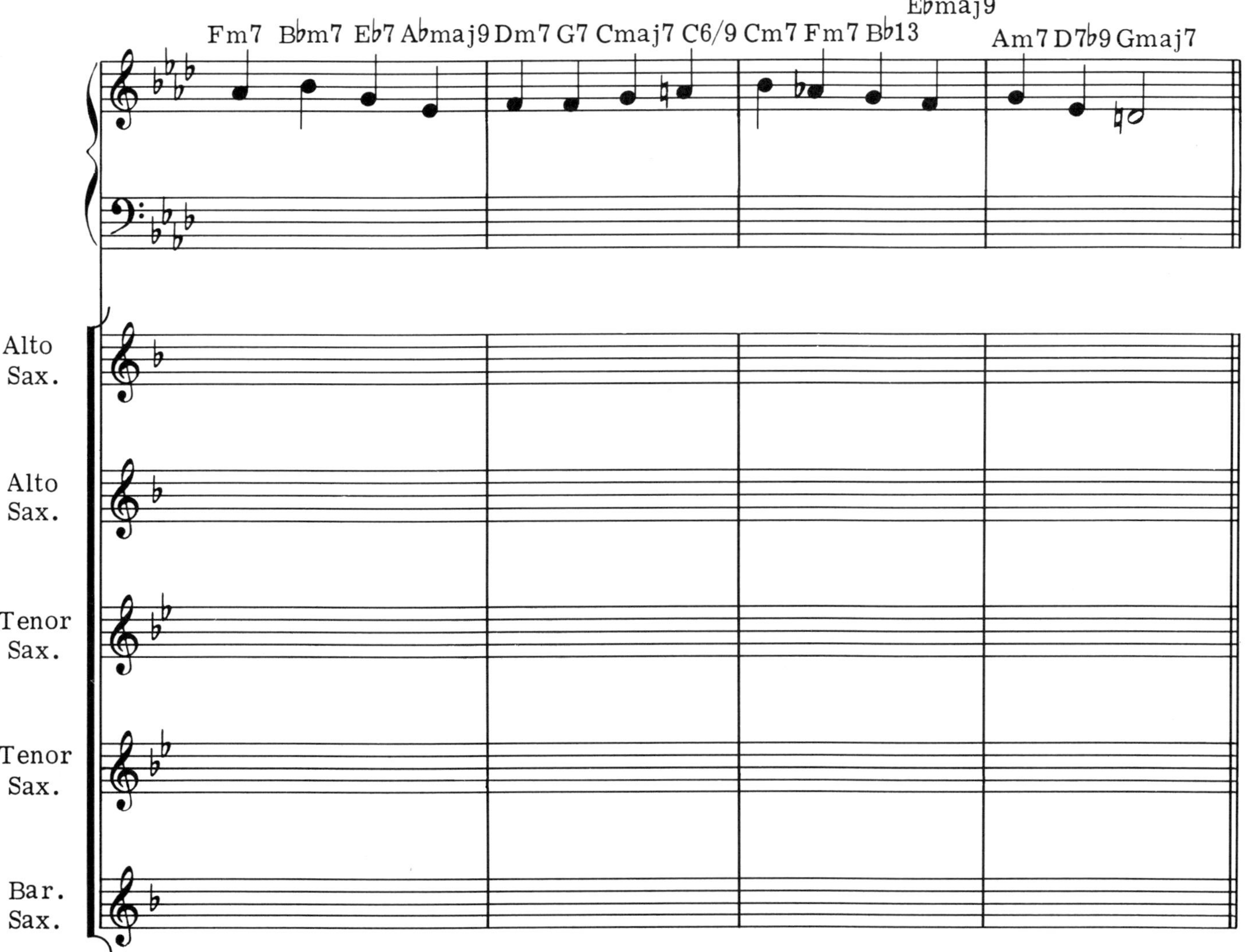

Exercise #90

Cmaj7 Cm7
Gmaj9
B♭m7
E♭9 Am7 D7♯9
F♯m7♭5 B7 Em7
A9
D13♭9
Tpts.
1
2
3
Trbs.
1
2

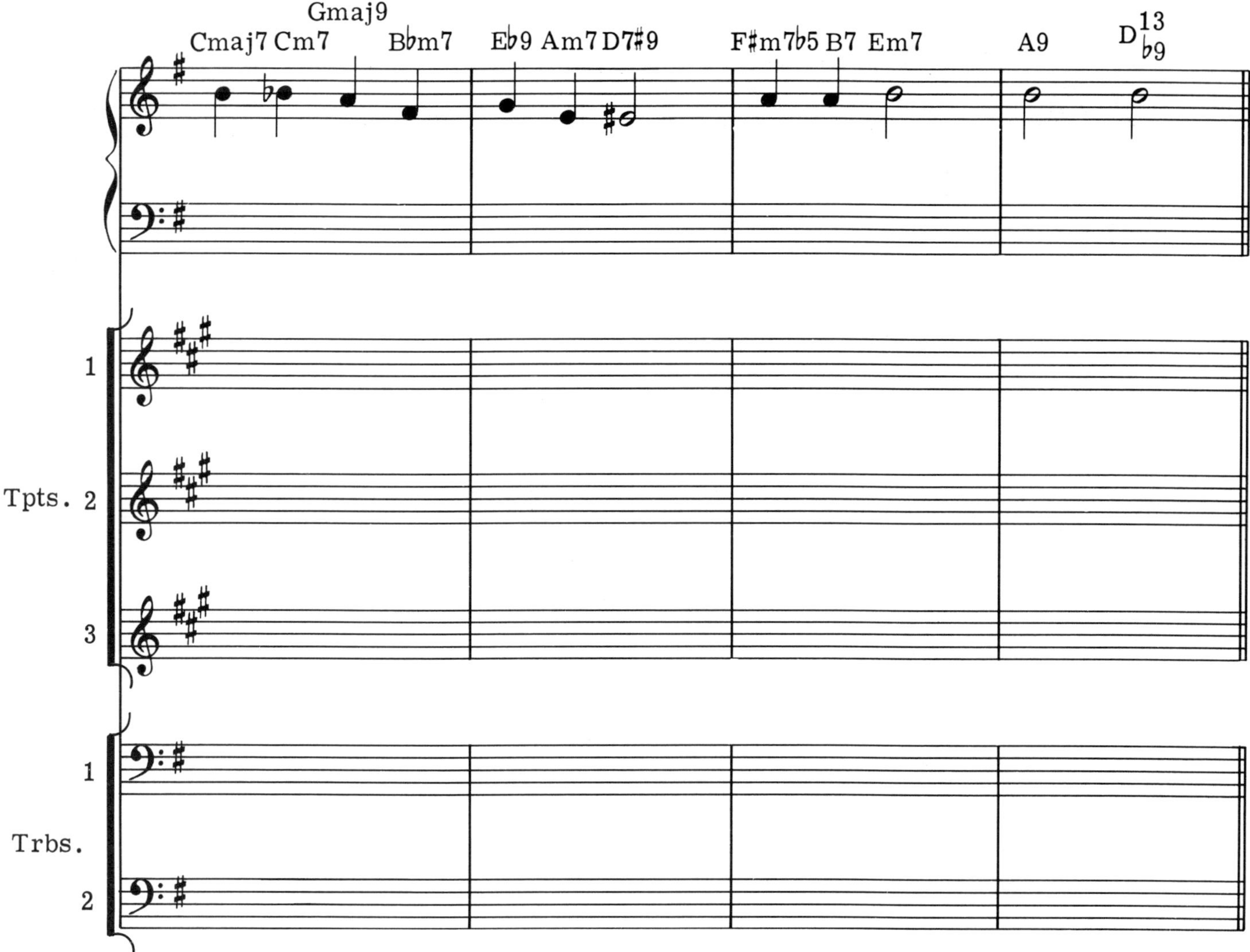

Exercise #91

Cmaj7 Cm9 E♭maj7
G7♭9
Cmaj7 C6/9 Dm7 G13 Cmaj7
Dm7 D♭9
Fm7 B♭13 E♭maj9
Alto Sax.
Alto Sax.
Tenor Sax.
Tenor Sax.
Bar. Sax.

APPENDIX

Here are solutions and answers to the exercises in this book. While sometimes there may be more than one solution to a particular exercise, (as in part writing) each answer should be looked upon as a good, "all around" solution to a musical problem.

Exercise #1

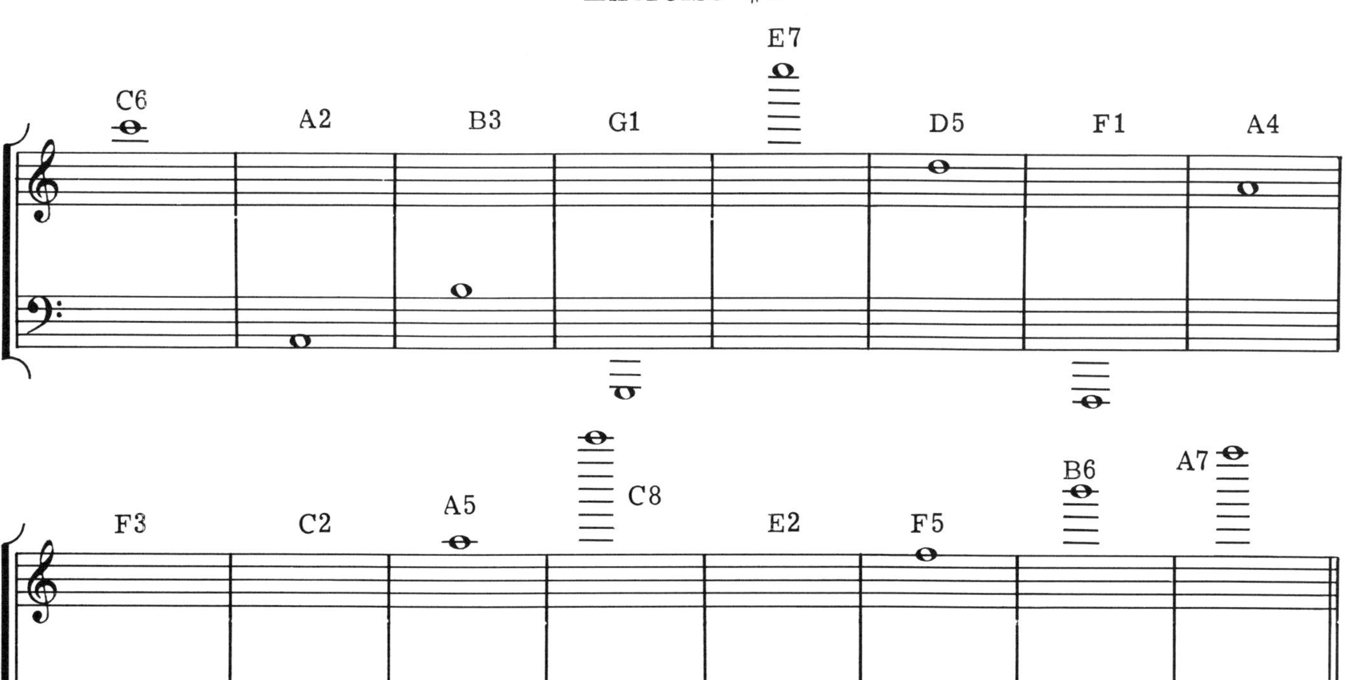

C6 A2 B3 G1 E7 D5 F1 A4
F3 C2 A5 C8 E2 F5 B6 A7

Exercise #2

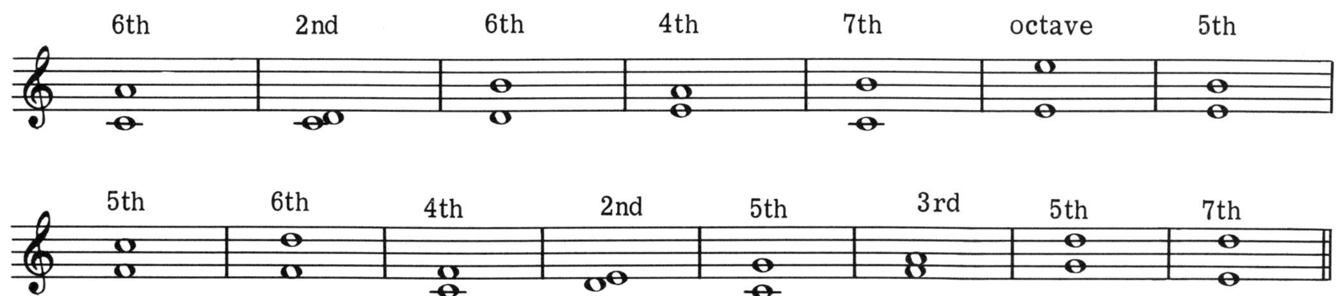

6th 2nd 6th 4th 7th octave 5th
5th 6th 4th 2nd 5th 3rd 5th 7th

Exercise #3

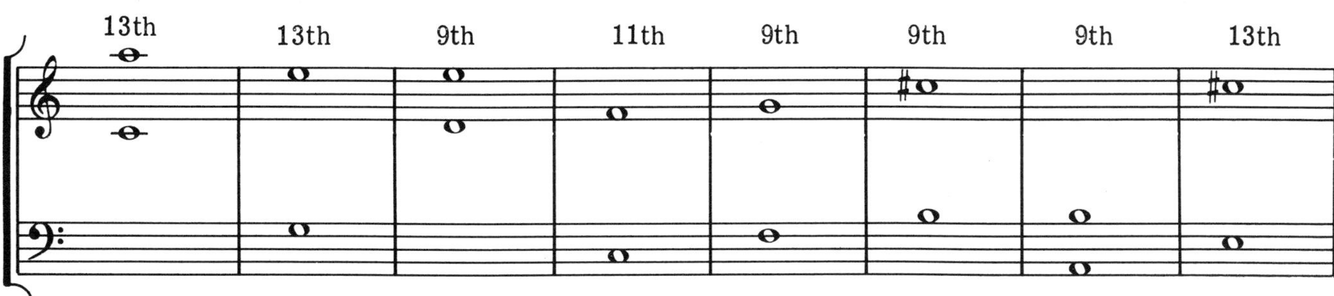

13th 13th 9th 11th 9th 9th 9th 13th

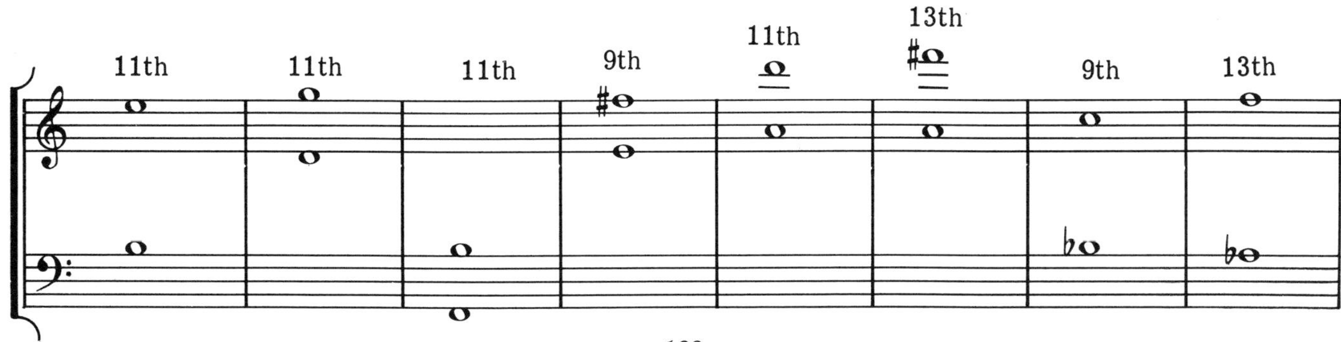

11th 11th 11th 9th 11th 13th 9th 13th

Exercise #4

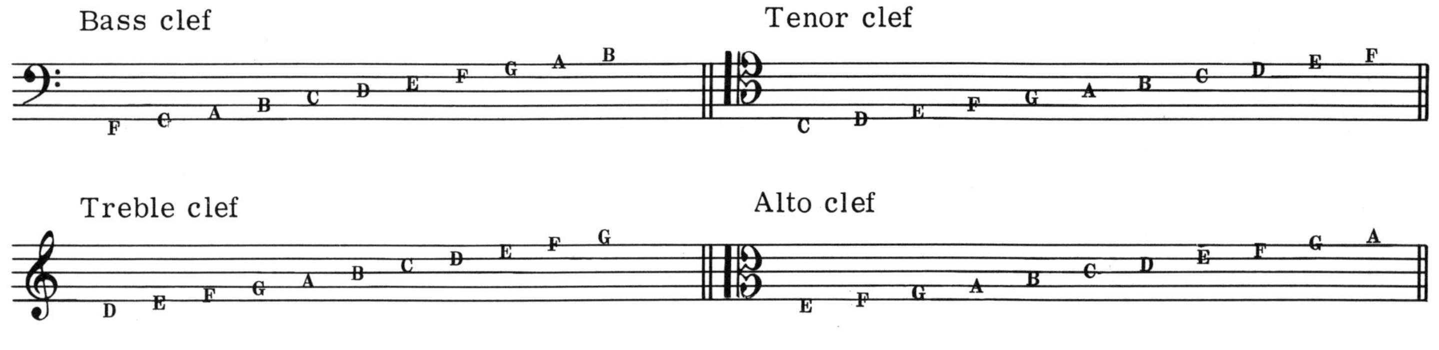

Exercise #5

Exercise #6

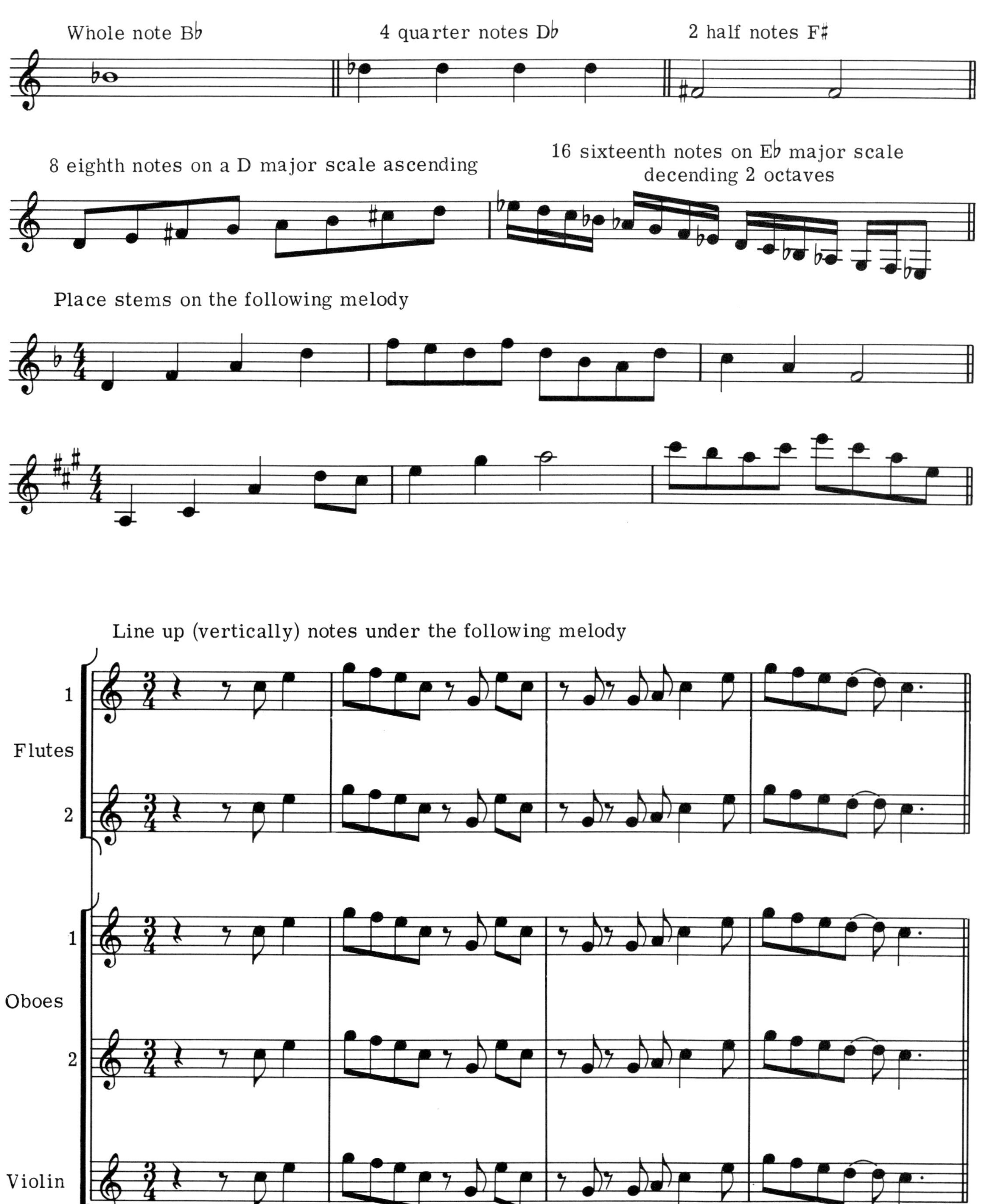

Write:
Whole note Bb
4 quarter notes Db
2 half notes F#
8 eighth notes on a D major scale ascending
16 sixteenth notes on Eb major scale decending 2 octaves
Place stems on the following melody
Line up (vertically) notes under the following melody
Flutes
1
2
Oboes
1
2
Violin

Exercise #7

Fill in the proper rest.
Whole rest
Equals
Fill in the
following
Equals
Equals
Equals
Equals
3
Equals____beats
1½
Equals____beats
3/4
Equals____beat

Exercise #8

Write the following intervals ABOVE the following pitches.

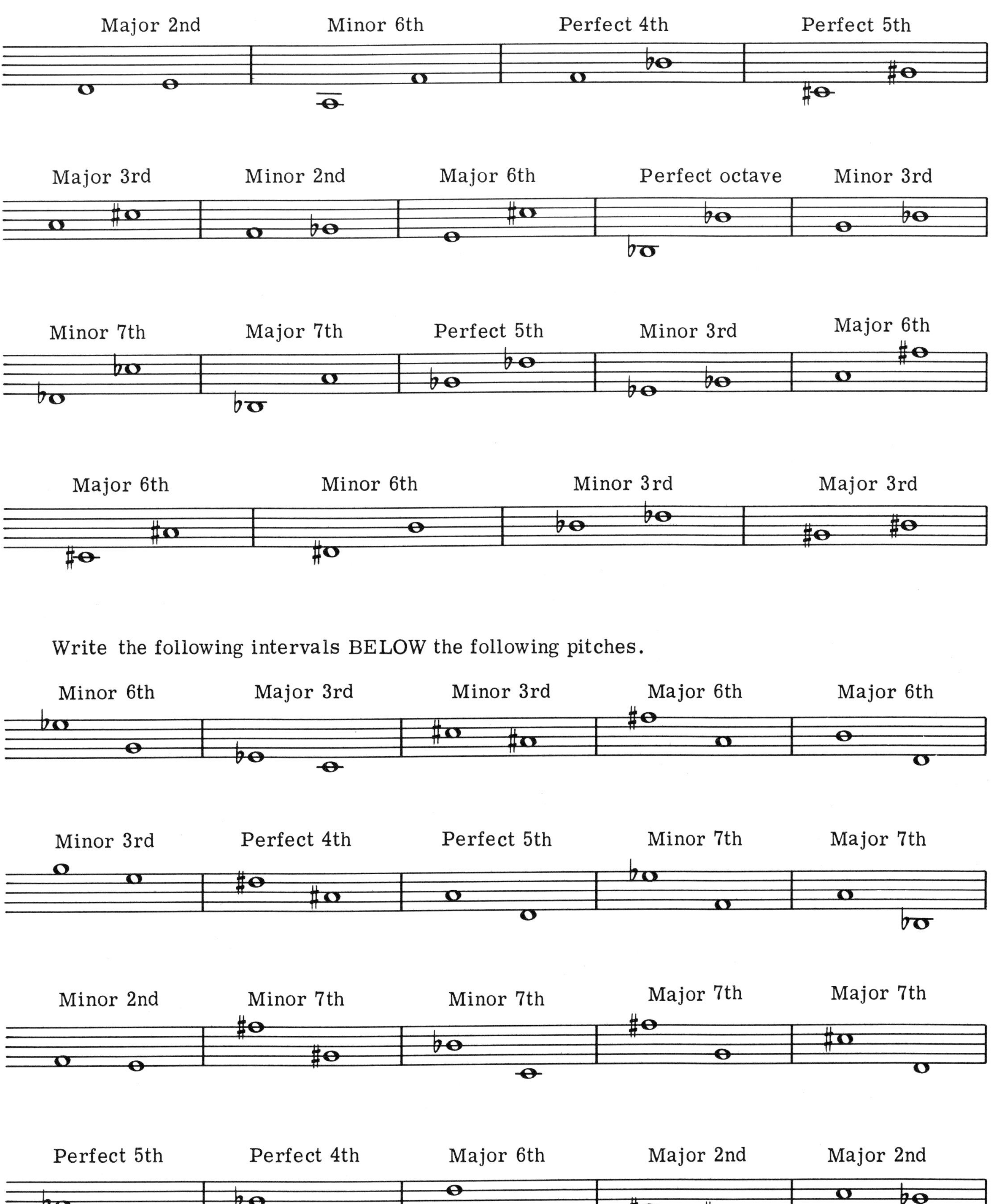

Write the following intervals BELOW the following pitches.

Exercise #9

Invert and name the following intervals

Major 3rd
Inverted Minor 6th
Minor 6th
Inverted Major 3rd
Minor 2nd
Inverted Major 7th
Major 7th
Inverted Minor 2nd
Minor 3rd
Inverted Major 6th
Major 2nd
Minor 7th
Perfect 5th
Inverted Perfect 4th
Major 6th
Inverted Minor 3rd
Perfect 5th
Inverted Perfect 4th
Minor 7th
Inverted Major 2nd
Perfect 5th
Inverted Perfect 4th
Perfect 4th
Inverted Perfect 5th
Major 3rd
Inverted Minor 6th
Minor 3rd
Inverted Major 6th
Major 2rd
Inverted Minor 7th
Minor 2nd
Inverted Major 7th
Major 7th
Inverted Minor 2nd
Minor 7th
Inverted Major 2nd

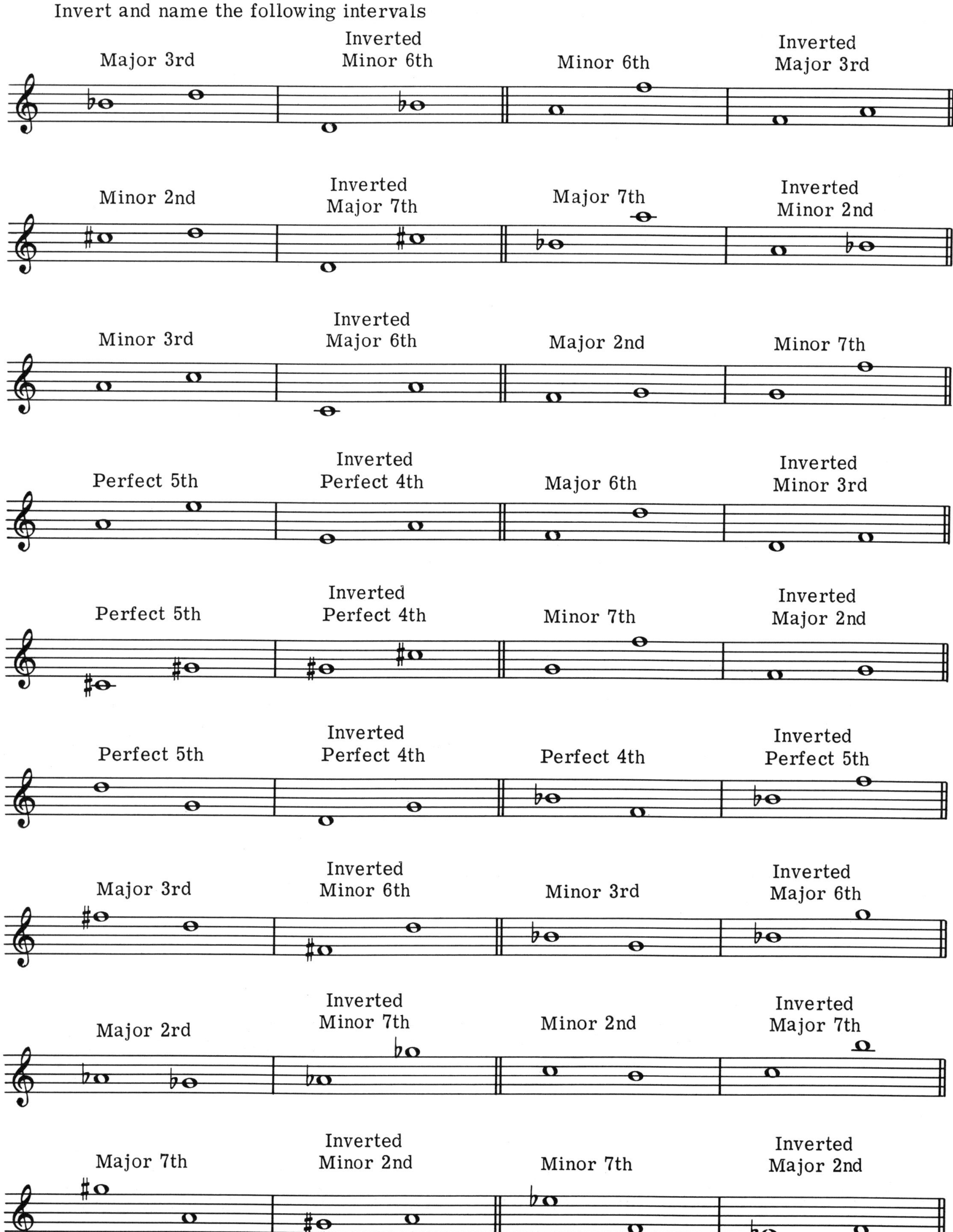

Fill in the proper key signatures.

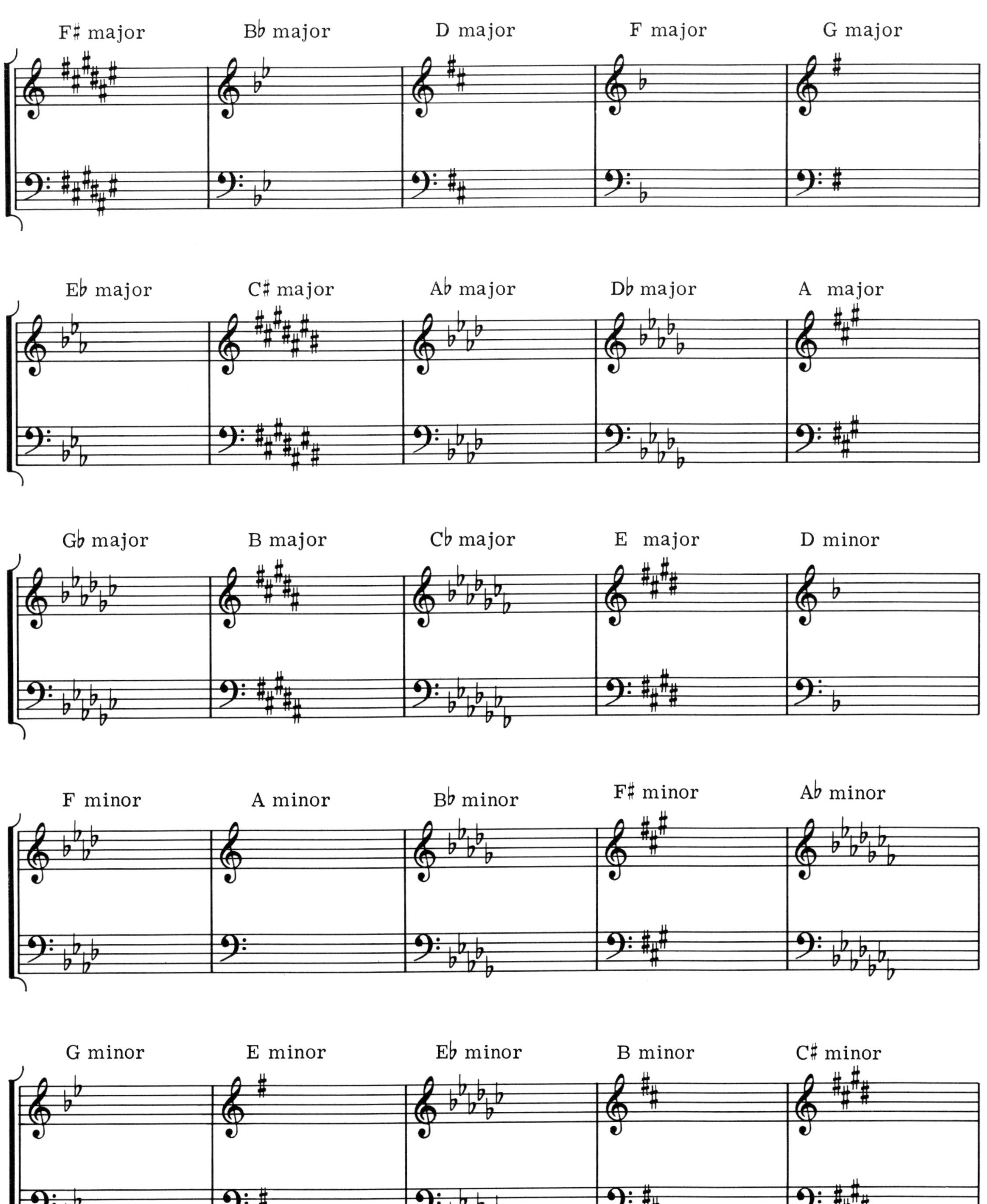

Exercise #10

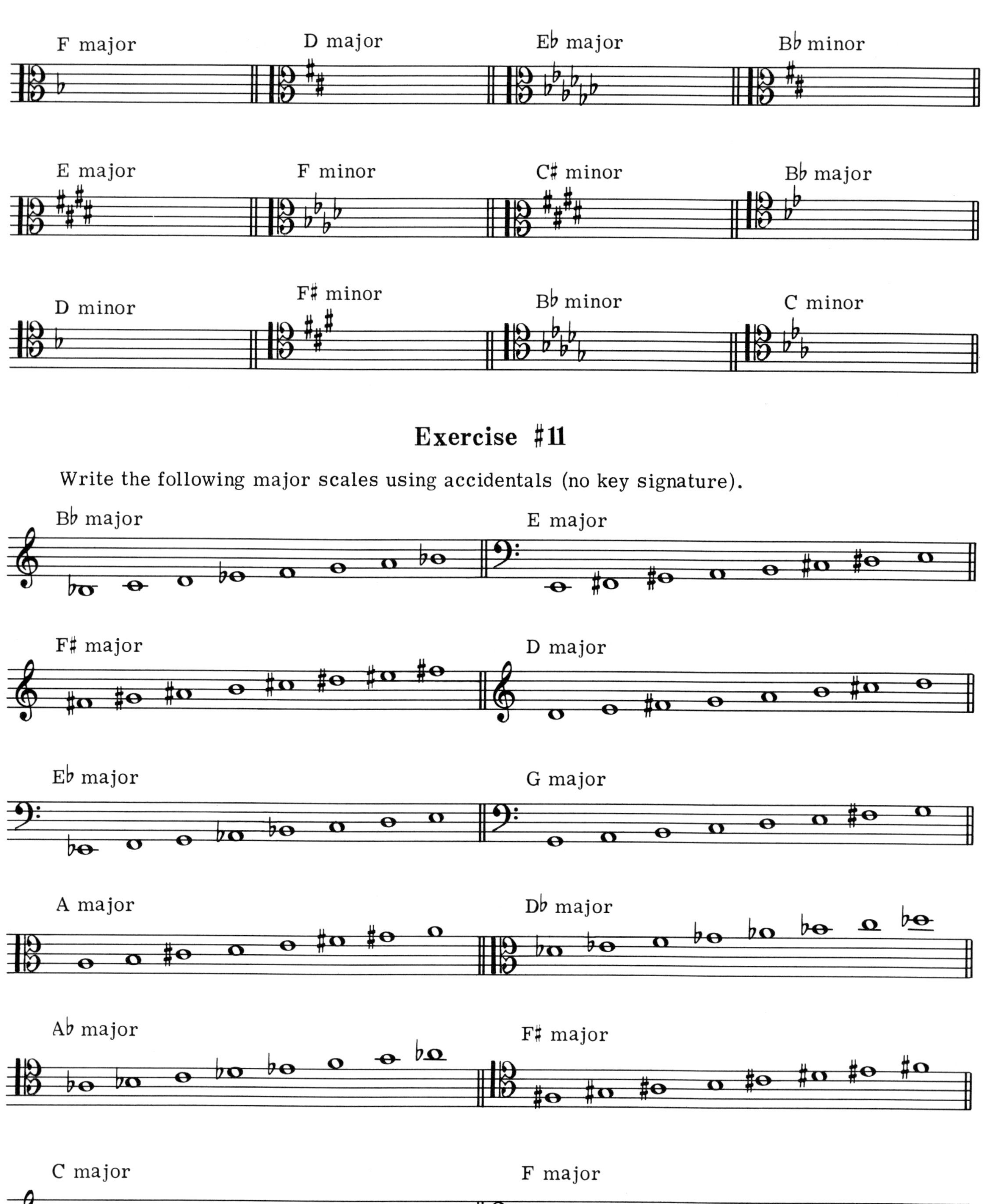

Exercise #11

Write the following major scales using accidentals (no key signature).

Write the following minor scales ascending & decending

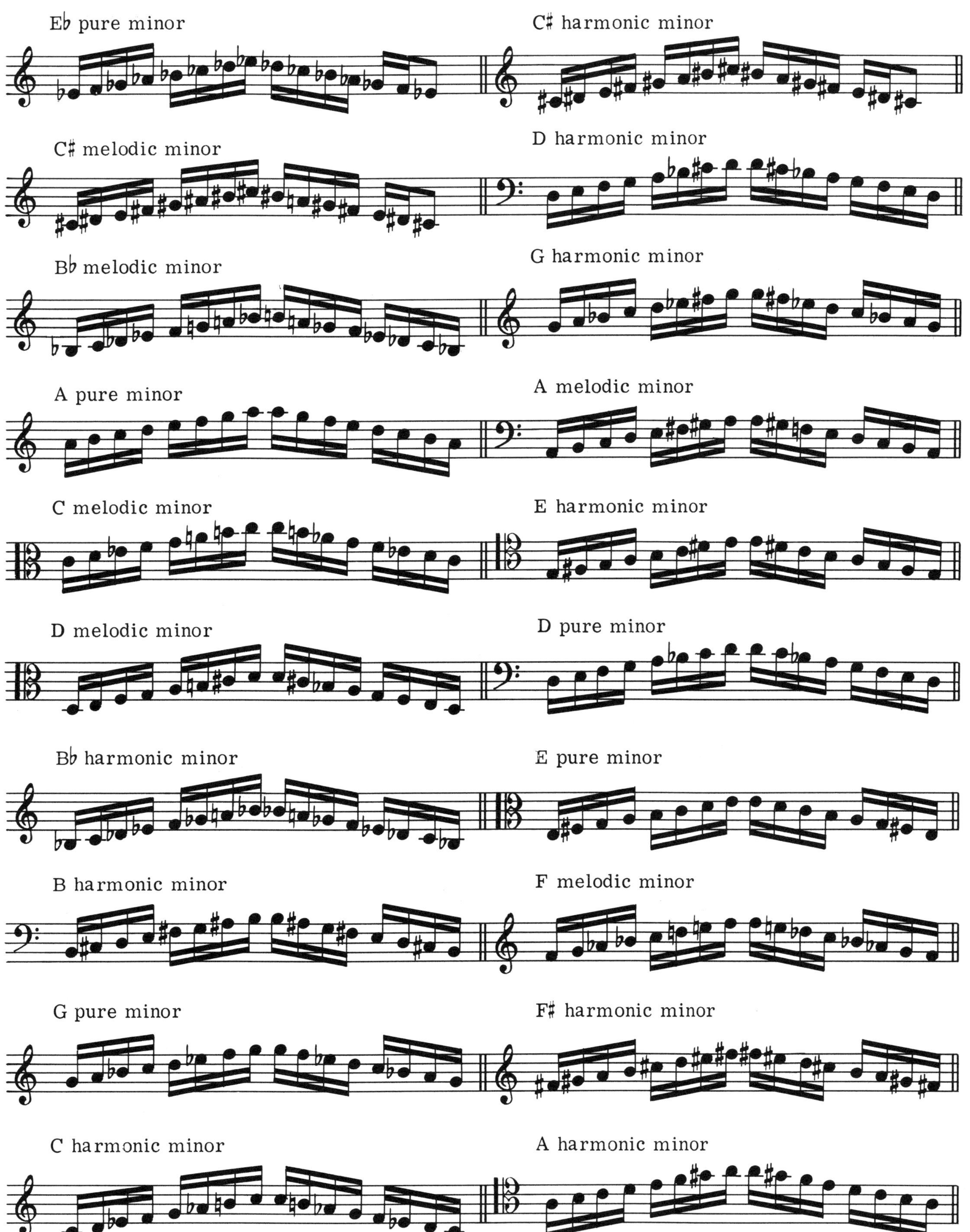

Exercise #12

Number and name the following scale step degrees according to the major key signature for each.

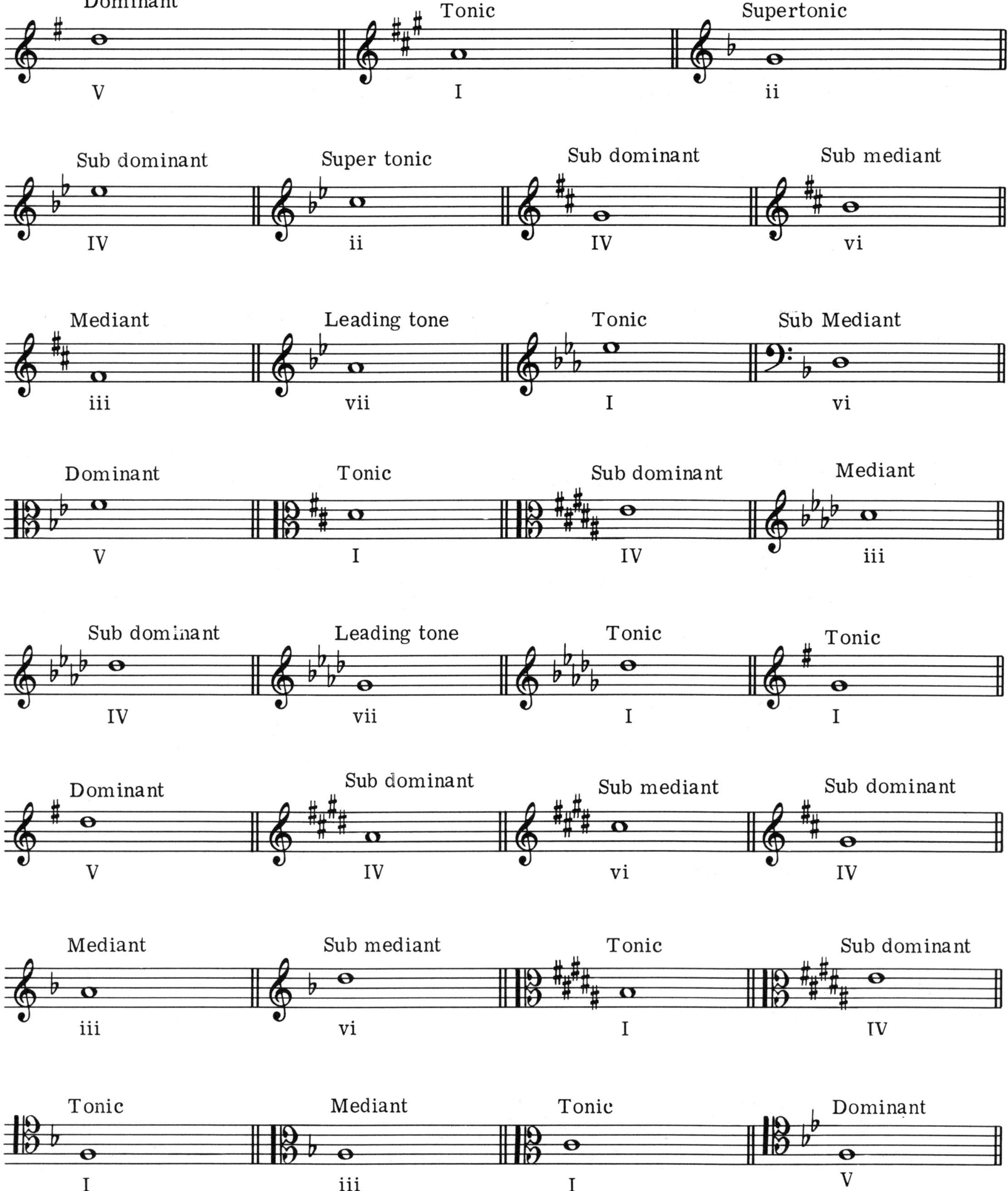

Exercise #13

Name and write the scale step number according to the major key signature for each and tell how each functions (major, minor, diminished, etc.)

Exercise #14

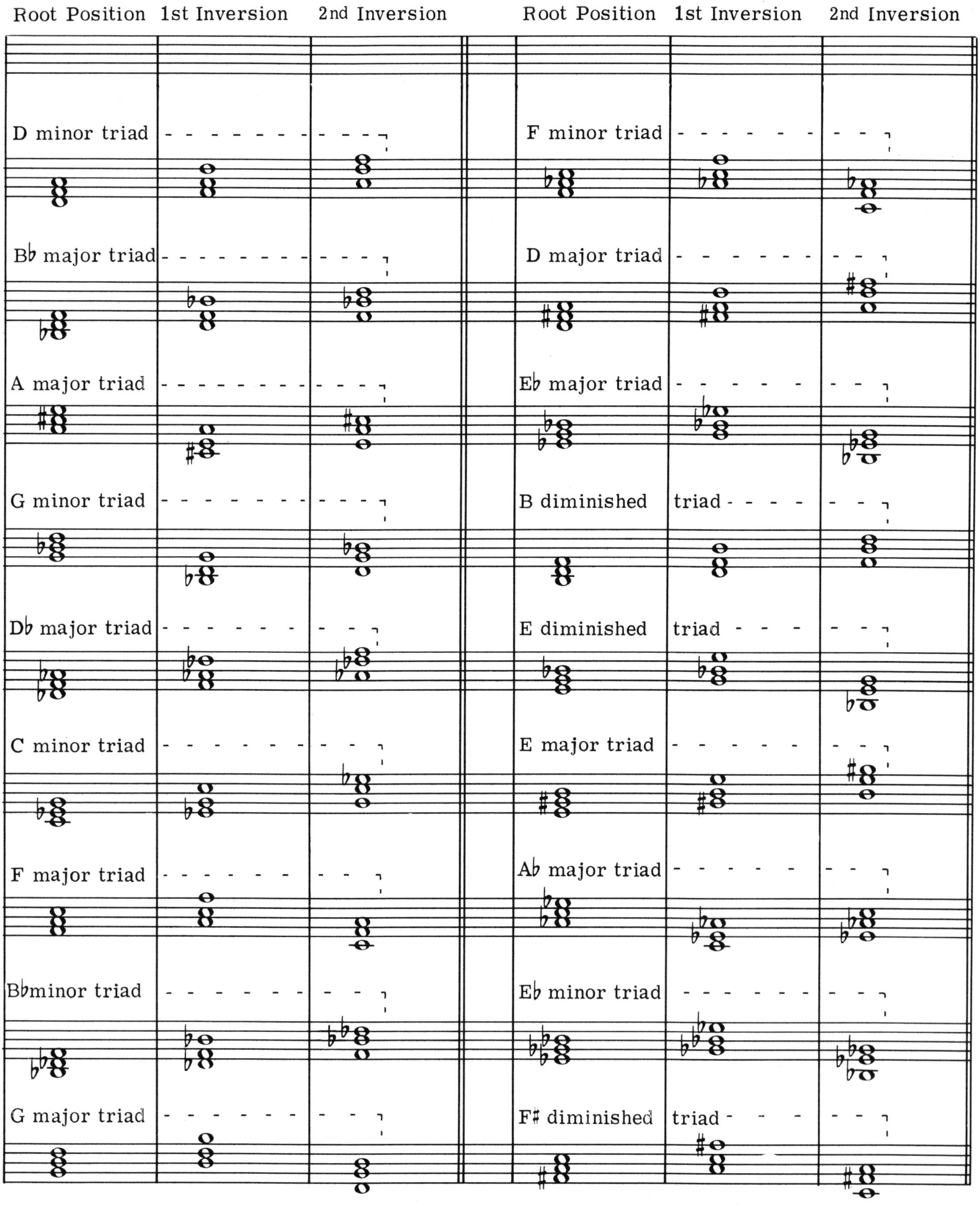
Root Position
1st Inversion
2nd Inversion
Root Position
1st Inversion
2nd Inversion
D minor triad
F minor triad
B♭ major triad
D major triad
A major triad
E♭ major triad
G minor triad
B diminished triad
D♭ major triad
E diminished triad
C minor triad
E major triad
F major triad
A♭ major triad
B♭minor triad
E♭ minor triad
G major triad
F♯ diminished triad

Exercise #15

Fill in the following circles in the cycle of fifths.

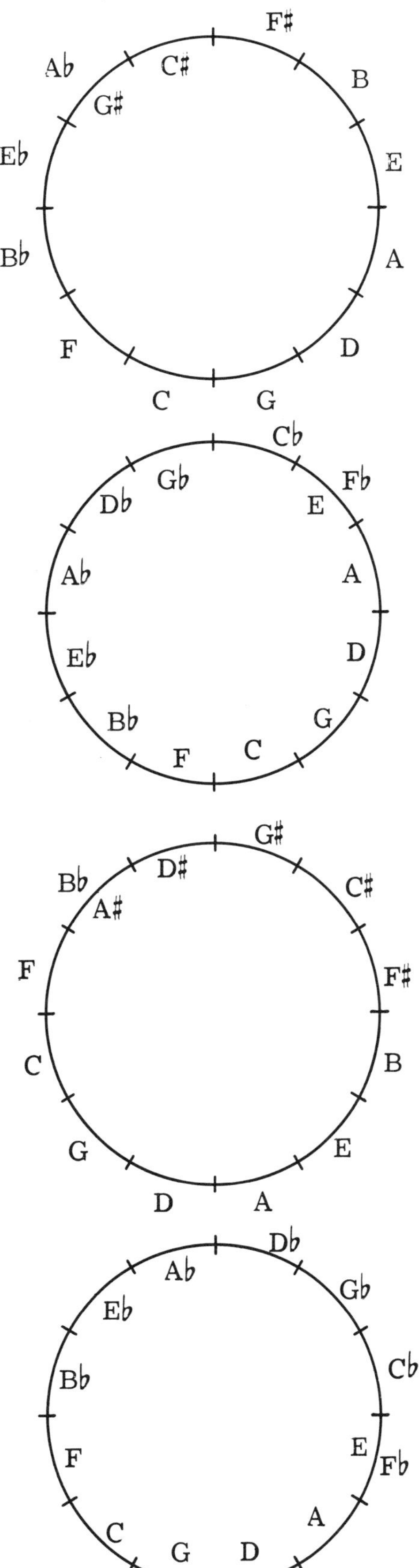

Exercise #16

Circle any chords chromatic to the key signature.

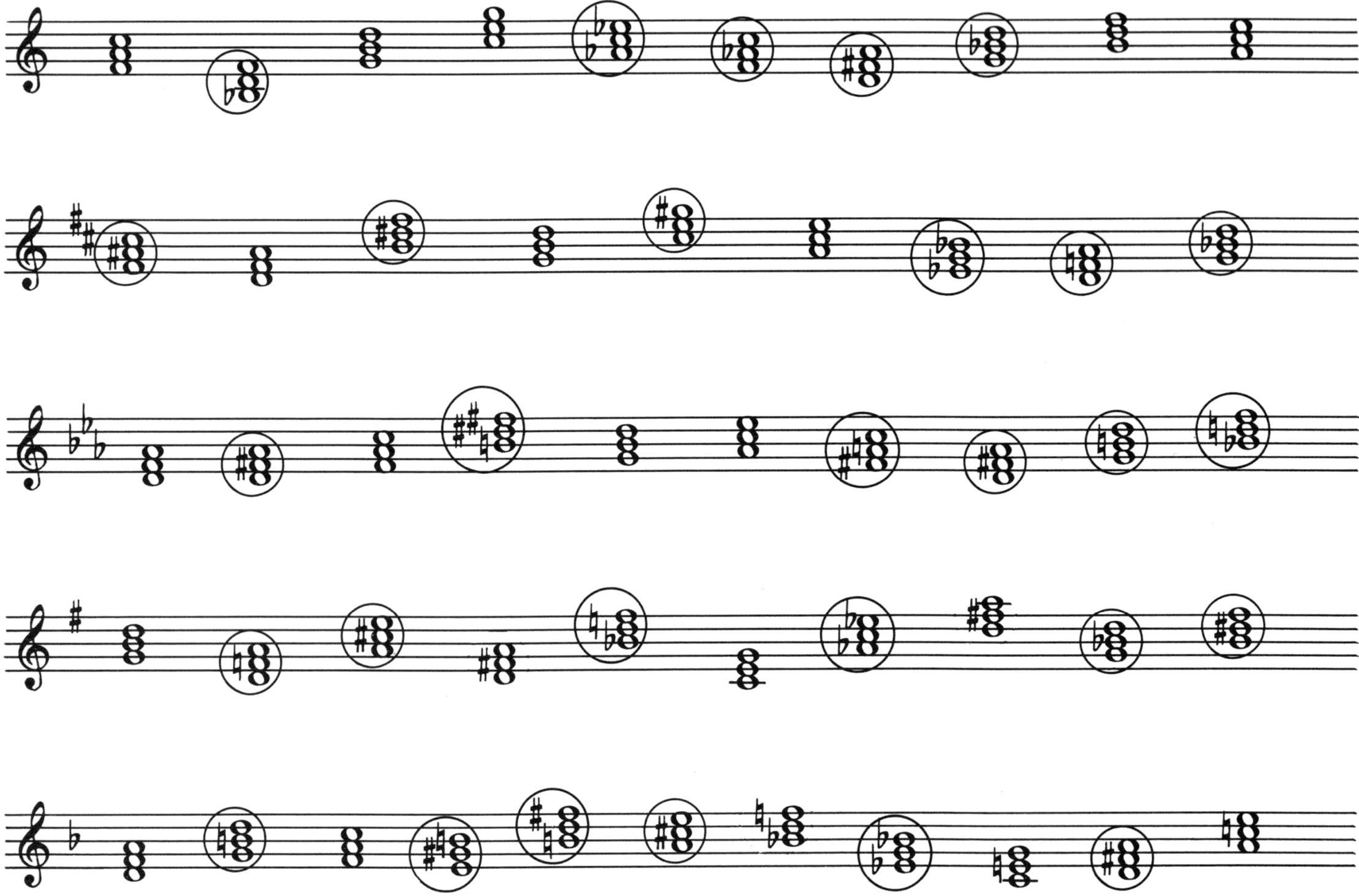

Exercise #17

Spell the following chords, making sure ALL accidentals are properly notated.

Exercise #18

Put the correct chord symbol above the following chord spellings.

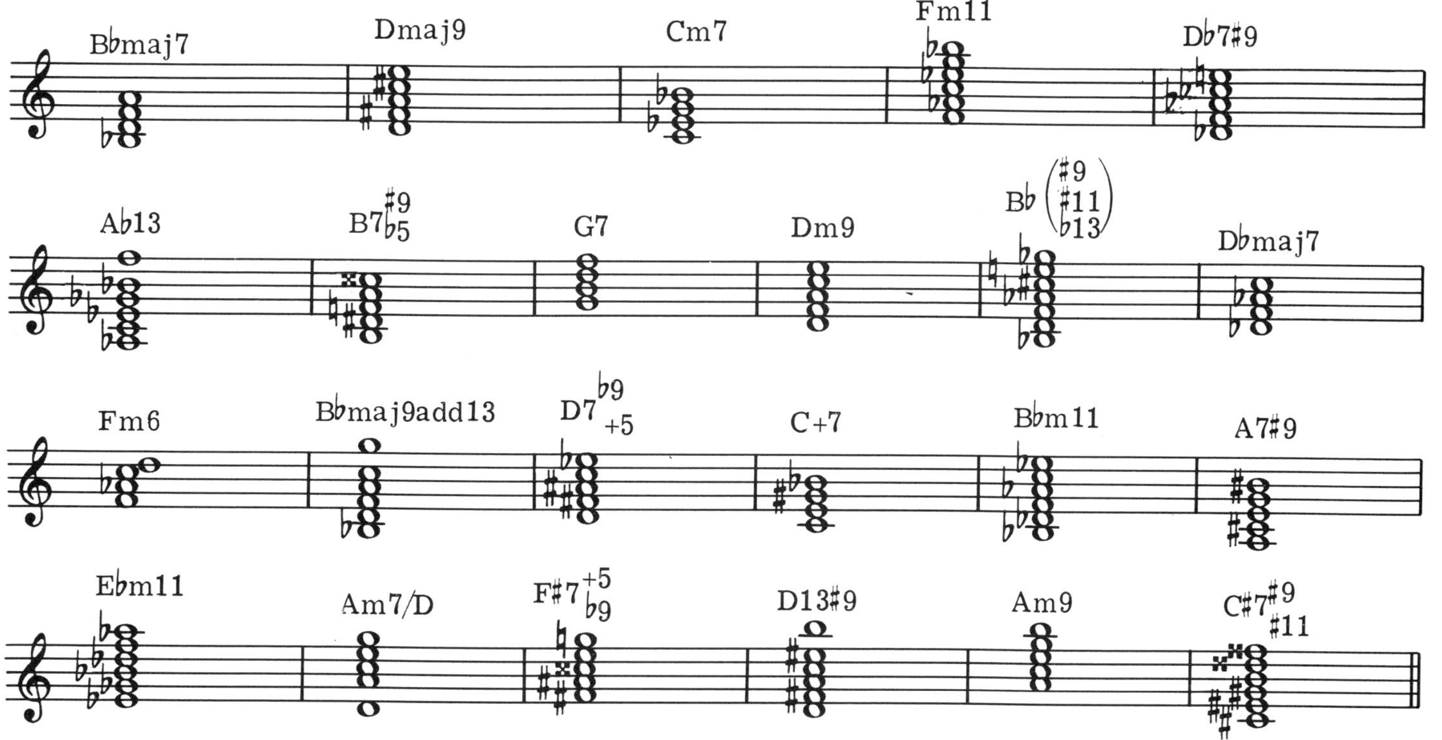

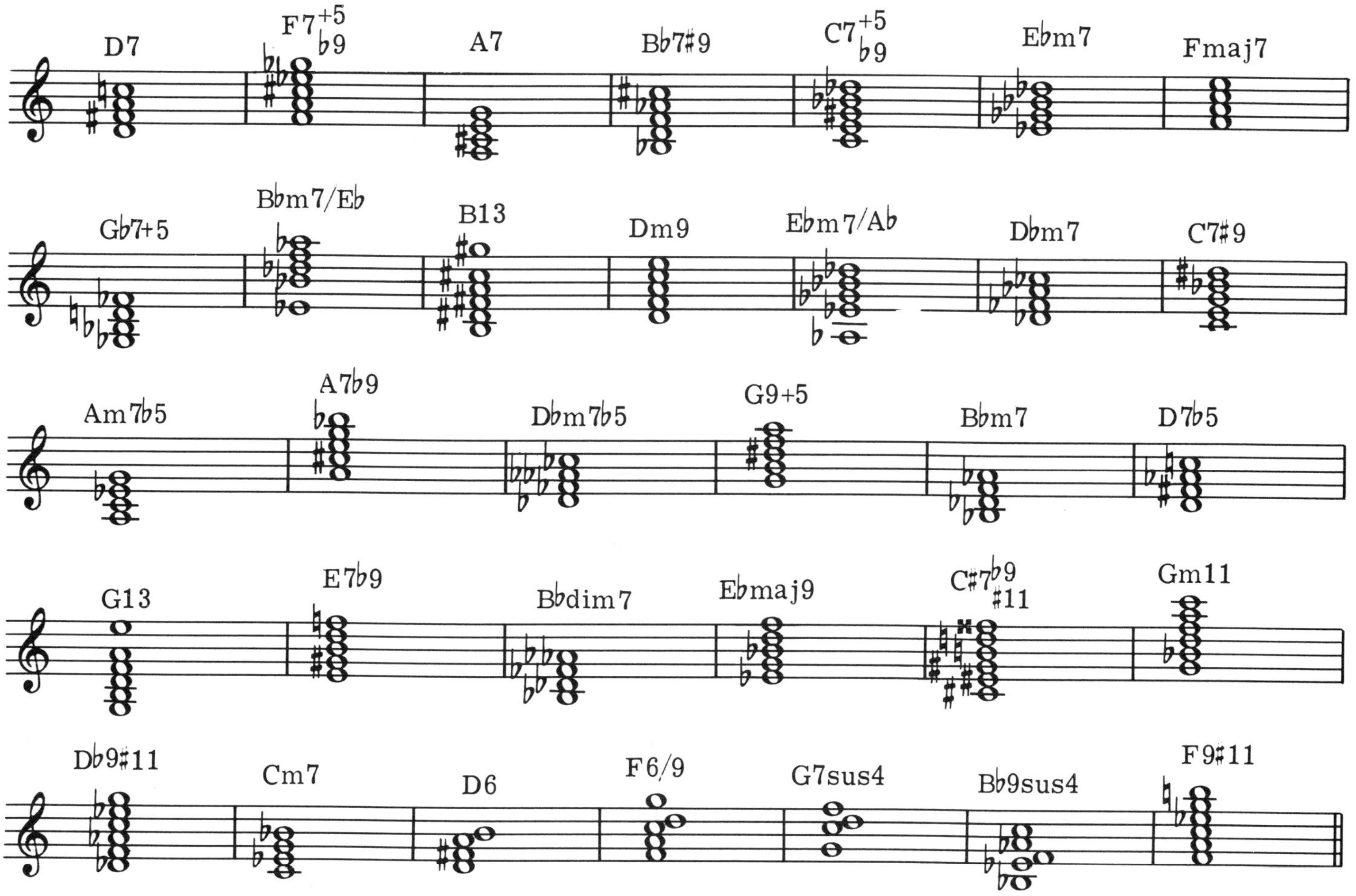

Spell out the following chord progressings in root position and name by number each chords function.

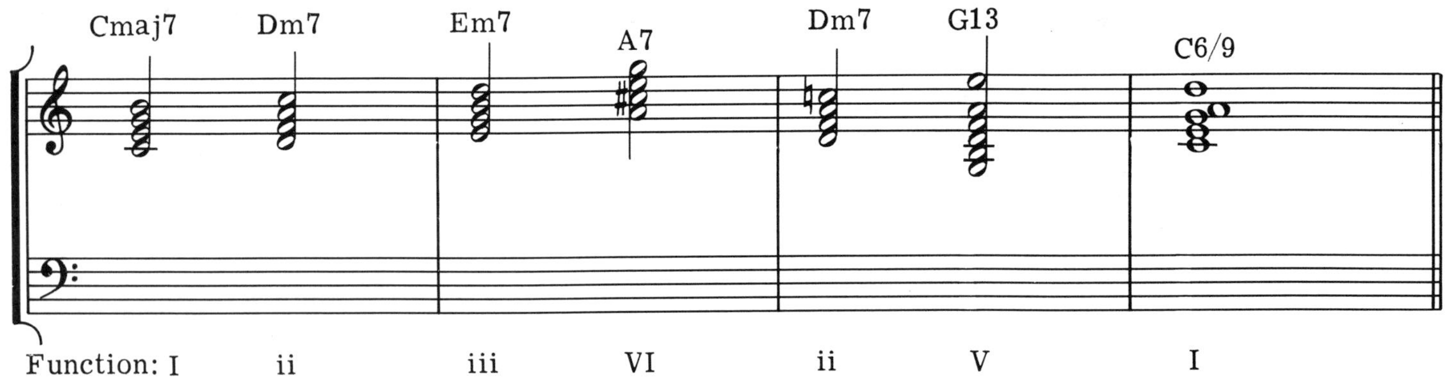

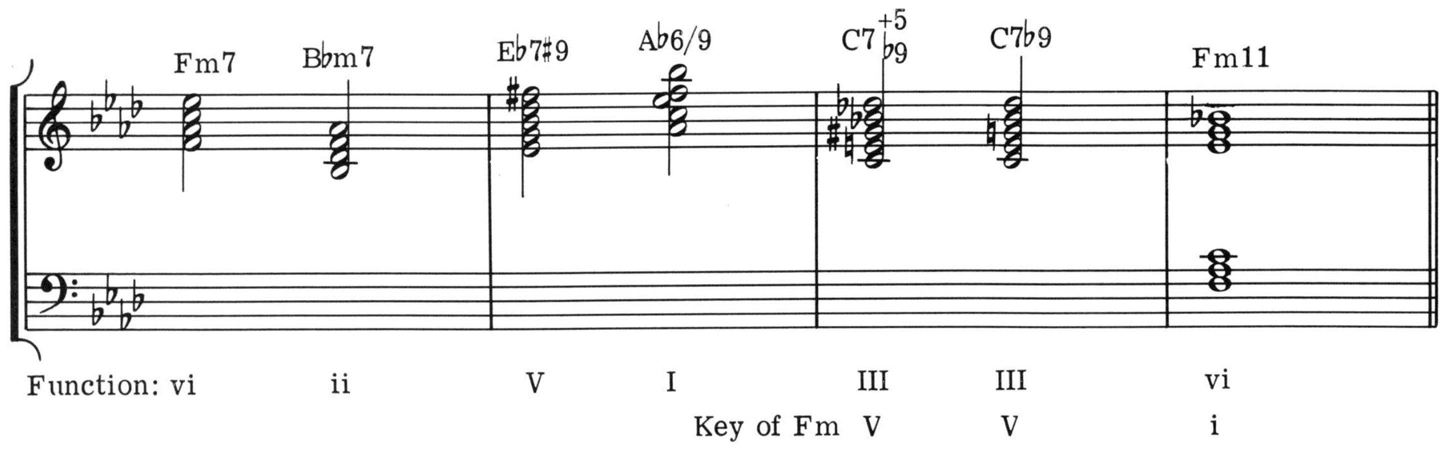

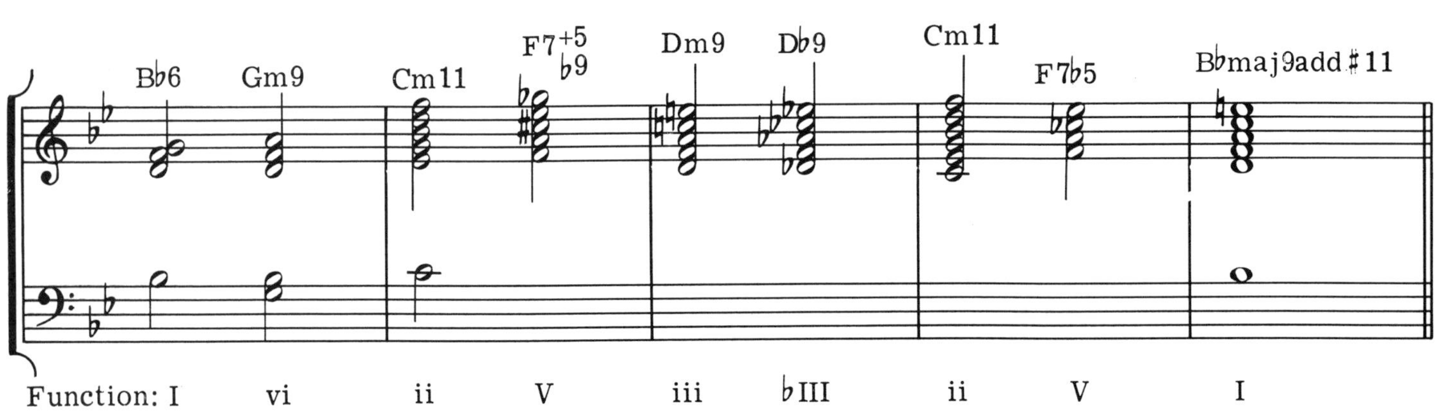

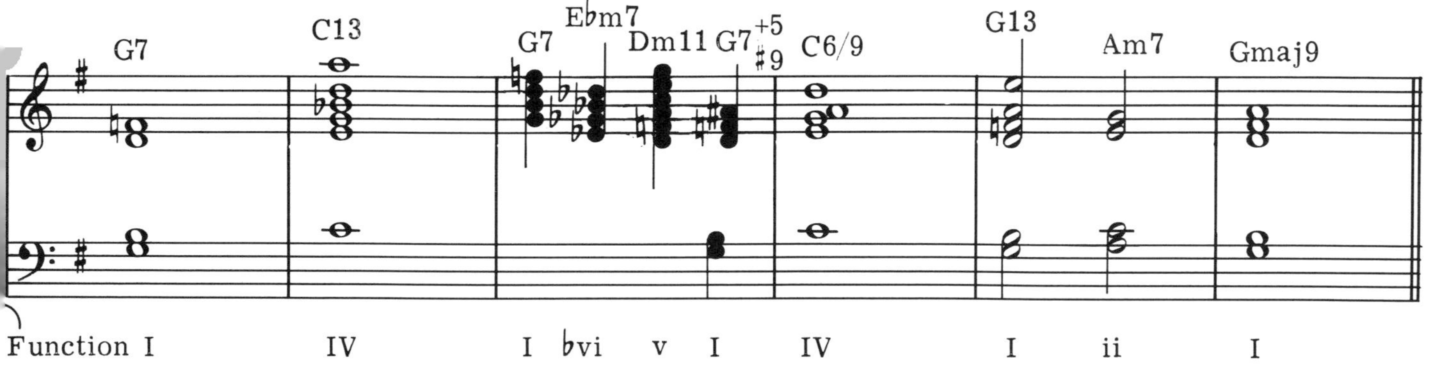

G7
C13
G7 Ebm7 Dm11 G7+5#9 C6/9
G13 Am7 Gmaj9
Function I   IV   I bvi v I   IV   I   ii   I

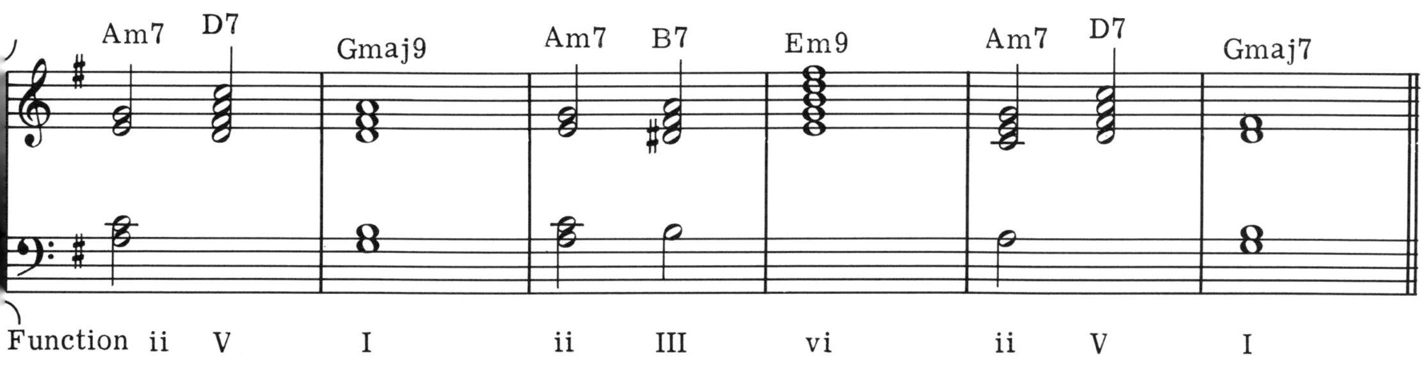

Am7 D7 Gmaj9 Am7 B7 Em9 Am7 D7 Gmaj7
Function ii V   I   ii   III   vi   ii   V   I

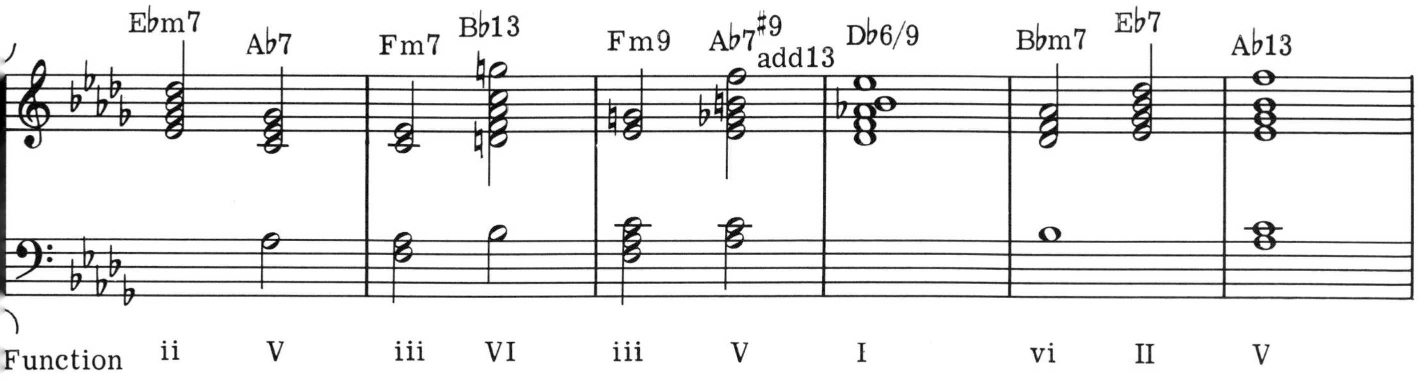

Ebm7 Ab7 Fm7 Bb13 Fm9 Ab7#9 add13 Db6/9 Bbm7 Eb7 Ab13
Function ii   V   iii   VI   iii   V   I   vi   II   V

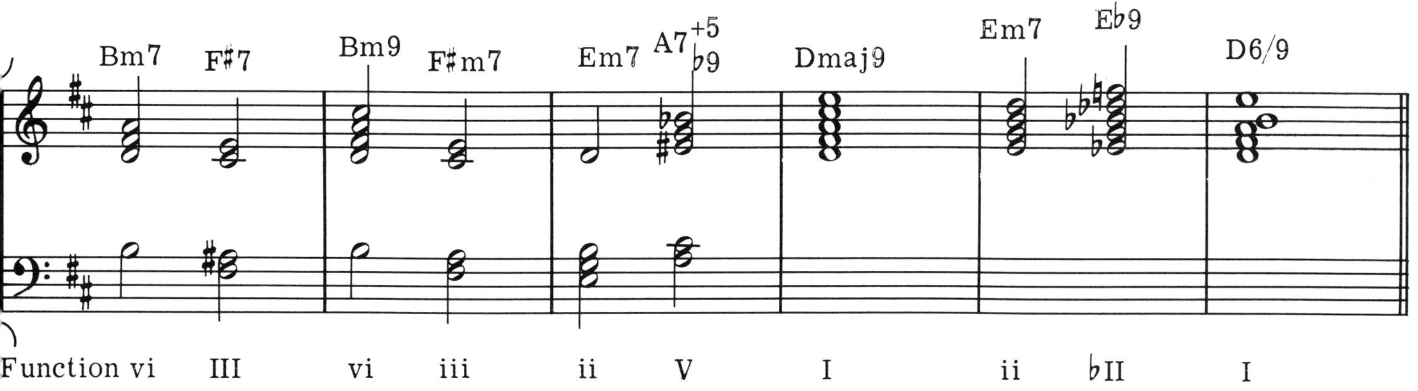

Bm7 F#7 Bm9 F#m7 Em7 A7+5 b9 Dmaj9 Em7 Eb9 D6/9
Function vi   III   vi   iii   ii   V   I   ii   bII   I

Exercise #20

Piano
Clarinet
Exercise #21
Piano
Clarinet
Exercise #22
Piano
Clarinet
Exercise #23
Piano
Clarinet
Piano
Clarinet

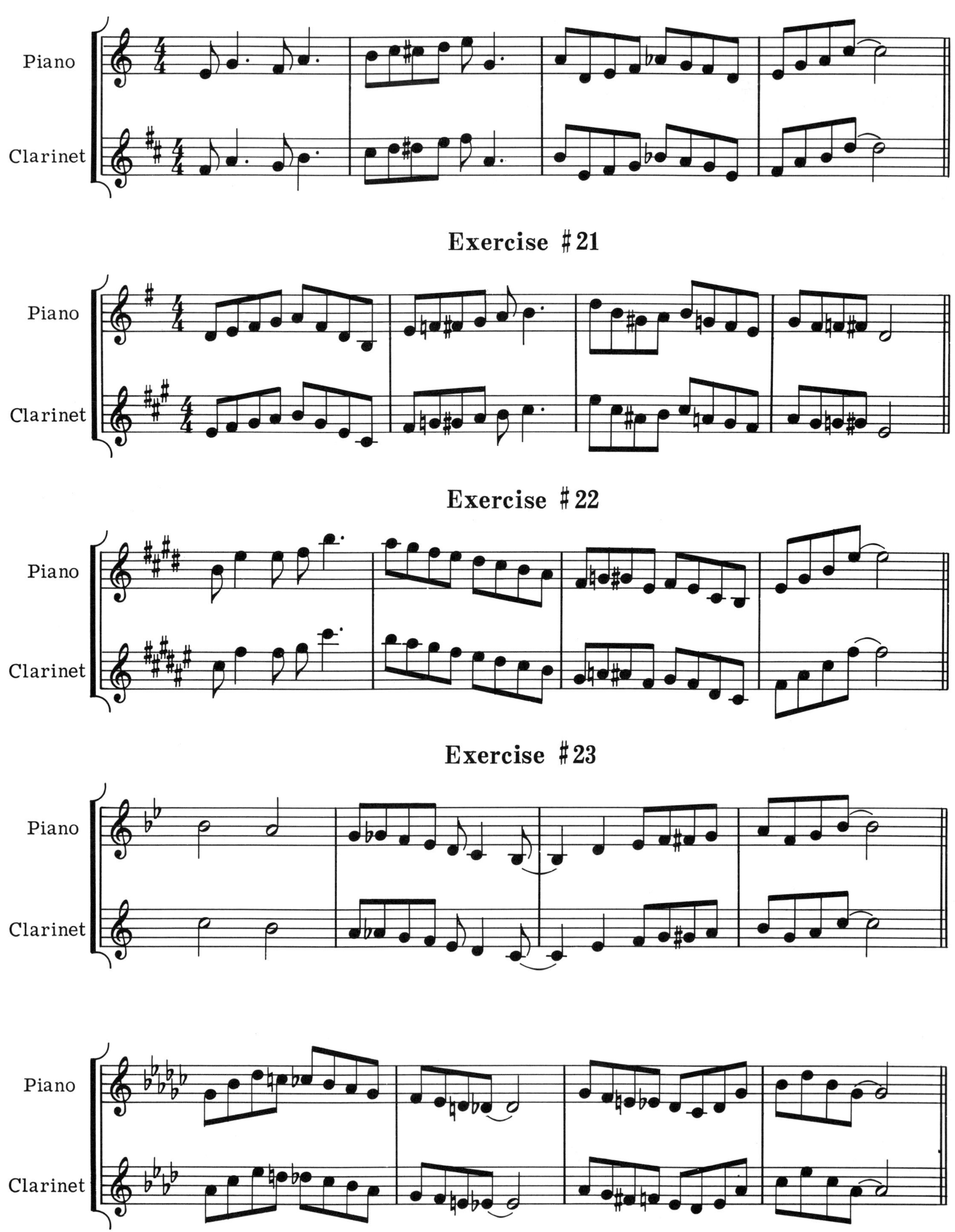

Exercise ♯25

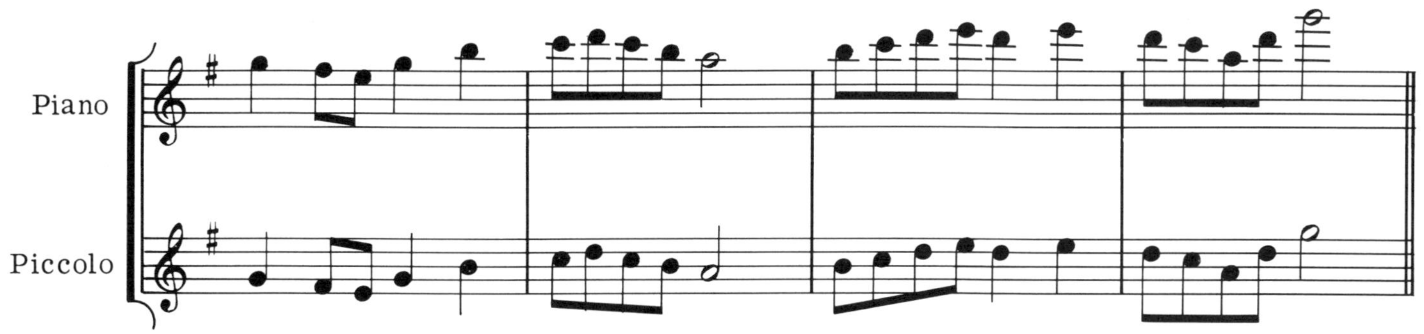

Exercise ♯26

Exercise ♯27

Exercise ♯28

Exercise #29
Bb Clarinet
Flute
Exercise #30
Piccolo
Bb Clarinet
Exercise #31
Piano
Alto Flute
Exercise #32
Bb Clarinet
Alto Flute
Exercise #33
Piano
Bass Flute

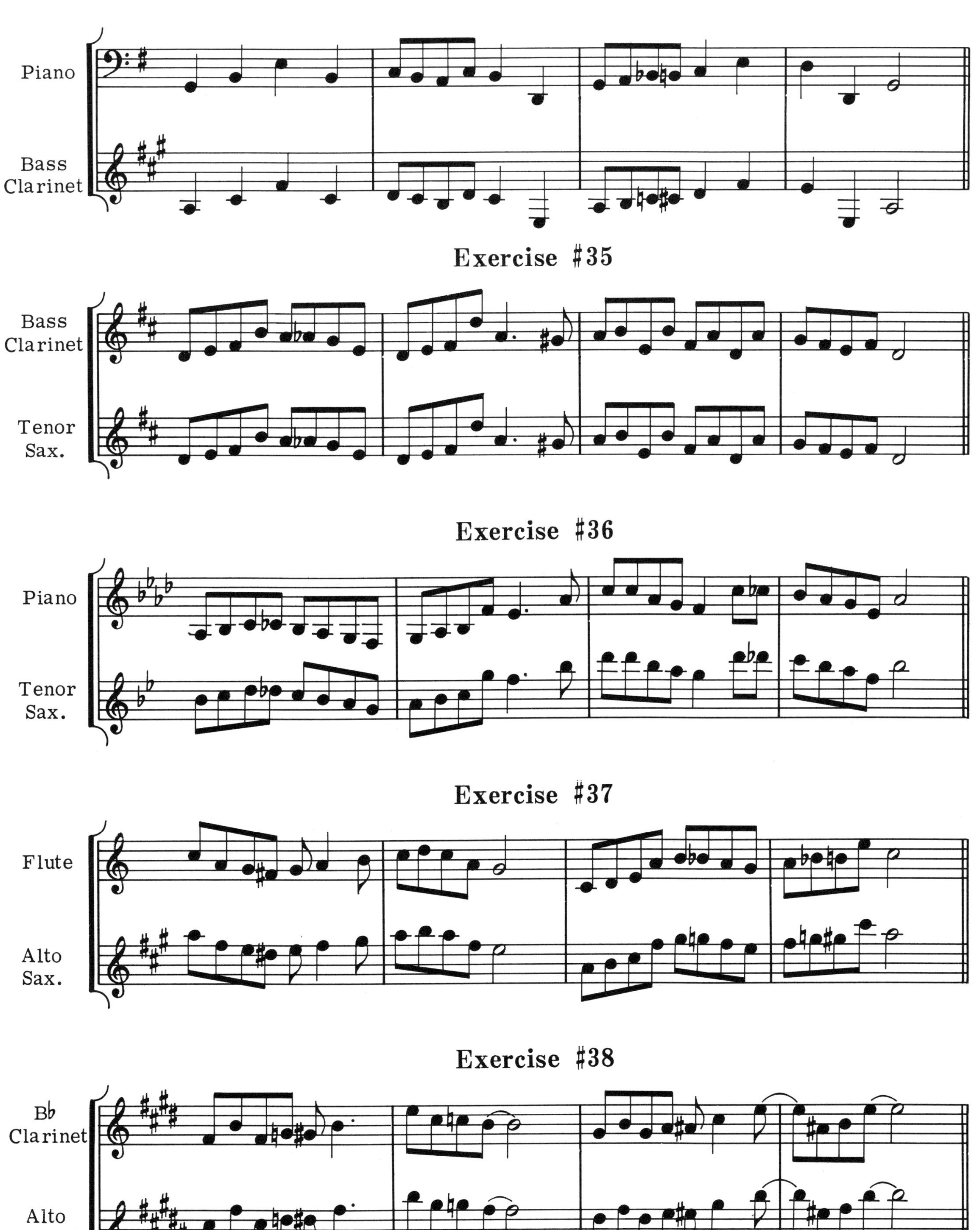

Exercise #34
Piano
Bass Clarinet
Exercise #35
Bass Clarinet
Tenor Sax.
Exercise #36
Piano
Tenor Sax.
Exercise #37
Flute
Alto Sax.
Exercise #38
Bb Clarinet
Alto Sax.

Exercise #39

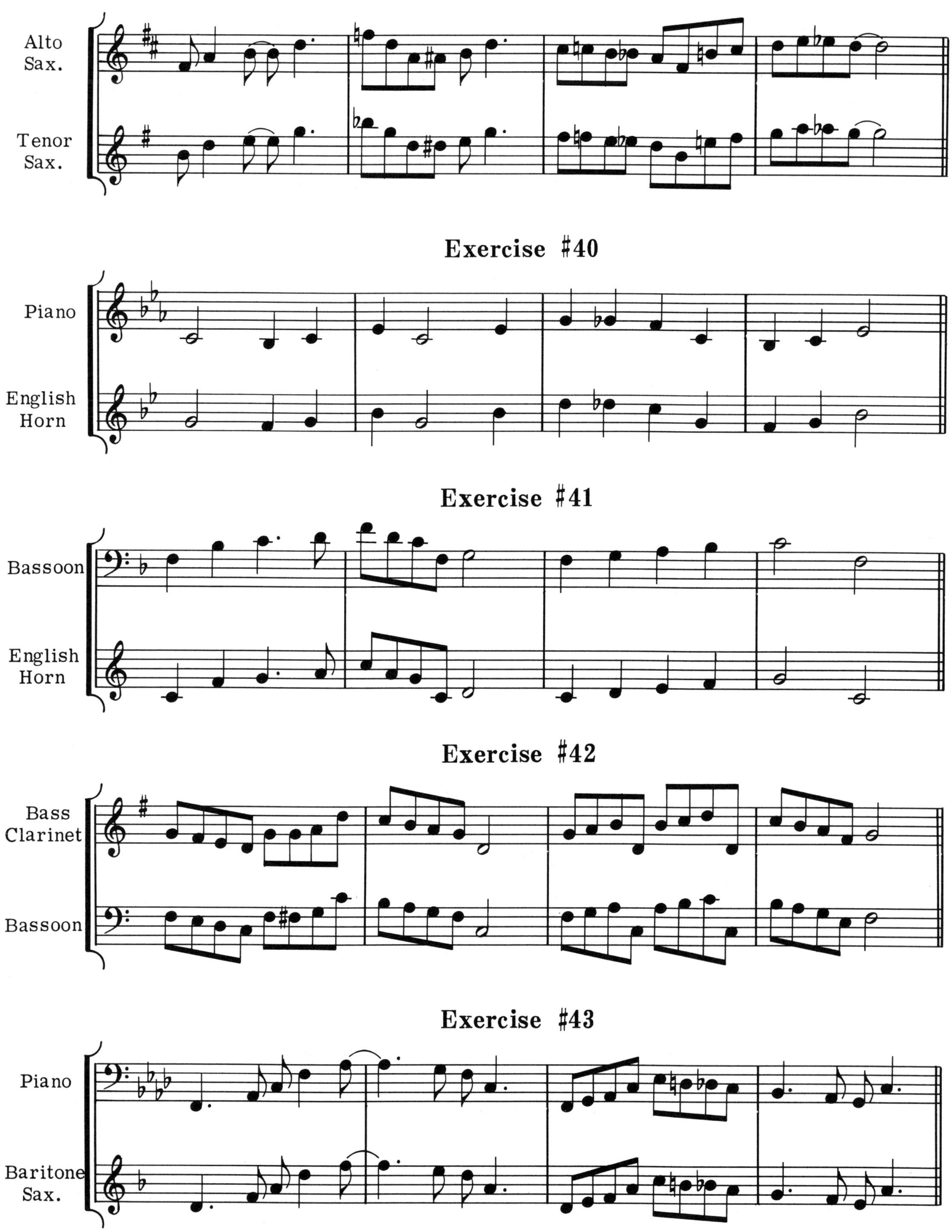

Exercise #40

Exercise #41

Exercise #42

Exercise #43

Exercise #44

Exercise #45

Exercise #46

Exercise #47

Exercise #48

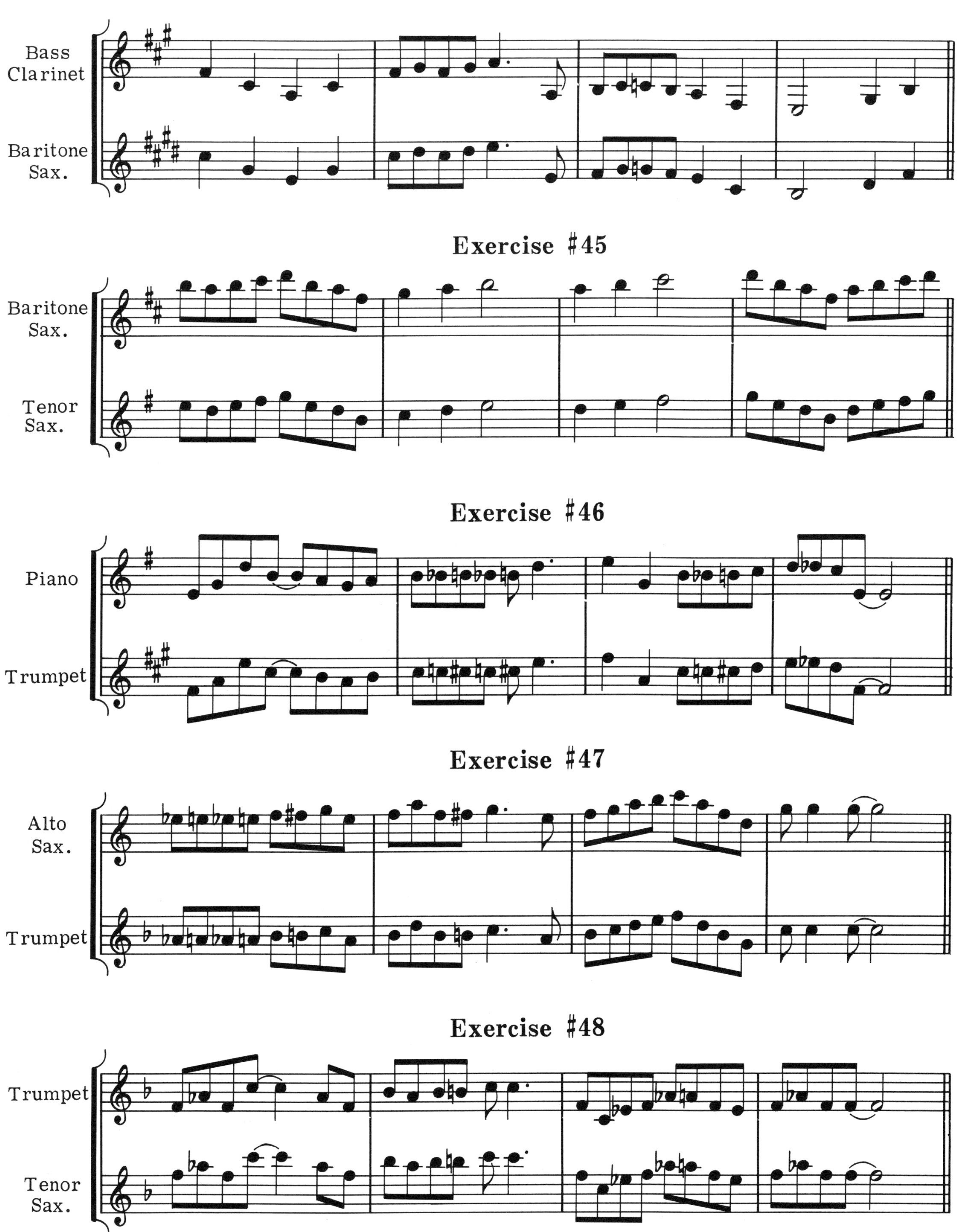

Exercise #49

Exercise #50

Exercise #51

Exercise #52

Exercise #53

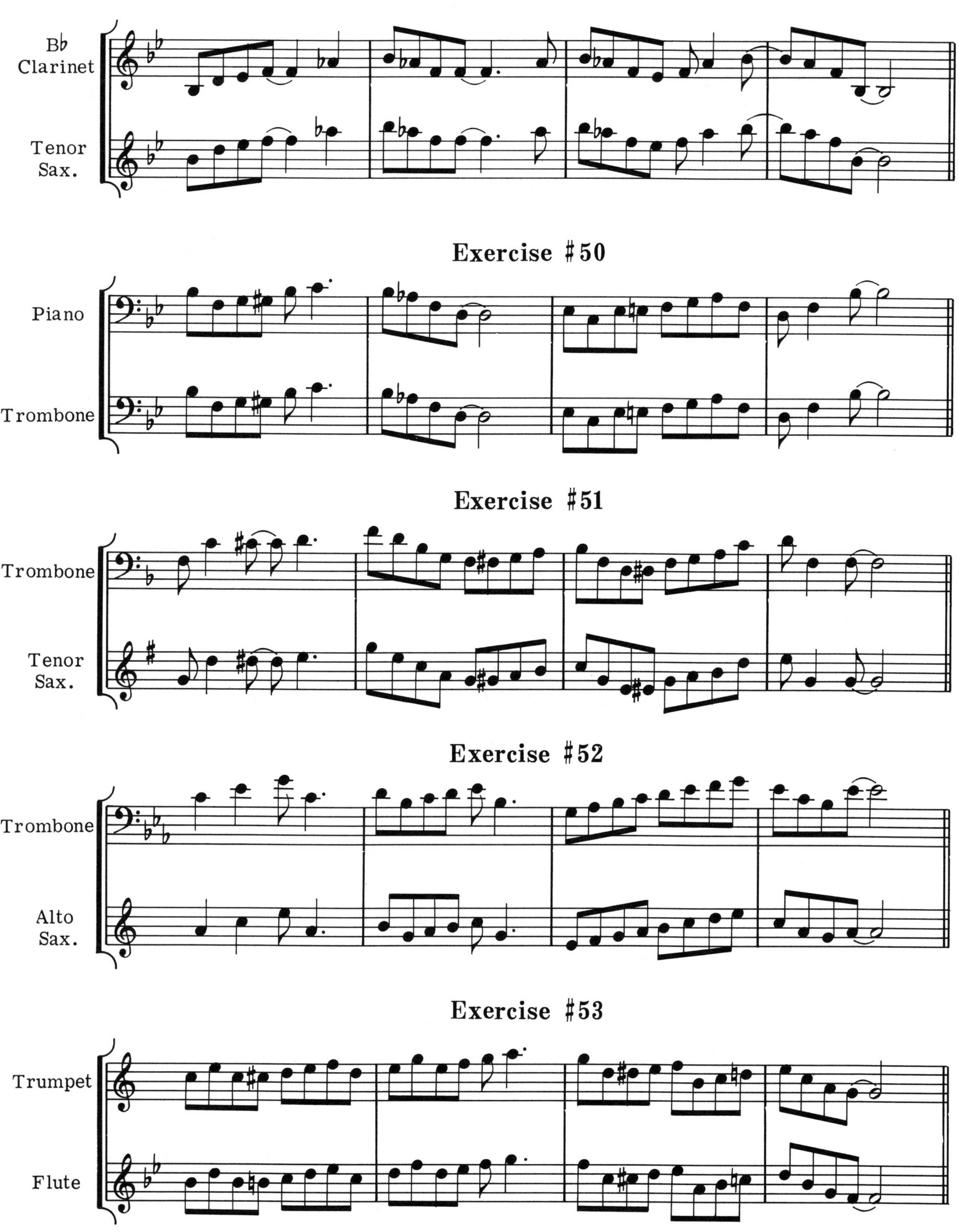

Exercise #54

Exercise #55

Exercise #56

Exercise #57

Exercise #58

Exercise #59
Flugel-Horn
French Horn
Exercise #60
French Horn
English Horn
Exercise #61
Oboe
English Horn
Exercise #62
Alto Sax.
French Horn
Exercise #63
Flute
Violin

Exercise #64

Exercise #65

Exercise #66

Exercise #67

Exercise #68

Exercise #69

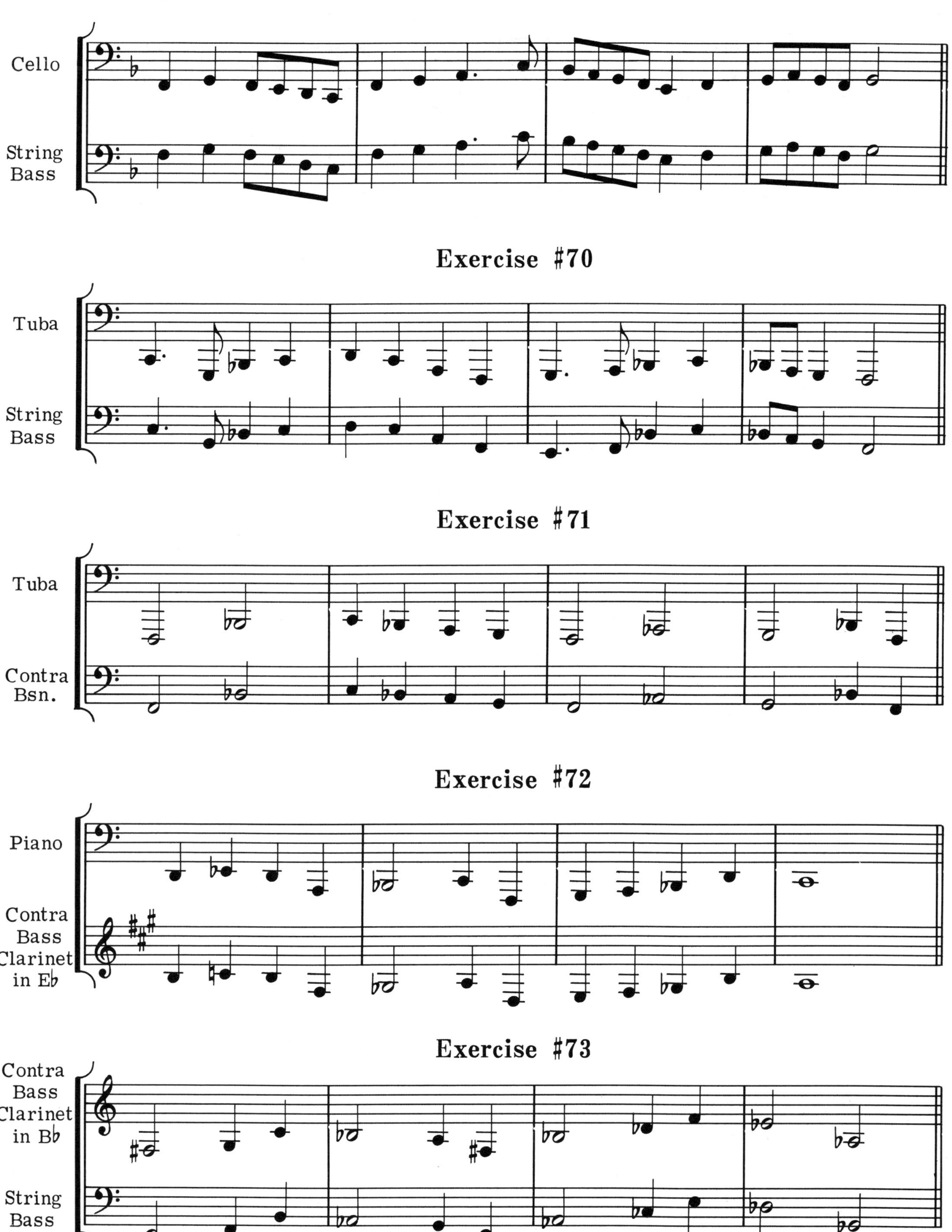

Exercise #70

Exercise #71

Exercise #72

Exercise #73

Exercise #74

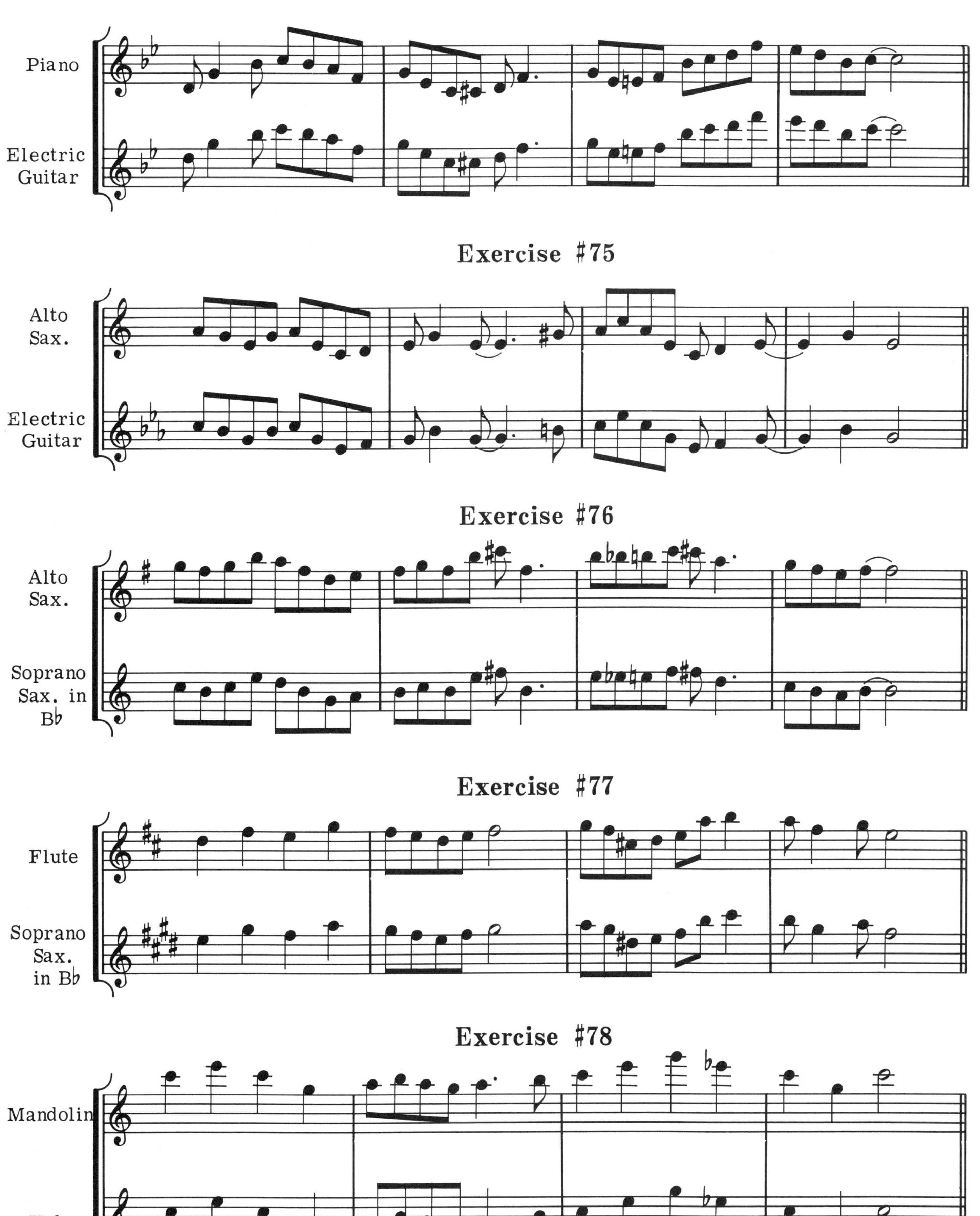

Exercise #75

Exercise #76

Exercise #77

Exercise #78

Exercise #79

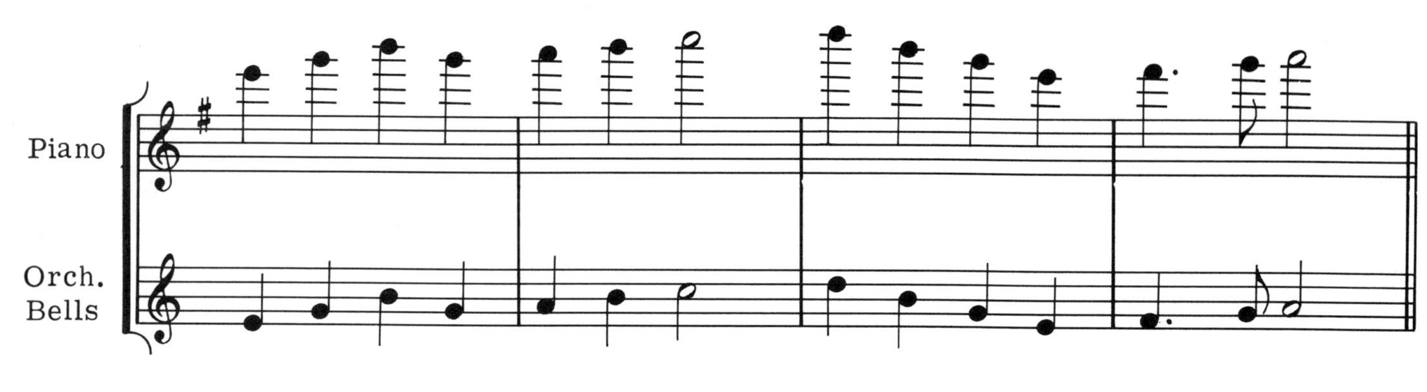

Exercise #80

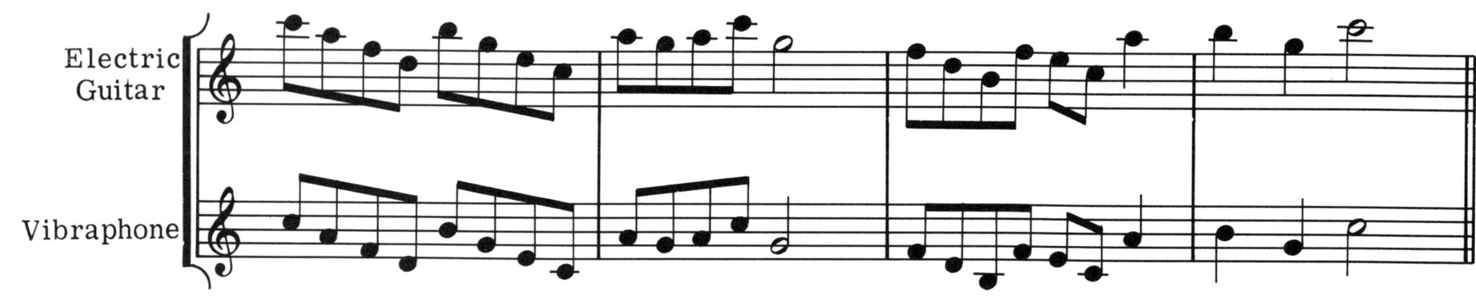

Exercise #81

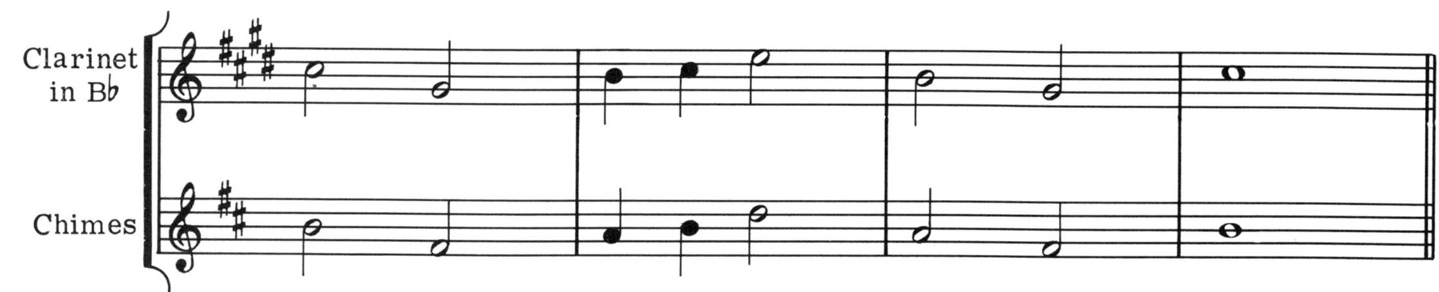

Exercise #82

Exercise #83

Exercise #84

Trumpet
Alto Sax.
Tenor Sax.
Guitar
Oboe
French Horn
Trombone

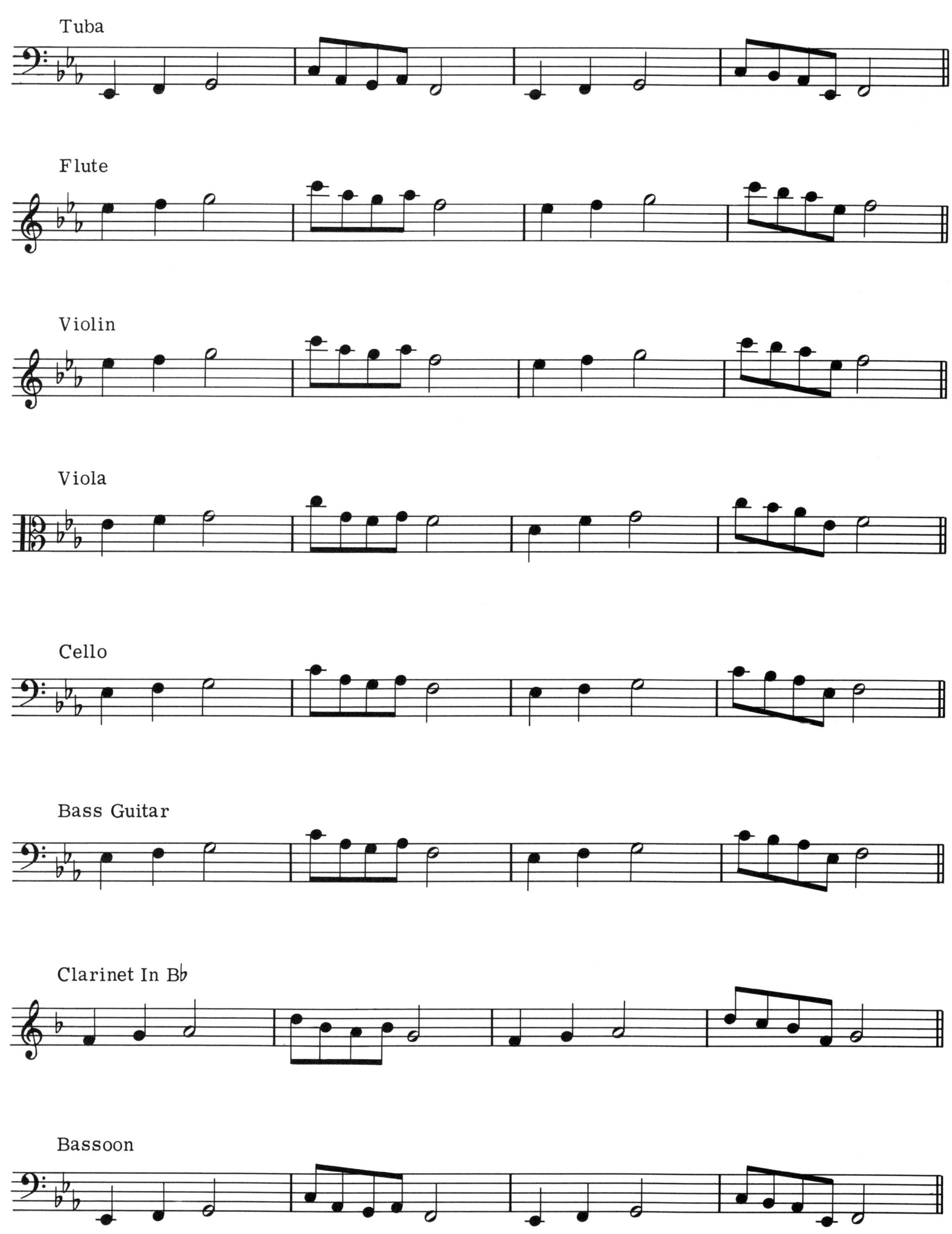

Tuba
Flute
Violin
Viola
Cello
Bass Guitar
Clarinet In B♭
Bassoon

Exercise #85

Exercise #86

Exercise #87

Exercise #88

Exercise #89

Exercise #90

Exercise #91

Cmaj7 Cm9 E♭maj7
G7♭9
Cmaj7 C6/9 Dm7
G13
Cmaj7
Dm7 D♭9
Fm7 B♭13 E♭maj9
Alto Sax.
Alto Sax.
Tenor Sax.
Tenor Sax.
Baritone Sax.

INDEX

Bayside
Press
®